What business leaders are saying about *Harmony at Work:*

"*Harmony at Work* is an enjoyable read that will improve working relationships between managers and workers at every level. With her charming musical analogies, Susan Spero has risen above bland business jargon to create a unique, comprehensive guide for anyone who longs to build rapport and compatibility in their workplace. Read *Harmony at Work* and sing a happy tune with your colleagues!"

Ken Blanchard, coauthor of
The New One Minute Manager® and
Servant Leadership in Action

"*Harmony at Work* is a valuable toolkit to help people understand and strengthen their relationships in any place of employment. My experiences as a social worker, politician, and author have taught me that technical skills and general knowledge are important but not enough. In order to succeed in our careers, we need to know how to manage the subtleties of interactions with others. The music metaphor is brilliant. It makes the book not only useful but delightful to read! It can't help but promote true harmony at work or elsewhere for anyone who reads it."

Dottie Lamm, MSW, freelance writer, former
First Lady of Colorado and *Denver Post* columnist

"Everything good flows out of effective relationships—from sales to marketing to engineering to accounting. *Harmony at Work* is a fresh perspective on leveraging relationships to create a better organization and a better life. This book is an unexpected and priceless gem!"

Steve Vannoy, CEO, *New York Times*
best-selling author, speaker, and Executive
Director of the 10 Greatest Gifts Project

"Spero's inspired metaphor of music harmony provides a unique window into the fine-tuning of our workplace relationships. Even people who are not musically inclined can follow the parallels and apply them to the 'choir' with whom they work. This book addresses the dissonance plaguing the 'music' in many organizations. Her lighthearted touches make for a fun but thought-provoking and practical read. It is a must-read for any young professional, be they new leaders or someone seeking to strengthen an established team."

Patrick J. Moody,
Assistant Attorney General, State of Montana

"Exceptional relationships don't just happen. They take care and maintenance, and they have seasons. The challenge is to know how to manage the ebb and flow that all interactions experience. Good communication is the thread that weaves and strengthens relationships, be they new or long term. Susan Spero's book, *Harmony at Work*, is a must-have tool for those who know the value of solid connections with others and want to increase their ability to sustain them."

Gina Hensrud, CEO,
Rocky Mountain Multiple Sclerosis Center

"Many books on organizational development have lots of theory but very few practical suggestions. Here's one written by a woman who has succeeded in the real world and has helped turn struggling organizations into first-rate performers! Read this book and keep it on your bookshelf to reread throughout your career. It will make you and your team more effective."

Craig O. Schaum, Colonel US Air Force (ret.)
and former VP, Northrop Grumman,
an aerospace and defense technology company

"A gifted songwriter uses rhythm, rhyme, lyrics, and experience to write a song that effortlessly rolls off the tongue and captures the human heart's journey. Susan Spero has placed her words and work on the pages of *Harmony at Work*. What leaps from these pages are the tools and experience she knows will help you create a workplace that sings like a great song. Memorable and moving."

Kerry Patrick Clark, singer,
songwriter, and professional musician

"In this engaging and inspiring book, Susan Spero takes us on an optimistic and uplifting journey through the world of interpersonal dynamics. Utilizing the metaphor of music combined with enlightening personal anecdotes, she draws upon years of consulting experience and wisdom to show the reader how to avoid clashing chords in relationships and strengthen the inspiring notes that lead to successful alliances. The result: *Harmony at Work* is a wonderful book that will help anyone interested in creating enduring music in the relationships that fundamentally influence their lives."

Donald H. Ruggles, architect, AIA; author of *Beauty Neuroscience & Architecture*; producer, *Built Beautiful*

"Susan Spero's *Harmony at Work* was both a wonderful refresher course and a 'songbook of new tunes' for me in relationship building. She draws on proven techniques and adds her years of experience as an executive coach to meet today's organizational challenges. CEOs and other C-suite executives need to effectively grow and deepen their key relationships. This book helped solidify and deepen the techniques I have learned and practiced with my board of directors, my executive team, our staff, and our business partners. I highly recommend this comprehensive yet accessible book for anyone who is serious about creating valuable, lasting relationships."

Tracey D. Campbell, CEO,
BRIDGE Healthcare Partners, LLC

"In our school, we bring families from different backgrounds together through the study and performance of music. Our main leadership challenge has been to set goals, earn trust, and support expectations. In the same way that music enriches the lives of our students and families, this book will enrich your relationships at work and provide the tools you need to succeed."

Peggy S. Wise, Founder,
Chicago Center for Music Education [ChiME],
formerly Suzuki-Orff School for Young Musicians

HARMONY *at* WORK

KEYS TO TUNE UP YOUR WORK RELATIONSHIPS

SUSAN SPERO

Harmony at Work

Disclaimer: The stories and information in this book are true and accurate to the best of the author's and publisher's knowledge. The names of specific people described have been changed in the interests of confidentiality. All recommendations are made without guarantee and should not be considered as advice for any particular business or reader's situation. The author and publisher disclaim any liability in connection with the use of this information.

ISBN (paperback): 978-1-7378680-0-2
ISBN (hardcover): 978-1-7378680-3-3
ISBN (ebook): 978-1-7378680-1-9
ISBN (audiobook): 978-1-7378680-2-6

Editorial services: Sandra Wendel, Write On, Inc.
Cover design: Miblart
Interior design: Megan McCullough
Author Photo: Victor Arango, Studio Candela

Published by Relationshift Publishing, Inc., Denver, CO
HarmonyAtWork.biz
Contact the author at Susan@HarmonyAtWork.biz

In memory of my parents,
Julie and Jerry Spero,
who created beautiful relationship harmony in
our family and fostered our love of music.

My life flows on in endless song;
Above earth's lamentation,
I hear the sweet, tho' far-off hymn
That hails a new creation;
Thro' all the tumult and the strife
I hear the music ringing;
It finds an echo in my soul—
How can I keep from singing?

"How Can I Keep from Singing?"
American folk song originally composed by
Robert Wadsworth Lowry in 1868

Contents

Stage 1
Auditions: Deciding to Join the Choir or Sit Out.. 21

Stage 2
First Notes: Starting the Song with Gusto 77

Stage 3
New Songs: Making Beautiful Music Together ..109

Stage 4
Clashing Chords: Resolving Initial Dissonance ... 137

Stage 5
Encores: Fine-tuning the Evolving Song 173

Stage 6

The Coda

The Overture:
An Introduction to the
Music Metaphor and Its Themes

- Your boss. She is an industry leader, but she drives you crazy.

- Your team leader is your best friend, but there's no way you can ever figure him out.

- Your staff works hard but is impossible to manage. It's like trying to nail Jell-O to the wall.

- Your vendors. You love them, but you want to strangle them at times.

- Your wacko colleagues across the hall. Even their manager can't motivate them to be more professional and considerate.

If any of these situations sound familiar, you are not alone. Unless we become hermits or lighthouse keepers,[1] all of us have ever-changing relationships at work. Our dealings with others take up much of our time and emotional energy, regardless of how productive or challenging they are. Some make us smile, while others make us gnash our teeth.

Maybe this interaction sounds familiar:

"Hey, George! Do you have a minute? I'd like some advice."

Juanita hovers in the doorway of George's office. George is the HR manager of the high-tech company where Juanita is a supervisor.

"Sure, Juanita," George says, as he sets a stack of files aside to clear his desk. "Come on in. Close the door and have a seat. What's up?"

Juanita slumps into the chair in front of George. "I have some static with three of the people I work with. I could probably handle one of them, but dealing with all three is a bit overwhelming."

"Tell me more." George leans forward. "Who's driving you nuts?"

"Well, our new programmer is really nice, but that's the problem: he's too nice. People see him as a doormat. He'll say yes to whatever people ask him to do just to avoid conflict, so he ends up overpromising and underperforming. The others on my team think he's weak and not smart. They've already made nasty nicknames for him and are sure he'll get fired soon. I think he has potential if they'd just cut him some slack."

"Okay. Who else?" George asks.

"You know our customer service coordinator?"

George nods.

"She's funny and high energy, but she creates chaos wherever she goes. She's quite distractable and usually late,

---

1   Which I wouldn't recommend: the job prospects for hermits and lighthouse keepers are rather bleak these days.

so she makes a lot of mistakes. She's likable, but I can't trust her to be accurate or to meet deadlines. Some of our customers say she's charming, but they don't want to work with her anymore." Juanita sighs.

George grimaces. "Sounds challenging. And if those two weren't enough, you said there is a third?"

Juanita sinks a little lower in her chair, like someone was letting the air out of her tires. "Yes, my manager causes me more stress than the other two combined. She's smart and really knows our department, but she's super critical and controlling. Her style is 'no news is good news,'" Juanita says, making air quotes. "So I never hear anything positive from her—just what I'm doing wrong. I cringe when I see her walking toward my office, and I brace myself to get interrupted or attacked in meetings."

George is thoughtful for a moment before responding. "Well, the good news, Juanita, is that you are paying attention. You've clearly identified three relationships that need improvement. From the accolades I hear about your team, it seems you're doing fine with the other folks. So let's sort out what your options are to help the programmer be more assertive and confident and the customer service coordinator to be more focused and organized. Then let's look at how you can create more trust and rapport with your boss. I also want to help you recognize what you're doing well with the rest of your team, so that you can leverage those strengths with these three people. Where do you want to start?"

Juanita's challenges exemplify how hard it can be to manage relationships effectively at work. It's not as if we walk into a room and think, "Let's see, who can I irritate today?" Each of us means well but lacks some of the skills needed to initiate and maintain productive interactions with others. Relationship friction in the workplace is inevitable.

Our ability to respond to it productively has a tremendous impact on our success, regardless of the type of job we hold.

Like Juanita and her colleagues, it is difficult to stop placing obstacles in our own path, often repeatedly. People also have trouble taking the insights from books, seminars, and prior experiences and applying them to current frustrations.

At your local library, bookstore, or on your favorite website, take a look at books on workplace communication and relationships. You are likely to find many options with a wide range of titles. You may see topics like these:

- How to get a job

- How to get away from your job

- How to get promoted

- How to survive when your best friend is promoted over you to be your new boss

- How to get along with the office bully

- How to communicate better with people who ignore you

Scores of books also exist on issues that arise from leadership challenges, team dynamics, generational profiles, gender, and cultural differences. They each explore a narrow slice of an extremely broad topic.

This Book Provides a Broader View about Relationships

Harmony at Work offers a different approach. You'll find three main benefits to looking at your relationships from a more global, 30,000-foot view.

First, we experience predictable stages of development as we interact with most people. This is true regardless of the nature of our contact with others. At times, it seems that you have just begun to figure out a person or situation, and then the relationship changes its tune, leaving you adrift.

Harmony at Work will help you notice those shifts and understand the characteristics of each phase. This awareness then makes it easier to navigate through each of those stages more successfully. It also reduces the tendency to feel resentment and fear regarding those inevitable changes.

Second, we all have some relationships at work that are more productive than others. You may get along well with your own team members but argue with people in other departments. You might be voted the Employee of the Month within the office but alienate vendors or customers. Often, you can be assertive with some people in your life but may get too aggressive or too submissive with others.

This book offers tools to recognize what you do well in your healthy relationships, as well as tuning into the recurring themes in difficult interactions. These tools will help you transfer your skills and insights from the successful situations to the ones that are more problematic. You may also find ways to apply successful approaches at work to your personal interactions and vice versa.

The third benefit relates to what my brilliant friend Karin often says: "We take ourselves with us wherever we go!" This is the most important value of examining the whole range of your relationships at work. No matter how fast you run or how well you hide, you take your own personality—assets, liabilities, needs, and interests—into every conversation in which you engage.

Sometimes you might try to disguise your true self by not saying honestly what you think or feel. You may be a clever poker player and not show others all of your emotional cards.

You may fool some of the people some of the time. Your real thoughts and feelings, however, usually leak through your pretenses: they often stand out awkwardly like an out-of-tune singer in a choir.

In the final analysis, we do take ourselves with us into each of our relationships. *Harmony at Work* suggests ways to be more conscious of your own patterns. You might notice that

- You often feel nervous around certain types of people and confident around others.

- There may be very few people with whom you can be totally honest and trusting.

- In specific situations, you repeatedly lose your patience or start to argue.

- Some circumstances may make you giddy and impulsively prone to bad decisions.

Armed with this knowledge, you may approach challenging interactions better prepared. You can anticipate how you might react and plan more constructive responses. You might even guide the conversation toward a more desirable outcome.

This type of insight encourages you to shift your own behaviors in order to compose more satisfying responses to the music around you. On a good day, it may also motivate others to act differently, thus improving their contributions to the overall sound of the music you produce together.

Even though some people appear to manage relationships more effectively than others, no one is immune from these challenges. We all have our own Achilles heels and blind spots. It is part of what makes us human. Think how boring our lives would be if we could definitively sort out all of this touchy-feely stuff[2] and know the punchline of every conversation. We'd be asleep on our feet and miss all of the excitement.

So why read another book on relationships? Anytime you get two or more people together in a room, there is the potential for disharmony.[3] Most of us have at least a few people in our lives who intimidate or annoy us, and we are not always sure how to respond to them.

In this book, I examine several current theories about interpersonal dynamics. The purpose of this exploration is to

- Boil down these concepts to a few, user-friendly ideas,

- Find ways that these basic notions link up with each other,

- Cite common examples of how these theories play out across the scope of our varied relationships at work, and

- Offer some tools and exercises so you can apply this information to the relationships that give you the most stomach aches, tears, or high blood pressure.

What Does Music Have to Do with Relationships?

The parallels between music and relationships first occurred to me during a meeting with one of my corporate clients. I was leading a strategic planning retreat for their senior management team. Each of the ten executives had different

---

2   As some of my clients lovingly refer to interpersonal issues.
3   Actually, I have the ability to have a juicy argument with myself when I'm alone in a room. When I lose those arguments, that's when it's most upsetting.

priorities and ideas for how to move the company forward. The familiar phrase "herding cats"[4] kept running through my mind. At one point, a vice president said, "I feel like Susan's trying to conduct a choir here, but we all have different pages of music, and we're all singing in different keys. No wonder we sound so awful!"

I had another experience several years ago that further highlighted the similarities between music and relationships. While working on a project in a local high school, I walked into a music class to give a message to the choir director. It was the second week of school, and the scene was controlled chaos.

The director calmly encouraged the students to focus on the music in front of them. A few of the kids were actually singing, watching him, or looking at the music. Most, however, were flirting, fidgeting, whispering, or staring into space. Several were blatantly texting on their phones. Many looked as if they had forgotten to brush their hair or put on clean clothes before coming to school that day.

When the director finally got the group singing, they were out of tune and behind the beat. There was absolutely no balance between the melody and harmonies. The sounds they made were painful to my ears, and I was amazed at the director's patience. I wondered if all choir classes were so ragged at the start of each school year. I also began to doubt that I would want to attend any of their performances.

Now fast-forward to their first concert three months later. The students wore suits and dresses. Standing tall on the auditorium risers, they had smiles on their faces and a sparkle in their eyes. They watched the director closely and followed his cues, hitting the correct pitches at the right

---

4   If you're a dog person, ask someone who owns a cat how impossible it is to get a dog to do anything it hasn't already decided it wants to do. Cats know they are not dogs and have no intention of being trained or herded like a dog.

times. The music was miraculously beautiful. The singers were obviously proud. The director was thrilled. The enthusiastic parents clapped wildly, some discreetly dabbing tears from their eyes with one hand while trying to record the moment on their phone.

What happened between that early September rehearsal and the first concert? The relationships between the director, the students, and the music had all evolved. The singers developed the skills to sing in tune. They had been trained to follow the director's cues. They noticed when they needed to adjust the tempo or volume. They listened carefully so they could blend with each other. The director had guided the choir to allow the repertoire and the relationships to develop. Everyone knew they had made progress, because the music sounded good, and they were having fun with the songs.

Like the high school choir, our relationships at work can evolve as well. Those interactions, like music, can be short, simple songs or long, complex masterpieces. They may sound harmonious or dissonant, lively or boring. Relationships, like music, fit into specific genres: boss, team member, customer, or vendor; classical, rock, jazz, or rap. They also become more interesting when we have the skills to vary their tempo, volume, and structure.

In many ways, the steps we go through to create the music of our professional relationships resemble the steps taken by that high school choir director. Whether we're conducting a choral group of staff members, or tackling a difficult duet with a colleague, we have the potential to sing harmoniously together *or* make a huge, discordant mess. Sometimes, we do both in the same day. Unfortunately, we may have no idea why it is so easy to make beautiful music with some people, and why other interactions sound so out of tune. We might not even be singing the right songs together.

What Are the Six Main Stages of *Harmony at Work*?

"Every exception proves the rule," according to an old adage. No matter how you define the structure of relationships overall, there will certainly be exceptions that challenge your definition. Nevertheless, *most* relationships will evolve through some predictable stages as they develop. Some of these stages may be skipped, repeated, or occur in a different order, depending on the context and the people involved. The duration of each stage will also vary.

When looking at interactions at work, it is helpful to understand, and thus anticipate, the six most common sequences that you may experience with others. In this way, you can prepare for, and more effectively manage, the dynamics at each juncture. Otherwise, the challenges will sneak up behind you and thwap you over the head with an interpersonal baseball bat! [5]

Every relationship stage has distinctive tempos, with highs and lows that are fundamental parts of the interpersonal music. These rhythms and the responses they elicit make the songs we sing with others more challenging. They also make them more interesting. As a result, certain resources are helpful to use with each stage.

Harmony at Work offers tools to help you conduct these six predictable stages of relationship evolution more harmoniously. These six stages form the structure of the rest of this book:

---

5   Physical abuse with an actual baseball bat is obviously illegal and morally wrong. Sadly, people often get away with using virtual interpersonal bats to verbally swat at their coworkers. While verbal abuse may leave no tangible evidence, it often has more long-lasting effects on the recipient.

1. *Auditions: Deciding to Join the Choir or Sit Out*

   When you contemplate finding a new job, accepting a promotion, or making a new contact at work, it helps to explore the variables that impact your initial decisions. It is important to first consider your needs, hopes, and fears. These, along with past work experiences, influence what you will look for if you decide to engage in a new relationship.

2. *First Notes: Starting the Song with Gusto*

   Once you decide to pursue a new job or relationship, it is helpful to review your options for initiating that new contact. You need to decide whom to approach, how to initiate contact, and how to best present yourself. When you begin composing new relationships thoughtfully rather than using your unconscious habits, you have greater success and make better music.

3. *New Songs: Making Beautiful Music Together*

   The beginning notes of the music you create with a new boss, team, vendor, or customer can be exhilarating. You need to examine the responses that you typically have to those new songs. That reflection includes what kinds of agreements you want to make and how best to leverage your strengths to address challenges. The way you begin these new songs often sets the tone for the relationship long term.

4. *Clashing Chords: Resolving Initial Dissonance*

   Eventually you need to deal with the emerging discord that may occur as the repertoire develops with colleagues. Once a new song becomes familiar, the tunes that initially attracted you to others may annoy you after a while. At this point, it is crucial to build your skills and confidence to address conflicts directly. It also helps to recognize what is causing the issues. It takes *courage* to share concerns frankly and resolve disagreements successfully. Your willingness to examine dissonance impacts how the song will progress long term, or if it will end prematurely.

5. *Encores: Fine-tuning the Evolving Song*

Once you have navigated through the first four stages, the next stage involves the ability to modulate and strengthen the music over time. Some of us are great musicians who easily compose new songs, but most of us need help finding ways to keep the music interesting over time. Clear roles, strong communication, and strategies to mitigate boredom all play a key role here. The tools and techniques used in Encores play a crucial part in determining both the tenor and the vibrancy of the relationship's music over time.

6. *Finales: Knowing If, When, and How to End the Song*

Some musicians are one-hit wonders: they have one memorable recording, making their success dazzling but short-lived. Others, like Bach and the Beatles, create music that survives and thrives for decades. It is the same with interpersonal dynamics. We need intentional strategies to maintain the harmony and commitment for relationships over time or figure out how to end them with grace and gratitude. Ironically, it is often the long-term management of individual and team interactions that is most challenging.

These six stages do not represent a simple, linear process. Sometimes, you may need to backtrack and revisit some of these stages whenever the relationship song shifts. You might have worked with someone for five years, but if one of you is suddenly promoted to supervise the other, you basically start all over with a new song. Someone may have been a close partner for decades, but with the occurrence of a birth, death, marriage, divorce, or job change for either person, the shift may cause both of you to revisit many of these six stages.

How Is Relationship Management a Recurring Theme in Most Careers?

All of my professional life has been focused on relationships of various kinds. My first six years after college were spent in education. I knew that my skills in teaching the core academic subjects were important. However, the strength of my relationships with the students, their parents, and other teachers had an even greater impact on how the kids grew and learned.

I then spent three years as a behavioral psychologist, working with chronic-pain patients. Again, it was evident that I needed to establish rapport with each patient, as well as with my professional colleagues, so we could help our patients achieve their therapeutic goals.

Since 1982, I have worked as a leadership consultant, corporate trainer, meeting facilitator, and executive coach. Ninety percent of my clients' requests are tied to relationships—how they communicate and resolve conflicts with the people in all facets of their lives. I often meet individuals who have superb technical skills for a given job but have such major interpersonal barriers that they cannot succeed at work. There are also many folks who are smart, attractive, and have interesting jobs but cannot maintain an intimate, long-term relationship in their personal life with a significant other.

I have learned that relationship management is often the unidentified elephant in the middle of the room.[6] People don't want to talk about it, don't know how it got there, don't like the mess it leaves on the floor, and can't figure out how to get

---

6   In Canada, they call it the moose in the middle of the room.

rid of it. They may fail to recognize that the elephant is in the room for a reason. Until they understand how to feed it, clean up after it, and then lead it gently back to its native habitat, it will make the music of their career difficult if not completely off-key and block their path to success and satisfaction.

This gap between technical and interpersonal skills is like an aspiring professional singer who has a fabulous voice, but terrible stage fright. Her fear causes awful performances in spite of her talent. My aunt Lilly was another example of this pattern. She trained to be an opera singer. But her performance anxiety made her choke and falter at every audition, which kept her from ever being hired for any professional singing roles.

Solid skills and strong material are necessary but not always sufficient for success at work. If I had a nickel for each time that I have met someone with such discrepancies between their specific job competencies and their people skills, I could donate large sums of money to my favorite charities.

Similarly, I have learned a great deal about relationships through my involvement with music. Singing has been a lifelong passion, and I have had the privilege to sing in some wonderful choirs and ensembles. I have also enjoyed conducting a small community choir for over thirty years. In all of these groups, the singers need to listen to each other and watch for cues from the director. At the same time, they must be aware of their own timing, pitch, and expression. I believe singing with others is a perfect metaphor for how we need to conduct our work relationships.[7]

---

7 Leading or singing in a choir is a lot like most day jobs: it's sometimes fun, exciting, and harmonious. Other times, it's tiring and frustrating, and you just can't seem to get the songs to sound right.

Earbuds, Surround Sound, and Streaming: A Balanced Relationship Diet

Music comes to us in many forms:

- Earbuds: our own carefully chosen playlists that only we can hear,

- Surround sound: big, loud sound systems at home or in a concert venue with lots of vibration that blast everyone's eardrums at once, or

- Streaming services: subscriptions that let us listen to whatever they decide to play for us.

The music of relationship comes to us via many channels as well:

- Earbuds: a quiet, intense one-on-one conversation in person, by phone, or online,

- Surround sound: a large, lively team meeting with lots of conversation, activity, noise, and energy, or

- Streaming services: the structure and timing of interactions is prescribed by others, when we need to sit back, observe, and respond to what comes our way.

In the same way that we can transfer relationship harmony skills from one stage to another, or from one person to another, the tools that we'll explore in this book can be applied to many different types of relationships, regardless of the channels through which they are delivered.

Applications: What Is the Best Way to Sing Along with This Book?

You might prefer to start with the Contents page and work your way through the book systematically. Some of you may want to look over the chapter titles and start with one that addresses where you are in a current relationship that is challenging for you. A third option is to glance at the anecdotes at the beginning of each chapter and see which ones sound most intriguing and relevant to you. Also consider how these stages and tools apply to your personal relationships outside of work.

Like a well-constructed musical composition, I have attempted to weave together

- Established theories,

- Familiar examples,

- Skill-practice exercises called rehearsals, and

- Suggestions for ways to apply these ideas in your current relationships.

By giving you several different tunes from which to choose, I hope that each of you will find ways to best link these concepts to the relationships in your life that you most want to tune up and rearrange right now. Some models apply to leaders, while others apply to anyone who works on a team. The first few stages are relevant for job seekers and people in new relationships. Later stages will help you to examine longer-term interactions that have either hit some sour notes or need some new energy. Human resources professionals and organization development consultants might find the ideas and exercises to be helpful to use with their clients.

You don't need to be a professional musician to enjoy this book. In fact, you might have been one of those embarrassed third graders whose crabby music teacher said to you, "Please mouth the words to the songs during our assembly. You really can't carry a tune in a bucket, and you'll just throw the other children off if you try to sing."[8]

There are no auditions required here: you are invited to hum along in whatever key you like. The important musical concepts that are used will be defined as we go. You will also find a glossary of key musical terminology at the end of the book.

The start of each chapter has a short dialogue among four friends: Juanita, Sally, Alex, and Omar. The intent of these conversations is to demonstrate how the characteristics and challenges of each stage of relationship evolution play out in real life. I hope you can relate to one or more of their experiences.

Where Are You Now?

Before we dig deeper into the six stages of relationship evolution that are covered in *Harmony at Work*, give yourself a quick rating for how well you think you currently manage each stage in general, using the following scale:

1= Not well: This stage is a struggle for me.

3= Fair: I have some skill and confidence, but I would like to improve.

5= Great: I feel comfortable and competent in this stage.

---

8   This really has happened to some people. Too bad that the kids who were subjected to those nasty, critical comments can't bill their former music teachers for the psychotherapy they've needed as adults as they try to rebuild their self-esteem.

		1	2	3	4	5
1.	Auditions	1	2	3	4	5
2.	First Notes	1	2	3	4	5
3.	New Songs	1	2	3	4	5
4.	Clashing Chords	1	2	3	4	5
5.	Encores	1	2	3	4	5
6.	Finales	1	2	3	4	5

How well do you currently manage each stage?

Then decide if you want to read this book in sequential order or start with the chapter that explains a stage in which you want to be more proficient.

Alternatively, you might think of a specific relationship that is causing you some angst. Consider which stage you believe you are now in with that person. You could start with the chapter that addresses that stage.

Final Notes: A Few More Suggestions before We Start to Sing

We often blame relationship problems on one of two assumptions:

1. We focus on our own defects, think they are all our fault, and believe we need to beat ourselves up for our failings, or

2. We assume that the other people involved are lazy, crazy, stupid, or evil (and sometimes all four).[9]

---

9   This one is much more fun but rarely creates harmony at work any better than the overuse of self-blame does.

While either of these two notions might be convenient, neither is productive. The reality of relationships is that they are hard to start and even harder to maintain. By now, you know that they are always shifting. Relationships require constant attention and frequent tuning, just like musical instruments. When the temperature in the room changes, I need to retune my guitar. When a piano is moved to a new home, it needs to be retuned. When the trust level with an individual or group changes, I need to retune the relationship.[10]

We each resemble the employees who will be described at the beginning of each stage in some respects at least some of the time. Fortunately, there are specific methods to help us improve our singing with others. As you learn more about how to compose, refine, and practice harmonious relationships, you will feel more confident about the interpersonal music you make at work. If you're not careful, you might also get more done and have more fun with your colleagues more of the time, regardless of which songs you choose to sing with them.

Managing relationships can be difficult. Our efforts to understand others and ourselves must be taken seriously. At the same time, I feel strongly that we need to be able to laugh at our own foibles. I sincerely hope that you find this book to be easy to use and occasionally worth a chuckle. The footnotes on many of the pages are intended to add some levity and can be ignored if they distract you. References to books, authors, and theoretical models can be found at the back of the book.

Your life and your relationships are a series of grand musical compositions. Some are carefully orchestrated, and others are full of improvised surprises. Each song has the potential to be either a source of great joy or profound pain.

---

10 Retuning guitars and pianos is *much* easier than retuning relationships.

Much of the time, though, relationships are just plain wacko.[11] The themes, harmonies, and dissonances that you hear with others are constantly shifting and evolving. Remember, that makes them more interesting.

So put this book on your metaphorical music stand, along with other musical scores that you have collected in your life. Use it to provide new perspectives about the people who cross your path at work. Let it empower you to conduct your relationships with more courage, creativity, and harmony.

From time to time, step back from the music. Assess what sounds good and try to improve what is out of tune. Remember to look for humor in at least some of the sour notes that you and others make. Take some calculated risks. Practice and rearrange your songs as much as possible. Raise the conductor's baton. Then start the music. See what you can do to create and enjoy more *Harmony at Work*.

Stage 1

Auditions: Deciding to Join the Choir or Sit Out

Juanita texts three friends: *Meet me for lunch. I need your help.* She is thinking of applying for a different job. She wants advice on whether it is worth the trouble to even start looking. Her buddies have all had different types of jobs and varied perspectives on work.

They meet up at Sammy's Sandwich Shop and grab the back table where they usually solve the world's problems. Today is Juanita's turn to direct the discussion. After all, she has sent the SOS text.

"Hey, everybody, thanks for coming at such short notice," Juanita says as she slides into the booth with her usual egg salad sandwich. She sighs. "Here's my problem: I have to decide if I should look for a new job with a better boss. My current manager messages me constantly and only focuses on what's wrong."

"I just wish my boss would spend less time sending texts and emails and more time actually *talking* to our team," Sally says. She sips her latte. "It would be nice if we had a face-to-face meeting once in a while to brainstorm ideas or collaborate on a project. For me, twenty emails a day don't count as meaningful communication, especially when her office is within shouting distance of mine, for Pete's sake." Sally is an IT specialist in a small start-up.

"Yeah, well, at least your boss is around the office," Alex says. "Mine spends so many hours in the field that, sometimes, I wonder if we'll recognize each other when he comes back in." Alex is a lead sales manager for a large manufacturing company. "I am also curious about what he's actually working on outside of the office, since all he seems to do is stop by, dump a bunch of work on the team, and then disappear again. Except for what he calls delegation (and we call passing the buck), he's really not managing us at all."

Omar holds up a hand indicating he needs to finish a bite of his sub sandwich but that he has something important to add. Finally, he says, "I'd gladly trade your email hermit or your absentee boss for the emotional abuse in our department. My boss is chronically crabby. He's either pouting or too upset to tell me what's wrong. Sometimes, he just nitpicks and micromanages me to death with trivial criticisms. The scariest part is that he absolutely refuses to get any help—either with the projects he's overwhelmed by or with the leadership skills he doesn't have. I'd give nearly anything to hear one positive, supportive comment out of him from time to time." Omar does fundraising for a midsized nonprofit agency.

Juanita considers all of their banter and remarks, "Listen to what you're saying here, friends. If it's not one kind of pathology, it's another. I'd just like to find some *normal* kind of job with a *reasonable* boss who knows how to lead and communicate like an *adult*. A little humor would go a long way too. Does that species actually exist anymore? How do I know if it's worth the effort to even look for a new job? Maybe the devil I know, as they say, is better than finding a new job that includes some new horror story."

"Don't let us discourage you, Juanita," Sally says as she finishes her lunch. "You're the first among us to find new jobs, get promotions, and even find new roommates. We'll help you figure out what you've done right in the past, so that you can repeat that process with this next job search. I'd call that leveraging your prior successes."

"And *you* taught *me* that you first have to get clear about what you most want and what you refuse to put up with," Alex adds, "like drafting a shopping list of must-haves and nonnegotiable deal breakers."

"Absolutely," Omar says, glancing at his phone. "I've gotta run. Mr. Micromanager will be watching to make sure I get back in time. But that's not all, Alex." He turns to Juanita, "You also have to think about what's going to be on the shopping lists of potential employers, or what they're probably looking for. That way, you can figure out how to highlight your skills and experience as they relate to what the prospective positions will need most. Am I right?"

Heads nod around the table.

"Okay, my loyal cheerleaders," Juanita says with a tight smile of determination. "This will take more than a lunch hour. Let's plan another get together, so you can help me sort all this out. Come to my place this Friday night at seven: I'll provide my famous lasagna and your favorite drinks."

"It's a deal!" exclaim Sally, Alex, and Omar in unison.

Assess the Effort to Start Singing

This first stage of relationship development, Auditions, happens whenever you consider changing jobs, seeking a promotion, or assembling a new team—as these employees were discussing. Several emotions characterize this phase.

Sometimes you are excited and confident. Other times, you're nervous and insecure. You may feel impatient, wondering how long it will take to find the right company, boss, project, or work group. You may tend to question whether it is worth the trouble to look for something new.

You might think, "Maybe I should just stay where I am and cope." When you feel discouraged or excessively fearful, you may not be able to engage in this first stage at all.

If, however, you can mobilize yourself to seek a new job or relationship, there are some predictable variables that influence the decisions you make in this stage. First, it is helpful to examine your attitude toward relationship initiation to see if it fits one of three familiar stereotypes. Often embedded in that attitude is another factor: the tendency to pack invisible baggage that might support or impede your search.

It can be helpful to look at one or more formal personality or work styles inventories. These can provide you with insights into your own preferences and patterns. The models they are based on also give tools to tentatively predict which organizations, departments, or projects might be the best fit for you. Generational differences may be something to consider when deciding with whom to build new work relationships.

Next, like Juanita, you need to draft a shopping list to help clarify what and who you are looking for. Then, you might begin by noticing how you sniff and wag, or start to check out people and situations, seeking ways to best meet your needs. Considering emotional intelligence competencies, both yours and those of the people you might work with, can play a role in your decisions about if and when you want to start a new song.

Finally, you have to consider the perspective that normal is a theoretical concept. The act of reflecting on these factors is a way to stop, analyze your reactions, and decide to sing or not to sing in a more conscious, focused manner.

Explore Three Common Attitudes toward Relationship Initiation

We are, by nature, social animals. In spite of individual differences, everyone seeks certain types of meaningful relationships in their lives. We are engineered so that we can survive alone for days, even weeks or years if needed. Generally, however, that is not how we thrive.

The need for meaningful connection with other human beings is a driving force in our lives. Considerable research documents how newborns who lack sufficient physical and emotional contact often fail to thrive as they grow up. Young children who are isolated by family or economic situations may miss the opportunity to learn the key social cues that others take for granted. As a result, they tend to have trouble developing the capacity for collaboration later in life.

Some people like lots of company and conversation. Others require more quiet, alone time. Even though our appetites for interaction and solitude vary greatly, adults who can form successful relationships report greater self-confidence. Increased productivity and happiness also result from better connections with others. No one gets all of their needs met 100 percent of the time, but some individuals seem to have an innate ability to establish rapport. They know how to promote respect and cooperation with others. The rest of us have to learn how to do this effectively. The good news is that it is a learnable set of skills.

Many people may appear to be quite outgoing but value independence and solitude. For example, I am often considered to be a raging extrovert who seeks out lots of contact with others. My work and life structure provide me with many opportunities for such interactions.

But I relish a fair amount of time alone, during which I can recharge and digest the experiences I have shared with others. Some folks find it difficult if not painful to be alone and seek to have people and noise around them as much as possible. Others, like some of my friends and family members, consider four people in the same room to be a huge crowd. They tend to choose jobs and hobbies that are more solitary.

The bottom line is that we all depend on communication with others, regardless of our preferences for solitude or companionship. The ways that we manage every stage of our relationships are profoundly impacted by early connections with family members and other key adults.

Some people are lucky enough to have grown up in a safe, loving home where cooperation and honesty are learned. Many others have negative patterns imprinted on their young, emerging personalities. Excessive criticism, conflict, or abuse may cause them problems later on, which include challenges such as addictions, aggressive behaviors, and self-esteem issues.

Even when we are raised in the best of circumstances with constructive role models to imitate, the successful care and feeding of relationships in our lives takes both effort and skill. When we have no effective examples to emulate, it is even harder to recognize a positive interaction when we see it or to figure out how to develop one.

Both our innate personality and our life experiences will color the ways we think about our interactions with others, especially during Stage 1 of relationship development. Most people exhibit one of three common attitudes toward the formation of new relationships:

The Adaptive Robot: When you adopt this approach, you don't think much about the quality of your relationships. This attitude resembles the arranged marriages in some cultures: the website said there was an opening, so I applied, got hired, and showed up. When you have this attitude, you rarely reflect on how things are going with the job itself or the team you're working with. You just go to work each day and cope as best you can. Some job seekers are comfortable with this attitude, just as people in some cultures find arranged marriages to be convenient and preferred. However, the risk here is that unless you are extremely tolerant, this coping approach may lead to resentment, frustration, or whining later on.[12]

You may have low expectations or none at all in order to prevent disappointment. You are unlikely to ask others about their needs. You ignore, and hence cannot easily articulate, your own wishes or concerns with current relationships. Perhaps you rely on TV or computer games at home to avoid reflections about your job. You may work long hours or use alcohol or drugs to suppress feelings about how the new relationship is progressing.

This attitude does not prevent you from finding and maintaining a healthy relationship, especially when someone else is pursuing you. As an Adaptive Robot, however, it can be more difficult to initiate Stage 1—deciding whether to sing or not to sing in a new relationship.

During periods of high unemployment, people may temporarily adopt the attitude of the Adaptive Robot in the interests of getting some job—any job—right now to pay their bills. Their behaviors are tied more closely to current economic necessities, rather than to their true core values and needs.

The Chronic Seeker: If you fall into this pattern, you are rarely, if ever, content with your current job, boss, or team for very long. The Chronic Seeker is best described by clichés such as, "The grass is always greener on the other side of the fence," and "I see the glass as half-empty, not half-full."

---

12 Occasional whining is cathartic—even fun at times, but chronic whining is never a good tool for creating relationship harmony, regardless of your attitudes, culture, or other aspects of your personality. Maybe there should be a bumper sticker that says, "Winners don't whine."

Your focus is frequently on the past, causing you to long for the good old days. You tend to feel guilty or resentful about what happened—or failed to happen. Just as often, you may worry about the future, considering what might or might not occur and fearing the worst. A friend of mine calls this "awfulizing."

As a result of this past or future focus, you are likely to be pessimistic. You may often fail to notice any positive events that do take place in the present. If you maintain this view of the world as a Chronic Seeker, you may be forever searching for the better boss, the higher profile team, or the more exciting project. You are convinced that you need to keep "shopping," that the perfect person or situation is just around the corner.[13]

Some people who fit this profile change their jobs or assignments more often than the rest of us change our socks. They may exhaust themselves, as well as the people they encounter. In some ways, the Chronic Seeker is the opposite of the Adaptive Robot. While Seekers are eager and skilled in the first few stages of beginning relationships, they usually are the first to flee in Stage 4, Clashing Chords, when the song hits some sour notes and conflicts need to be addressed.

The Student of Relationships: Those of us who fit this profile are most likely to step back from a given relationship and look at what is or is not working. We watch nonverbal cues. We listen to what is really being said. Tuning in to the possible tensions, we check out our own and others' feelings about the interaction. Here's an example of this attitude: if you have chosen to read this book (versus being commanded to read it by a boss, coach, or relative), there is a good chance you fit into this category.

---

13   The expression, "When the going gets tough, the tough go shopping," is amusing when you're talking about shoes or electronics. It has much different implications for relationship shopping.

When taken to extremes, this type of person comes across as tedious or intrusive.

People give them labels like armchair psychologist or process junkie. However, as long as these behaviors are not overused, they are more likely to help you thrive where Adaptive Robots and Chronic Seekers tend to struggle or just cope. The introspection encourages you to find and maintain healthy relationships while leaving behind the ones that cannot be improved. These behaviors are especially useful in Stage 1 when initiating contact with others.

The Student's approach to relationships takes the most skill. It also takes commitment. It is, unfortunately, not often demonstrated effectively in many workplaces. The more that you engage in this type of reflection without overdoing it, the greater are your chances of success. This applies when singing through all six stages of harmonious relationship development, especially in Stage 1, Auditions.

At the end of this stage, we'll assess which type of attitude you most often adopt.

Unpack the Invisible Baggage

The second factor that impacts the decisions we make in Stage 1 of creating harmony at work is the behavior I call packing invisible baggage. Part of what makes the human species both intriguing and challenging is the well-established existence of our unconscious mind.

In addition to our overt actions with others, there are several subterranean levels of thoughts and emotions that influence our behaviors. Those unconscious layers are operating every moment of every day whether we're asleep or awake. These are linked to our brain's hard wiring, our overall health, and the lessons that we have learned—intentionally and unintentionally—from others.

As a result, we engage in Stage 1 to sort out *if* we should sing and *with whom*. When we do, we are influenced by several types of unconscious luggage. We might not realize that we are dragging these bags around. While they come in many varieties—carry-on bag, 26-incher, hanging bag, duffel, footlocker, with or without wheels—they often fall into one or more of the following categories:

Innate Physical, Intellectual, and Emotional Makeup: From birth, each of us is neurologically engineered to be more

- Calm or anxious,

- Focused or scattered,

- Optimistic or pessimistic,

- Open or resistant to change,

- Introverted or extroverted, and

- Driven more by logic or by values and emotions.

We typically have default settings for these qualities, which represent our preferred ways of responding to people and situations. We may, however, shift our patterns depending on our circumstances—that is, calmer sometimes, more anxious at others. Life experience and changing priorities also play a part in modifying our patterns.

For example, someone might be extremely outgoing by nature, but after experiencing a sudden death in their family or being diagnosed with a serious illness, they might need to withdraw from others while they deal with their own shock, grief, and fear. Once they recover from the trauma, they might return to their more extroverted patterns.

Similarly, consider a person who is often nervous and disorganized. They might rise to the occasion to act strong and calm during a crisis while everyone around them is falling apart. When the crisis has been resolved, they might revert to their previously rattled state of mind, or they might be able to incorporate the new, focused behaviors into their standard repertoire.

Even when we strive to use behaviors that are the opposite of our core personality, these innate traits play a definite, if unconscious, role in all six stages of *Harmony at Work*. They are especially influential in Stage 1. They may cause us to either amplify or tune out the music we are considering as we seek a new relationship.

One of my clients is a successful real estate attorney. When initiating conversations with others, she is articulate, witty, and confident. While it seems that extroversion is her innate preference, she is clearly an introvert who has learned how to excel in an extroverted profession. She once told me, "I've always been an introvert and always will be. At the end of each day, after negotiating with staff and clients, I can hardly wait to go home, withdraw, and not talk to anyone else—even my kids. That's just who I am at my core."

Role Models: Parents and other early caregivers often leave the most indelible marks on our psyches since they structure and control our environment when we are most impressionable. If we are asked to name someone who has had a major impact on our approach to life, a spouse, teacher, or boss might also be on the list, along with other family members.

It is often harder to recognize the people who have indirectly influenced how we function. Sometimes, a single comment or action can have a profound effect that stays with you for the rest of your life.

A friend told me about a beautiful letter her boss wrote her after her brother had died in a plane crash. This correspondence significantly affected how she viewed her brother's death. It also affected how she mourned and how she prepared to return to her job. It has continued to impact how she reaches out to others when they experience losses of their own.

The opposite is also true. I distinctly remember a few one-line comments people made to me after the deaths of some of my family members. Rationally, I knew they were not trying to be nasty, but their words cut me to the quick. For example, when my mom passed away several years after my father's death, three different people each said to me, "Well, I guess you're an orphan now." Each time I heard that comment, I felt like I had been socked in the stomach. These emotional punches taught me a lot about how best to respond to others and what not to say when they are grieving.

Our unintentional role models can make strong negative impressions on us. As a result, we may consciously try to avoid acting like them or being in situations that recall the discomfort they caused us. Ironically, we might keep telling ourselves, "I won't ever be like that boss," "I will never say that to my team," and "I will never treat my customers like I have been treated." However, we often end up mimicking the very behavior patterns that we most despise and want to discontinue.

It is almost as if our role models are whispering in our ears, especially during Stage 1, giving us good and bad suggestions about how to proceed. Robert Dubac wrote and performed the one-man play, *The Male Intellect: An Oxymoron*. While the title sounds like the plot will be full of male bashing, Dubac actually does a brilliant job of making fun of both men and women and how we interact with each other.

In the play, there are six roles. In addition to being his own confused self, Dubac plays five alter egos or role models: the tough military Colonel; the romantic Frenchman, Jean-Michel; the uber-cool Fast Eddie; the passive, idealistic Old Mr. Linger; and Ronnie Cabrezzi, the gangster. Each of these characters is giving him conflicting advice about how to manage his love life. Their suggestions are quite varied and, for the most part, all rather pathological.

In addition to being hilarious caricatures, each is a terrific example of the many twisted advisors we may carry around in our heads. We can get ourselves into a great deal of trouble when we choose our songs and fellow singers based on bad advice from our negative role models. For example, what if one of your cerebral advisors keeps telling you that you're not smart or skilled enough, and that you need to work harder than everyone else? If you believe that message, it might cause you to speak up too often in meetings or become a workaholic.

Regrets, Expectations, and Assumptions: The lower down you go on the food chain, the more likely an organism is to be focused only on the here and now.[14] By contrast, we humans have enormous capacities to look back and look forward. We then draw conclusions that may or may not be helpful. They might not even be tied to reality.

That's the good and the bad news. Sometimes our lives are enriched by our abilities to feel regret, hang onto expectations, or make assumptions. Other times, this capacity just makes us miserable. We may make exaggerated assessments of both ourselves and others. We all know people who frequently say things like this:

- I should never have left my last job. I'll never find a boss as good as Matilda again. (regret)

- I just know this new job I have is going to be my dream job. My boss and I are perfectly compatible, with so many common interests. Even though we've

---

14 We can't be sure, since we can't interview them, but it's a fair guess that spiders don't spend a lot of time or brainpower on guilt about past actions or worry about the future.

only known each other for five days, I can already see many happy years of working together. (expectation)

- I couldn't possibly work on that team. They're all (engineers, social workers, IT geeks, men, women, old codgers, young pups, foreigners, PhDs, uneducated, fill-in-the-blanks), and I just know they'd be impossible to work with. (assumption)

These types of regrets, expectations, and assumptions can sometimes help us decide whether or not to sing in a new relationship. They also have the potential to discourage us from even participating in Stage 1, thus eliminating options that might have been viable.

A specific type of assumption influences our expectations and may be tied to some regrets or fears that we've tucked into our invisible luggage. It's called a self-fulfilling prophecy, and it often packs a wallop. It becomes a dog chasing its own tail. It is a prediction in which the interplay of beliefs and behaviors causes the prophecy to come true, even when the expectation is based on incomplete or wrong data. It works like this:

Self-Fulfilling Prophecy

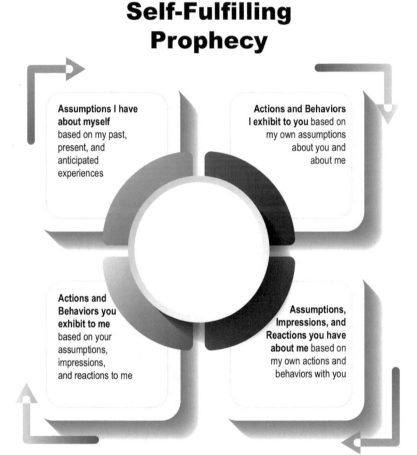

A self-fulfilling prophecy is a prediction in which the interplay of beliefs and behaviors reinforces the expectation, even when it's based on false data.

Self-fulfilling prophecies can be either positive or negative. They can be about me, another individual, or a group. Let's say I'm about to present a report to my colleagues that I've worked on for weeks. One possible scenario would look like this:

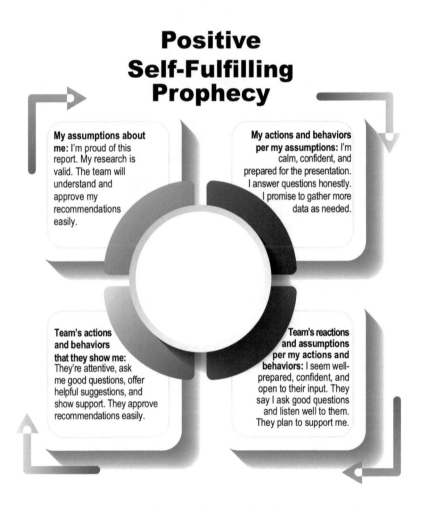

Positive Self-Fulfilling Prophecy

My assumptions about me: I'm proud of this report. My research is valid. The team will understand and approve my recommendations easily.

My actions and behaviors per my assumptions: I'm calm, confident, and prepared for the presentation. I answer questions honestly. I promise to gather more data as needed.

Team's actions and behaviors that they show me: They're attentive, ask me good questions, offer helpful suggestions, and show support. They approve recommendations easily.

Team's reactions and assumptions per my actions and behaviors: I seem well-prepared, confident, and open to their input. They say I ask good questions and listen well to them. They plan to support me.

My positive assumptions and actions about myself or others encourage others to think and act positively toward me, thus supporting my initial positive belief.

But if my initial assumption had been negative, the outcome of the meeting could be quite different.

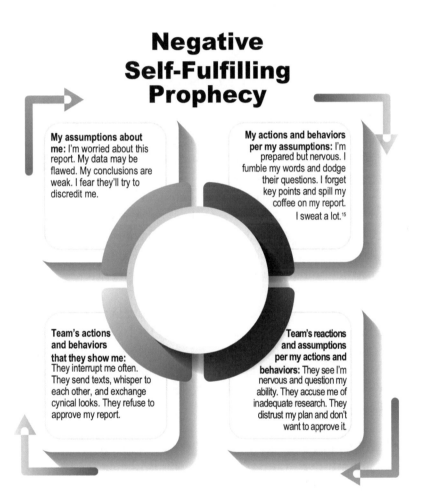

Negative Self-Fulfilling Prophecy

My assumptions about me: I'm worried about this report. My data may be flawed. My conclusions are weak. I fear they'll try to discredit me.

My actions and behaviors per my assumptions: I'm prepared but nervous. I fumble my words and dodge their questions. I forget key points and spill my coffee on my report. I sweat a lot.[15]

Team's actions and behaviors that they show me: They interrupt me often. They send texts, whisper to each other, and exchange cynical looks. They refuse to approve my report.

Team's reactions and assumptions per my actions and behaviors: They see I'm nervous and question my ability. They accuse me of inadequate research. They distrust my plan and don't want to approve it.

My negative assumptions and beliefs about myself or others predispose others to think and act negatively toward me, thus reinforcing my initial negative belief.

Generally, each step in the cycle influences the next. When I get a positive response from the team, as in the first example, it reinforces my initial positive assumptions about myself, my report, and how my colleagues view me. This, in turn, builds confidence and trust, making it easier for me to succeed the next time I have the same task or work with the same people.

Similarly, if I get a negative response from the team, like in the second example, it fortifies the negative assumptions on my part. What results is more relationship disharmony and greater difficulty in my subsequent efforts. Either way, it's a self-fulfilling prophecy that repeats and reinforces itself unless someone consciously interrupts the cycle. I once heard someone say that a self-fulfilling prophecy "perpetuates a reign of error." There can be much terror and disharmony embedded in that error.

Obviously, I don't have total control of the situation in either example. I only have control over the first two parts: my own assumptions and my own behaviors. It is possible that I could have a positive starting assumption and engage in constructive behaviors and still not get the positive reactions that I seek from others.

But behavioral research has documented that the more I can maintain positive expectations and behaviors, the more likely I am to get the desired responses I seek from others. Similarly, the more I expect the worst, the more likely others are to deliver my negative expectations to me, often on a silver platter.

Emotional Scar Tissue: If I have a physical scar on my hand from the bad burn that I got at age twelve, it serves as a reminder of how I got hurt. It also helps me prevent future accidents. In the same way, we all bear emotional scars, even though they may be harder to acknowledge. They result from the challenging experiences we have had in the past. Sometimes that scar tissue strengthens us, giving us new insights and confidence. Other times, it is a barrier that prevents us from noticing or facing what we most need to address in the future.

Consider the young man I know who had just found a new job after being fired from a previous position. He brought all kinds of emotional scar tissue with him. Still angry from what he saw as an unfair critique by his prior boss, he walked into the new company with a defensive attitude. The chip on his shoulder was palpable. He was immediately on guard, ready to find fault. His self-fulfilling prophecy was strong and quite negative.

What a surprise: he found lots of faults. The new company was not much better than the old one and was, in some ways, worse. He saw his new boss as incompetent. The senior managers said they expected quality and valued their employees, but their actions did not support their words. This new hire's scar tissue—the emotional damage from his previous firing—served as a significant barrier to success in his new situation. It caused him to come across as an arrogant know-it-all who was quick to criticize others.

It is often true that the people who are really skilled and successful don't need to tell you—repeatedly—just how skilled and successful they are. They just quietly demonstrate it. People who brag about themselves or criticize others liberally are often telegraphing their lack of confidence in their own skills.

It's certainly possible that his current boss was inept. But his scar tissue kept him from feeling confident. He was unable to listen to others with an open mind. He couldn't be optimistic or build rapport effectively with his new colleagues. Sadly, his tenure was short-lived in his new job.

Collectively, our innate hard wiring, combined with a lifetime of role models, regrets, expectations, and emotional scars, are all packed into our invisible baggage. We drag that luggage with us as we head into Stage 1, making decisions about how and with whom to start new relationships at work. Positive or negative, this hidden gear influences each of the six stages of *Harmony at Work*. Yet, it may have the most potent impact when we're deciding whether or not to sing in the first place.

Understand Personality Types and Work Styles

Most people who have been in the workforce for more than thirty minutes have had their boss administer some type of personality or work styles assessment. This is mostly good news, with a side order of bad news.

The advantage to using these types of inventories at work is that they can give you additional insights into your individual preferences and innate styles. This provides greater awareness of your own behavior patterns, allowing you to analyze what works well for you and what might be a barrier to productivity and healthy relationships.

It also gives you an alternate lens through which to observe the people around you, helping you to understand how their perspectives and strengths may be different from yours. In that way, when they say or do something that is 180 degrees from your own inclinations, you're less likely to take it as a personal affront and more likely to say, "Yes, of course, they come at this issue from the opposite direction than I do." [16]

The downside to these types of evaluations is that people often misuse the data. If a manager or peer does not realize the intent and value of these assessments, they may be tempted to unfairly judge or critique fellow workers. They are likely to pigeonhole people and make unfair assumptions.

---

16 They still might be wrong or drive you crazy. But at least you start out from a more positive position and might even give them the benefit of the doubt—on a good day.

Some resistance to these assessments comes from the reality that none of us is static. We change and grow over time. Our mood or current situation may cause us to act differently from day to day, or even moment to moment. That said, these measures can give us an idea of our innate tendencies and most common patterns. They are a basis for awareness and conversation, not a finite, immutable calculation.

When teams or leaders have not been adequately coached about how to use the information about types and styles, they sometimes do and say outrageous things. I've heard comments like this:

- "Oh, you're an XYZ type. I bet that's why you weren't promoted!"

- "Well, since you're an XYZ type and I'm an ABC type, there's no way we'll ever be able to get along."

- "There are so many ABC types on this team. No wonder we're so dysfunctional!"

I was once hired by a company to train and coach their younger managers in how to create more relationship harmony with customers, peers, and direct reports. This group of leaders had much in common: their average age was thirty; they had MBAs from distinguished grad schools; they were high achievers who accepted the need to work sixty to eighty hours a week; and they often treated their clients with arrogance and condescension.

In addition, 90 percent of them had the exact same profiles on the personality and work styles inventories that we gave them in the training program. As a result, the minority of people who had different profiles felt ostracized. The different perspectives these outliers brought to the workplace were neither understood nor valued. That 10 percent often felt like aliens from another planet. The training and coaching helped them to validate their unique approach to work tasks and relationships as well as to advocate for their own views.

We also sought to help the majority understand that not all of their coworkers or customers saw the world exactly as they did. The dominant group made most of their decisions based on logic and rational standards. They looked down on people who used values, emotions, and relationships as part of their decision-making criteria. This correlates with the Thinking-Feeling dimension on the MBTI described later in this section. *Feel* was practically a dirty word with these managers. So during the weeklong workshop, every time I used *feel* in a sentence, someone would shout out, "Susan used the F-word again!" While this provided some comic relief, it was a perfect example of people carrying weighty biases and assumptions around in their invisible baggage.

That dominant group had to acknowledge that their ways of working and interacting were not the only ways to function in the world. If they wished to create relationship harmony with diverse colleagues and customers, they had to learn to appreciate and communicate with different styles.

When you have a clear grasp of the theory upon which a personality or work styles inventory is based, you can more successfully use the data it provides to strengthen rapport. This, in turn, allows you to make better music with others, which is part of the intent of the assessments.

From the plethora of personality and work styles tools on the market today, two of my favorites are the Myers-Briggs Type Inventory (MBTI) and the Kolbe Indexes. They measure different aspects of the personality that we take to work each day. They are similar in that they can bring valuable insights about ourselves and others when used responsibly. These insights come in handy at each of the six stages of relationship evolution, especially during Stage 1 Auditions.

Myers-Briggs Type Inventory (MBTI)

The MBTI has been around as an inventory since the early 1950s. It is based on research done by the mother-daughter pair, Katherine Briggs and Isabel Briggs Myers. They used the theories of the Swiss psychologist Carl Jung as the basis for observations they had made and recorded about patterns people exhibit relating to their preferences for four types of behaviors:

1. Where people focus and get energy from

2. How people take in information

3. How people make decisions based on the information they take in

4. How people structure or organize their external world

These four categories became the basis for the four dimensions that make up the MBTI assessment. It has been revised and updated numerous times in the last sixty-plus years. It has been translated into twenty-nine foreign languages and has been given to millions of people worldwide. The model seems to work cross-culturally. Many people find that if they retake the test ten or twenty years later, their designated profile type remains the same.

The four dimensions are as follows:

Extrovert—Introvert (E and I): where people focus and get their energy from

Sensing—INtuiting[17] (S and N): how people take in information

---

17 N is used for Intuiting, to distinguish it from the I used to denote the Introvert preference.

Thinking—Feeling (T and F): how people make decisions based on the information they've gathered

Judging—Perceiving (J and P): how people organize their external world, their time, and their priorities

These four dimensions are continuums. No one is all one side or the other—just more of one attribute than its opposite. These preferences indicate what your first inclination often is, where you tend to go first. When you take the MBTI, you get a four-letter code, one for each of the four continuums. This code is one of sixteen possible combinations of the eight different attributes that you would have received based on your responses to the questionnaire.

For example, if you answered more Extroverted items than Introverted items, you'd show an E (vs. an I) preference in your four-letter profile. If you answered more Thinking items than Feeling items, you'd show a T (vs. an F) preference.

Let's say that I am trying to initiate a relationship with you at work. If I know that my preferences map out as an ENFP, or Extrovert, INtuitor, Feeler, and Perceiver[18] and your preferences are ISTJ, or Introvert, Sensor, Thinker, and Judger,[19] then I have some useful information about how we might interact.

- As an **E or Extrovert**, I'm more likely to be comfortable initiating conversation, brainstorming things aloud with others, reacting spontaneously to comments and questions in a meeting, and increasing my own energy based on the ideas and enthusiasm of others.

---

18   As mine do!
19   Some of my closest friends and relatives are ISTJs, polar opposites of me.

- As an **I or Introvert**, you're more likely to hold back, hear what others say first, sort ideas out in your own mind before sharing them, and feel put on the spot if someone asks you, "What do you think?" before you've had time to reflect. You may need time away from the team to recharge your own battery and clarify your ideas.

- As an **N or INtuitor**, I am prone to focus on the big picture, the final result, and future possibilities. I'm more likely to trust my gut or sixth sense when gathering information.

- As an **S or Sensor**, you're more likely to focus on specific details that you can see, hear, feel, touch, and maybe even taste,[20] noticing what's happening right now and what is concrete, measurable data.

- As an **F or Feeler**, I'm more likely to base decisions on personal values, emotions, and how I anticipate a decision might impact a given relationship.

- As a **T or Thinker**, you're more likely to decide something based on objective, rational criteria as well as policies and concrete standards.

- As a **P or Perceiver**, I may prefer flexible formats and time frames. I might be more willing to change approaches midstream and be less bothered by surprises. I could be less disciplined about deadlines and more prone to keep my office messy. It will be important to me to keep my options open regarding plans and strategies. Rigid protocols and premature decisions may make me uncomfortable.

---

20 Hopefully you won't be using your sense of taste if you are making decisions on toner cartridges for your office printer.

- As a **J or Judger**, you'd prefer more structured schedules, procedures, and goals. You're more likely to organize your workspace well and have clear to-do lists to help you check off completed tasks. You're more likely to value closure, for example, to complete one task before starting the next or making a decision and then moving on. Flexible plans, missed deadlines, and ambiguity are more likely to rattle your cage. Work relationships, not to mention marriages, between people with strong preferences in Judging and Perceiving are interesting, to say the least! I believe it is one dimension that is most likely to cause angst and disharmony between people with different profiles.

When people are trained in how to use the MBTI effectively, they also look at the combination of the four specific preferences. Obviously an ENFP (extroverted preference) might present quite differently than an INFP (introverted preference). The relative strength of each preference also influences how each person demonstrates it. For example, a clear preference in Sensing will look and sound different from a slight preference.

In addition, people need to remember that these four preferences are only one aspect of someone's personality. Given attitudes, values, background, and experience, two people with the exact same MBTI profile might demonstrate vastly different behaviors at work or at home. The understanding of our own and others' preferences may increase the harmony between us and reduce the chances of our getting defensive or annoyed when others' reactions differ from our own.

While this is just a brief definition of the four MBTI dimensions, it makes a relevant point. There are so many ways that we act differently from the people around us. If you and I vary significantly in any of these four measures, there are at least two possibilities:

1. We can complement each other, form a strong team, and learn a great deal from each other, at least on a good day, or

2. We can misunderstand each other, criticize each other for not doing things "the right way," namely *my* way, and drive each other nuts on a daily basis. Sadly, this happens more often than not. However, with increased self-awareness, open communication, sometimes coaching, and usually a great deal of patience, people can change the dynamics from conflict to collaboration with their opposites so that they learn from each other and make more harmonious music together.

Kolbe Indexes

Kathy Kolbe's tools, which look at our innate talents, measure how each of us is hardwired to problem solve, make decisions, and complete tasks at work. She began developing her materials in the 1970s based on her work in education. She sought to help kids identify their innate strengths. Kolbe then made the connection between those instincts and how people can be optimally efficient and motivated at work.

While the Kolbe Indexes look at a different part of our personality than the MBTI does, they are equally powerful in allowing people to recognize their own and others' natural, instinctive abilities. This, in turn, helps people seek out for themselves and delegate to others the right types of work situations and duties that leverage everyone's greatest strengths.

When you are working in concert with how your brain is hardwired, you spend less time and effort working against the grain. You can also understand what does and doesn't work well for others. You can leverage your strengths to shore up areas where you may struggle. As a result, you are more likely to increase your energy, productivity, job satisfaction, and ability to create harmony at work.

Kolbe's model is based on three parts of the mind:

1. The *cognitive* part of the mind, related to thinking, that accounts for our intellect, as measured by IQ tests, standardized school achievement tests, and industry-specific skills tests that assess the knowledge we have acquired in particular subject areas;

2. The *affective* part of the mind, related to feeling, that includes our emotions, preferences, values, and interactions with others, as measured by the MBTI and other similar inventories; and

3. The *conative* part of the mind, related to action, that describes our ability to problem solve, make decisions, and get things done. To date, the Kolbe Indexes are the only ones that measure our conative abilities. [Conative comes from an obscure word, *conation*, that means "the area of one's active mentality that has to do with desire, volition, and striving. The related word, *conatus* [koh NAY tus], comes from the Latin verb *conari*, to try." From *1000 Most Challenging Words*.]

The Kolbe A Index is one of many Kolbe tools, but it is the starting point for assessments of conative talents. The Kolbe A has four modes to describe four types of instincts:

- The **Fact Finder** mode measures how we gather, analyze, and share information.

- The **Follow Through** mode measures how we arrange or structure time, data, procedures, and materials.

- The **Quick Start** mode measures how we deal with risk, uncertainty, and change.

- The **Implementer** mode measures how we handle physical space and tangible objects.

One of the important benefits of Kolbe's model is that whether you have a one, a five, or a ten [on a ten-point scale] in each mode, it is considered as one of your strengths. It's just that a one in Fact Finder is a different kind of talent or way of approaching data than a ten is.

When you are going through the Auditions stage of initiating a new relationship at work, think about the value of knowing your own and others' Kolbe profiles. If I know you're a two in Quick Start, and I'm a nine, I can make some educated guesses about how we might complement each other and how we might annoy each other. If we both know the Kolbe model and can discuss our differences and similarities openly, we have a much better chance of jumping into the new relationship with more confidence and getting that song started out in the right key.

The Kolbe materials have a wide range of applications. Besides increasing your own self-awareness of how you're hardwired and can best use your instinctive talents, they impact your relationships in a number of ways. They can be used for

- Helping to screen final applicants in a hiring process,

- Improving team collaboration and understanding of team dynamics,

- Strengthening communication between a supervisor and his or her direct reports,

- Performance appraisal and improvement, and

- Career counseling and succession planning.

Both the MBTI and Kolbe Indexes are examples of how you can use formalized personality and work style inventories to understand yourself better and anticipate how you might react in certain work situations with various types of people and work duties.

These are just two of many personality assessments on the market. During the Auditions stage of relationship development, this is especially useful information to help with your decisions about whether or not you want to sing a particular song in a new context with other singers.

Obviously, you may know only your own profile on any assessment. That self-awareness, plus the understanding of the model that the assessment is based on, may help you make educated guesses about the styles and approaches of others you hope to work with. That insight may then help you decide how best to interact with those potential colleagues.

Acknowledge Generational and Cultural Differences

There have always been variations of perspectives and priorities from one generation to the next. Since the 1960s, however, the term *generation gap* has become popular in Western cultures. This gap is tied to the increasingly rapid rates of change in technology, communication, and lifestyles during the last fifty to seventy-five years. There has also been extensive research on the impacts of each person's generation on their behaviors and values.

While various monikers and dates have been used, the generational groups from the last hundred years are often labeled as follows:

- The Greatest or GI Generation (born 1901–1924)

- The Silent or Traditional Generation (born 1925–1945)

- The Baby Boomers (born 1946–1964)

- Generation X (born 1965–1980)

- Generation Y or Millennials (born 1981–1995)

- Generation Z (born 1996–2009)

- Generation Alpha (born 2010–2025)

In addition to significant differences in their views on marriage, family, sexuality, money, recreation, and music, people in each of these generational groups bring widely varied perspectives to the workplace regarding ethics, communication, loyalty, work hours, technology, and authority.

When you are in the Auditions stage of relationship development, your own generational influences and those of the people you consider working with are yet another element in the music you might potentially create together.

People in similar age groups sometimes have an easier time establishing rapport and communicating well. They also may miss out on a wider range of experiences because of their uniformity. Conversely, relationships among people with different generational blueprints might need more time and effort to establish trust and collaboration. If you are willing and able to communicate your diverse views to each other, you may be able to create more harmony at work by leveraging the benefits of your unique approaches. By recognizing the impacts of these generational factors, you can use yet another lens through which to view any given situation, make better decisions, and hopefully make better music.

A parallel type of cultural lens is based not on when you grew up but where and how. Consider a team made up of two people from New York City: one is a person of color who grew up in Harlem, while the other is White and grew up in a wealthy New York suburb. Now add to the team someone who moved to the US from the former Soviet Union when he was thirty, someone who grew up in a small rural town in Mississippi, and someone whose family worked in an auto plant in Detroit.

Each of these team members brings a whole set of cultural experiences, values, and biases that will influence the ways that they approach work tasks and relationship harmony. Again, there is the possibility, with strong, insightful leadership, that their varied backgrounds will enrich the team and add to the texture of the relational music among them. Similarly, it may be difficult, if not impossible, for these coworkers to build trust and cooperation without good communication and overt efforts to bridge their differences.

While generational, ethnic, socioeconomic, and cultural factors have an impact in all six stages of relationship evolution, these factors play an extremely important role during Auditions when you are deciding if you want to join the choir or not.

Draft Your Shopping List

Drafting your shopping list is another behavior that influences the initiation of Stage 1. If you decide, "That's it—I've had it with this job/boss/department/company/project—it's time to move on," it is helpful to start by creating what resembles a list for the grocery store. Try to identify the types of people, characteristics, and situations that you are looking for. In other words, you are deciding what kind of song you want to sing. You also consider with whom you are willing to sing. This is an important aspect of Stage 1 when determining if you will seek a new relationship of any type.

Once you say that you're in the market for a new relationship, you need to sort out what you most want and need to find in order to identify your wish list of preferred qualities. Then you might make note of what you expect you're most likely to find. It may be helpful to articulate what you may be worried about or afraid of in your search.

Finally, you should identify the nonnegotiable conditions that have to be there for you to proceed, as well as deal breakers or conditions you are not willing to put up with at all.

One example of this kind of shopping list was for a young man who was moving from a retail sales job to starting his own business with pianos. He had small children, didn't like dressing up, and being an introvert, he got tired of talking to lots of strangers every day. So when he decided to leave sales, his list included

- No evenings and weekends, so he could spend time with his kids,

- No requirement to wear a tie, and

- The chance to work alone or mostly talk with individuals he knew.

Another aspect of this sorting process is to ask

- How might my prior work experiences help or hinder my efforts now?

- Where should I look, how should I research options, and whom should I approach first?

- How might my personal preferences, skills, and styles color and shape the music I hope to create in a new position?

Some people do this list-making very consciously, as if they were filling out a survey or registering for wedding gifts.[21] Often, however, this list is formed intuitively in their heads

---

21 Some couples find making the decisions for a wedding registry to be harder than deciding what job to apply for. If they can't agree on towels and kitchen utensils, this could be a bad sign for their upcoming marriage.

and hearts, where it serves as a subliminal assessment tool to use when they encounter new people and opportunities.

Still others never get clear about their minimum requirements and needs. As a result, they are more likely to bounce from one job or project to the next, acting surprised and confused when they haven't met their goals. If you know what you are looking for, with or without a formal list, you're more likely to have a successful search. It's the interpersonal equivalent of using a map or GPS: the list clarifies where you want to end up and how best to get there. It's just like the list Alex suggested to Juanita during their lunch together.

A person who fails to identify their expectations is like a composer who thinks up a new melody, never writes it down, and then gets frustrated that it can't be recalled or developed. This shopping list type of prioritization can be quite easy for some people and extremely overwhelming for others. When people stall out with this step, they usually need assistance from a neutral third party like a manager, external coach, or employment counselor. That person can help them clarify their needs and wants—a crucial element of Stage 1.

Appreciative Inquiry

When determining how to proceed in Stage 1, it's helpful to look through a forward-thinking lens as much as possible. David Cooperrider developed a revolutionary approach to change and innovation called Appreciative Inquiry. It focuses on strengths and possibilities more than problems and repairs. This methodology helps you leverage your prior successes to address current frustrations and challenges.

One of the Appreciative Inquiry techniques is to

- Identify an earlier time when you were in a positive relationship or role, articulate what was happening at the time and what made it rewarding for you,

- Consider what an ideal new scenario would be like for you and your colleagues, and

- Articulate what advantages might occur for you and others if you were able to achieve, or at least approach that ideal, and what steps you would need to take to get there.

The mindset created with Appreciative Inquiry tools is helpful during Stage 1 when deciding if you want to sing and with whom.

Sniffing and Wagging

Of all the common behaviors that influence Stage 1 decisions, sniffing & wagging is one of the most interesting. I once had a boss who used this none-too-elegant metaphor to describe what people often do in the early stages of a relationship. In some ways, we resemble dogs that meet at the park.[22]

We humans, however, tend to have subtler methods for checking out potential employers or job opportunities. Much of the sniffing involves reading nonverbal cues. Sometimes we engage in casual small talk to get an initial read on the other person. In this way, we begin to size them up vis-à-vis our own shopping list and previous experiences.

Our sniffing then influences any subsequent wagging. It can often be the smallest detail that either piques our interest

---

22 Please remember that this is just a metaphor: I'm not suggesting that you literally imitate how dogs sniff and wag around each other at the park! As one of my clients said, it's good that humans have evolved to shaking hands.

or sends us running in the opposite direction. It might be that the person reminds us of a relative, a prior love, or a former boss—any of which could be a huge plus or a minus. Their weird way of talking or an overbearing personality might bother us. They might wear clothes or a hairstyle that are either a giant draw or a major turnoff. This holds true whether we're looking for a job, an insurance agent, or a new love interest. Regardless of the context, this is an important aspect of Stage 1, as we decide if, how, and with whom we wish to make music.

A colleague once scheduled an interview for me with one of his business partners. They ran a consulting firm and were looking for some additional contractors. My friend and I had a cordial lunch with his partner, John, during which John read over my résumé and asked me predictable questions about my experience. We seemed to establish a good rapport, and John promised to call me in a week to let me know if I could work with them.

After John avoided my calls for two weeks, I finally reached him and learned that I would not be hired after all. When I asked why, his only response was, "I don't know. I just didn't feel the right chemistry with you!"

I told one of my employees about his response, and she said rather angrily, "What's WRONG with him? He was interviewing you for a JOB, not a DATE!"

Unfortunately, I'll never know what I did or said that didn't work for him. It may, in fact, have been some subtle nonverbal cue or association that turned him off when he was sniffing and wagging around me. As arbitrary as it seemed at the time, it's a powerful and often unconscious element of Stage 1.

By contrast, some people are so desperate for new connections that they will sniff for two nanoseconds, wag enthusiastically, and quickly accept the first job they are offered. This may be an indication of low self-esteem or fear.

The relationship seeker thinks, "They've shown a little interest in me; I guess I'll find a way to like them as well. I might not get any other offers. I better take this one."

Others have such a long stringent list of requirements that they sniff and wag incessantly. They eliminate one prospect after another, wondering why they are still not employed or promoted. These people tend to appear to others as being overly perfectionistic and critical, acting as if nobody is good enough for them.

There are people who find job hunting, sales calls, and interviews to be wonderful entertainment. Still others would rather have a root canal without novocaine than go through what they consider to be this extreme form of torture. However, when we want to start a new relationship, this stage of checking others out must happen to some degree, even when someone else initiates the contact and seeks us out.

In addition, there are now many ways to research people and their backgrounds online. Someone's electronic profiles and accounts can either be immensely helpful or damaging. Sometimes people don't realize that photos and posts of them at a bar or on a beach may not be positive motivators to make others want to sing with them at work. The more consciously and clearly we can sort out our ideals, our perceptions of reality, and our must-haves and limits, the more likely we are to succeed in Stage 1 and start the song off harmoniously.

Emotional Intelligence

One of the factors that influences your ability to sniff and wag effectively is your level of emotional intelligence. Your EQ or Emotional Intelligence Quotient represents how adept you are at noticing and responding appropriately to emotions—both your own and the emotional reactions of others.

While there are many EQ materials on the market today, I consider the Genos Emotional Intelligence materials, developed by Benjamin Palmer and Associates, to be the most useful in the workplace. After reviewing some of the other EQ models that had been published, Dr. Palmer identified specific behavioral skills that showed up consistently in the EQ literature. He then designed an assessment based on the following six skills:

1. Emotional self-awareness

2. Emotional awareness of others

3. Authenticity

4. Emotional reasoning

5. Emotional self-management

6. Inspiring performance

One of the advantages of Genos's behaviorally based model is the focus on how to increase your EQ. If you can acknowledge which skills you demonstrate at work with some frequency and effectiveness, then you can strategize how to use those strengths to shore up the skills that you need to strengthen.

Another benefit of the Genos inventory is the opportunity to get a 360 assessment from your colleagues. Their 360 feedback tools allow the people around you in all directions—your boss, peers, direct reports, and sometimes others such as customers and vendors—to give you anonymous feedback. As a result, you can compare not only ratings among the various people giving you feedback, but also contrast your own self-perception with the degree to which others see you using these six emotional intelligence skills at work.

In a perfect world, the way I see myself matches how others perceive me. It's so reassuring (albeit rare) when this occurs. In the real world, we often judge ourselves either more harshly or give ourselves more credit than others do. When this happens, our self-assessment varies greatly from the perceptions of others.

If you want to raise your EQ and hence increase your ability to create harmony at work, you have to do a great deal of difficult soul searching and goal setting and practice new responses. This may be way less fun than having everyone's assessments align, but in the long run, you're much better off knowing where you stand. That way, you can think about what you are able and willing to change.

Emotional intelligence plays a role in every phase of relationship development. While its impact might be louder in some of the later stages, it is another factor to consider when you contemplate auditions, deciding if you want to sing and with whom.

Checking Out the Team

Sometimes, when you are being considered for a new job, a promotion, or inclusion on a project team, you meet with the entire team or department. These interviews can be one-on-one or talking with the whole group at once.

One advantage to these group meetings is your opportunity to interact with several of your potential peers, not just with the leader. You can observe how similar they are to each other and to you. You may also notice significant differences among the team members, as well has how they may differ from you. In addition, it is an opportunity to notice their group dynamics:

- How do they interact with each other?

- Are there unofficial or informal leaders who dominate or influence others in the group?

- Is there any apparent tension between team members? If so, are there indications of the source of those existing conflicts?

- How do they feel, individually and collectively, about adding you into their team?

An advantage for the team leader is their ability to get a read on how the team members react to you. Often, after a group interview like this, the leader will solicit feedback about each candidate from the group. If the group is unanimously in favor of Person X, that helps with the onboarding and integration of that new team member.

The downsides of involving the whole team in the Auditions stage include

- The possibility of disagreement, where some team members like Person X and others can't stand X and lobby hard for Person Y;

- The risk that the whole team rallies behind Person X, but the leader prefers Person Y, dislikes X, or knows some reason that X can't be hired (background checks, drug tests, bad references); this leads to disappointment or resentment when Y gets hired; or

- If team members are resistant to the inclusion of anyone new for a variety of reasons, they could be confrontational during the interviews and hostile when the new person is hired.

Savvy leaders make a judgment call about the pros and cons of having team input into the hiring or promotion decision. Observant candidates can learn a lot about their future peers when team interviews are part of the Auditions.

Normal Is a Theoretical Concept

Finally, we must realize as we make decisions in Stage 1 that normal is a theoretical concept. This phrase, in fact, has become a personal joke between one of my sons and me. Whenever we hear someone try to assert that a certain behavior is normal, whereas other options are not, we both smile. It is true that statisticians can mathematically define the mean, median, and mode of a group of numbers. Many scientists will then proceed to identify what is associated with these measures as normal, given its numerical significance.

Fortunately, human behavior does not fall into such neat and tidy categories. Life would be very boring if it did. As Paul Simon suggests in the song, "One Man's Ceiling Is Another Man's Floor," what seems like the floor or the bottom of the barrel to one person might be the ceiling or best possible situation to someone else. The cliché "One person's trash is another's treasure" gives the same message.

At Google, employees are encouraged to dress in jeans and play games during work hours if they wish, to promote creativity and commitment. In other companies, this would be grounds for discipline or firing. In some cultures, it is normal to give every person a kiss on both cheeks when you enter a room; in other places, this would seem bizarre and inappropriate at best, if not considered sexual harassment.

Webster defines *normal* as "conforming to a standard or common type; usual, regular, natural; approximately average in any psychological trait such as intelligence, personality or emotional adjustment; free from mental disorder, sane."[23] When applied to interpersonal contact, normal really means what we're familiar or comfortable with.

---

23 I once bought a T-shirt that had a funny cartoon of a guy hanging upside down, and it said, "Normal is boring." I wish I had bought one for every member of my family.

When people are asked why they stay in abusive jobs or marriages, they often say, "I'm used to it. At least I know what to expect. Doesn't everyone act this way?" It is either the only reality they know, or they believe it is the best option available. Normal is also a relative measurement: what seems natural and appealing to me at one point in my life might seem strange and off-key at another time.[24]

The subjective, variable nature of the concept of normal makes Stage 1 of *Harmony at Work* even trickier. Except for certain legal boundaries and company policies, there is no universal template or rulebook that applies to all situations and tells you:

- "All job interviews should include—"

- "All bosses need to —"

- "All employees will —"

- "Anyone who is married is required to —"

- "Any friend you have known and liked for more than a week must —"

Once we get past the laws, policies, and contracts that address basic rights, we are singing improvisationally, without many formulas or background supports, trying to decide what is normal and sounds good for each of our own musical compositions.

Sometimes, that sorting out process is fun. It can be exciting and lyrical. Much of the time, however, it is just plain annoying and confusing. It can, on occasion, create scary, harsh sounds as well. That is part of the challenge as we search for a new job, new team, or new friendship. We must sort out what we want and need, what we will settle for, and what is normal for us in each situation.

---

24 As a kid, I thought that a Hostess Twinkie was one of the best desserts on earth. Now, the idea of actually eating one makes me gag.

To Sing or Not to Sing

Many of us struggle to figure out what is normal or how things are supposed to be with the other people in our lives. We may be searching for something without clear definitions or parameters. Especially in the absence of positive role models and healthy experiences, our efforts to find normal relationships are a bit like describing chocolate to someone who has never tasted it.[25]

The longer I observe relationships, the more I'm convinced that normal is definitely a theoretical concept, an arbitrary point on a statistical bell curve. What is status quo for me might trigger a heart attack for you. What is typical and comfortable for you might put the next person to sleep. And what is an acceptable scenario for me today might be totally inappropriate for me next week or next year.

Our assessments of our relationships are relative and based on a range of variables. The tunes and tempos are always shifting. This is part of what makes the music of relationships both interesting and challenging.

Two friends of mine moved to a large US city to start new jobs. Their normal routine involved getting up at 4:30 a.m. each weekday, getting dressed, fixing breakfast, and packing lunches for themselves and their two young sons. Then they woke the boys at 5:30 a.m., got everyone dressed, fed, and out the door by 6:00. They arrived at day care by 6:30 and made their separate commutes to work by 8:00. The return trip included picking the kids up by 6:00 p.m., having dinner by 6:30, baths and jammies for the boys by 7:00.

They would put the kids to bed by 7:30, fall into bed themselves at 8:30 or 9:00, and start all over again the next day. Many of us would consider this abnormal and abusive. We would agree to such a lifestyle only if we had to. For

---

25 Which, as a confirmed chocoholic, I would find extremely sad indeed.

this family, it became their concept of normal for several years, because it was what they had to do to survive. They were, however, ecstatic when they could move back to their hometown with more manageable work schedules and close-in childcare. Sometimes you don't realize how badly your head hurts till you have the opportunity to stop bashing it against a brick wall.

Similarly, some couples manage commuter marriages in which one or both travel for work four to five days every week. Then they commute home on Friday, do laundry, get reacquainted over the weekend, repack their suitcase Sunday night, and begin again on Monday. If they get used to this arrangement, it becomes the norm and may even be comfortable. For other couples, it would bring an end to their relationship song.

The good news is that regardless of how we negotiate the human interactions in our lives, some patterns can help us muddle through the music. If I get along well with my boss, but can't finish a calm sentence with my spouse, there might be something in the work relationship that I could bring home to help me communicate better in my personal life. If I know how to mediate conflicts between my children, how can I transfer those skills to bickering staff members on my team at work? If I keep having the same kinds of problems with every boss I work for, what can I learn from the repeating patterns that can help me try out new behaviors and seek different types of work relationships?

Some people say that life is a journey, not a destination. If we choose to, we can view it as a fascinating trip whose itinerary holds many surprises, joys, disappointments, and lots of interesting music. Other people compare life to a series of classes we attend that provide us with opportunities to grow and change.

Sometimes, I say to myself, "I don't remember signing up for this class to learn about anger or patience. In fact, I thought I already took that course to learn how to stay calm under fire. Actually, I thought I got a passing grade. Why do I have to take it again?"

Life rarely follows a logical trajectory like a school curriculum. If it did, it would be easier, but we might be bored out of our minds.

Final Notes

The journey of our lives offers us all of these lessons, sometimes in the form of multiple refrains. The next five stages will provide you with guidance and support on that journey.

If you choose to accept the challenge, you can be enthusiastic observers of yourself and other people. If you pay attention, ask questions, take risks, and reach out to others, there's a boatload of information you can learn. If you aren't careful, you might even get better at creating relationship harmony with others. If you aren't careful, you might even be happy and satisfied, at least some of the time. If you aren't careful, you might even have fun making beautiful music with others. Look out—let's start the music!

Rehearsals:

Application Exercises for Auditions

Choose one of these exercises to help you apply the Stage 1 information to your current experience. Then decide if it would be helpful to try a second type of rehearsal.

1. **Identify your dominant attitude.** Consider the three common attitudes that people tend to adopt when considering the start of a new relationship—Adaptive Robot (who accepts what's available and doesn't worry much about the fit or quality of the new role), Chronic Seeker (who is rarely content and always looking for something better), or the Student of Relationships (who is prone to observe and analyze what does and doesn't work, sometimes constructively and other times obsessively).

    -   Which one is most like you?

    -   What do you tend to do, say, think, and feel most often as a result of being more of a Robot, Seeker, or Student?

    -   Jot down your thoughts about the impact of those behaviors and expectations on your prior success record in managing harmony at work, especially in the Auditions stage.

    -   Finally, make note of some possible benefits and downsides for you if you could consciously adopt one of the other two attitudes in an effort to create more harmony at work when faced with potential new relationships.

2. **Inventory your invisible baggage.** Think about both the positive and negative aspects of any unconscious luggage you may be schlepping around as you consider new work relationships.

- Make a list of

    ◦ Relevant qualities in your physical, intellectual, and emotional makeup, and how you view each one,

    ◦ Role models—both positive and negative—who have influenced how you look at potential bosses, coworkers, family members, mates, and other friends,

    ◦ Any fears, regrets, expectations, and assumptions that are tied to new relationship formation, and

    ◦ Emotional scar tissue you may have that is linked to prior Stage 1 efforts.

- Review the list you have just drafted and put a plus sign by any items that you think are positive and help you form better relationships, and a minus sign by any that might be detrimental or limiting for you. Put an asterisk by the ones that you think have the loudest and most significant influence on your upcoming auditions.

- Make notes of the specific impacts that the positive and negative items in this list might have on your current and future efforts in Stage 1, as you consider when and with whom you want to sing.

- Consider what benefits you might reap if you could discard any of the negative baggage just listed, even if you could only put it in a figurative storage locker for a short while. What, if anything, could you do to repack and better utilize the positive items? What would need to happen for you to lighten your luggage and discard some of the negatives in the interests of making better music with others?

3. **Consider taking personality inventories to learn more about yourself.** Psychological tools like the MBTI and Kolbe Indexes are excellent resources to give you more insight into how you move through the world and make music with others. They do not measure your how smart you are or what skills and experience you have gathered.[26]

Emotional intelligence (EI) inventories also provide useful feedback that directly applies to Auditions and the five stages that follow it. For more information about the MBTI, Kolbe, or Genos Emotional Intelligence tool, check our website at HarmonyAtWorkTheBook.com.

People have found these inventories helpful in deciding if they want to sing or not participate in the auditions:

- DISC (everythingdisc.com)

- Enneagram (tallonconsultinggroup.com or enneagraminstitute.com [RHETI test])

- Emergenetics (emergenetics.com)

---

26   They also don't show if you're crazy or if you're a nice person. Mental illness is measured by other tools with a licensed psychologist or psychiatrist. Niceness is too subjective and variable to be squished into a psychometric measurement. You can measure niceness by paying attention to how people respond to you or by assessing what impact you have on others. If people don't give you direct feedback, you have to pay attention to nonverbal and other more subtle cues.

- Herrmann Brain Dominance Instrument (thinkherrmann.com)

- PDP ProScan Survey (pdpglobal.com)

- Hogan (hoganassessments.com)

What is most important about any inventory that you choose is to have a licensed, experienced practitioner set up the tool(s) for you, and then work with you to explain the results. In that way, you can talk about how to apply the data to your current situation and goals. You may miss the real value of these resources if you just take an abridged knock-off version in a magazine or online.

4. **Review books and articles about generational and cultural differences.** Morris Massey did original writing and training about generational differences in the 1970s. Read some of what has been written on this topic since then. Consider the generation in which you grew up and the influences at play during your formative years. Find out what you can about the ages of the people with whom you are considering the formation of a work relationship.[27] If they are close to your age, consider how your common generational influences might support or impede harmony at work among you.

If the others are significantly older or younger than you are, think about what generational gaps might exist.

- As a result of those gaps, how might your work values, perspectives, and styles differ?

---

27 However, it's considered improper at least and, in some circumstances, illegal to directly ask a person's age in an interview situation, due to EEOC concerns about protected classes and age discrimination potential. My grandmother would have just considered it rude.

- How might those possible differences enrich your relationships or make them more challenging, should you decide in this audition stage that you do, in fact, want to join the choir and sing with them?

Also find out what you can about the cultural backgrounds of the people you are considering working with. Think about how similar or different they are from you. Check in with your own experiences of working in heterogeneous environments.

- What, if any, overt or implicit biases might you have that you would have to work through or let go of?

- Are there any biases or assumptions they might make about you and your background that would add to or detract from the potential music you could create together? If so, how can you respond to those without being defensive or critical?

Again, be careful in interview situations when asking about race, religion, and culture to avoid appearing to discriminate, per EEOC guidelines.

One caveat here: broad generalizations about any group of people are easy, tempting, and sometimes entertaining to make. That said, not all [millennials, baby boomers, people from X country, X religious group, people with a college degree in X, fill in any group name] are created equal. In seminars and coaching conversations, I often hear people say things like, "Of course he's lazy and comes to work late—he's a millennial" or "Of course she's rigid and stupid about technology, she's a boomer who was born before computers were everywhere."

Be careful that you don't make assumptions about people or blame their behavior based on when they were born, where they were born, or the culture in which they were raised.

5. **Make sniff and wag observations.** Think about the last time you participated in any of the following activities. For each one, make note of as many sniffing and wagging examples as you can think of. They may be behaviors that you have used yourself or have noticed in others. If you have not participated in one or more of these activities recently, jot down what you expect people would do if you were to find yourself in that situation. One example is given for each situation.

   Job fair: Company representative nearly tackling anyone whose eyes glance toward their company's booth; talks loudly, nonstop, leaves adrenaline stains on your shirt; is clearly too enthused, too insecure, too bored, and/or too caffeinated.

   Singles bar: Both men and women dressed suggestively and/or with the latest styles; lots of posturing, bragging, clichéd pickup lines; either very intense eye contact with the person they're talking to or limited eye contact, looking past the person they're talking with for other opportunities in the room.

   Job interview: Candidate fidgeting nervously with pen, button, or hair; avoiding eye contact with the interviewer; searching for answers to questions; not posing any questions to the interviewer; apologizing for mistakes; discounting past accomplishments in other jobs; perspiring heavily in a cool room (or the same behaviors from the interviewer).

   Cocktail party or open house (where most people don't know each other): Lots of visual scanning of the crowd, sizing up who would be good to approach and talk to; often in the corner or at the bar, avoiding conversation; making awkward or inappropriate comments when actually talking to others; either mumbling or dominating the conversation about boring, arcane topics.

New employee orientation: Some people looking like second graders on the first day of school—well coiffed, sitting up straight, asking lots of questions, while others hang back shyly, only speaking when spoken to; some people talking a lot, seeming to show off their knowledge, experience, or finesse, possibly interrupting others; some whispering, texting, or passing notes to people near them, seeming to evaluate others in the room.

6. **Examine past beginnings.** Think of two kinds of Stage 1 experiences that you have had in the past, one of which was easy and successful, and one that was stressful or unproductive.

   • First consider a time when you effectively began the search for a new professional relationship (Situation A). Jot down when, who, and what you were looking for. Then identify at least three attitudes, actions, or other factors that helped you successfully decide what you wanted to sing, where, and with whom.

   • Now record the main details of the other Stage 1 time (Situation B) that you considered to be at least difficult, if not a total failure. Make a list of what you were thinking, feeling, saying, doing, and not doing that might have kept you from effectively deciding whether to sing or not. What were the barriers? What, if anything, did you do well, in spite of the ultimate difficulties?

   • Finally, ask yourself if any of the attitudes, skills, and approaches you used in the successful Situation A would have helped you in Situation B. If you could rewrite the music and conduct it differently now, jot down what you would have to do to make Situation B sound better and evolve even a little more harmoniously. How could you have made it more enjoyable to sing through Situation B like it was in Situation A?

7. **Develop an Appreciative Inquiry attitude.** Think about a time when you were excited, challenged, and energized in a job. You felt like you were at your best and loved the high-quality work you were engaged in. Ask yourself these questions and make some brief notes:

   - What was happening in that role, and why was it a peak experience for you? Identify some of the mindsets and behaviors that you and others displayed that helped to create your success and satisfaction.

   - Imagine what would be the best possible outcome if you accept this new job or position that you're contemplating. Describe what might be happening and how you would be feeling one year from now if you and your colleagues were thriving and creating great harmony at work.

   - Consider how it might benefit you and others to achieve this ideal vision of your potential new work relationship, and what kinds of things you would have to do to make it happen.

8. **Draft your shopping list.** Reflect on the type of relationship you may be ready to pursue at work. Be as specific as possible.

   - First make a list of two to four characteristics you would most like this new relationship to have, if it were with the ideal boss, team member, company, customer, or vendor, for example.

- Next jot down one to three qualities that you know you will not tolerate in this person or the relationship overall, in other words, your nonnegotiable deal breakers.

- Now make note of two to three bottom-line considerations for this new relationship that you must have in order to proceed, or your minimally acceptable limits.

- Finally, record what you think you're likely to find in this search for a new job, new staff, new client, and where you are most likely to find the right people and situations—that is, what is likely to be available where you plan to shop.

The following example might apply when you consider looking for a new job with a compatible boss:

- *Ideal boss*: Direct and honest; supportive and encouraging; interested in challenging me and promoting professional growth; sense of humor—especially in times of stress; willing to admit own faults.

- *Deal breakers*: Talks nonstop during the interview (and doesn't listen); avoids direct answers to my questions during the interview; shows disinterest or lack of focus by taking phone calls or answering emails and texts during the interview.

- *Minimally acceptable limits*: Shows interest in my skills and background; describes the position and related staff as interesting and relevant to me and my goals; sees potential for me to make a difference in this role.

- ***What I'm most likely to encounter***: High-level managers who often don't return calls and emails from job candidates; first interview probably with HR person or recruiter; have to find a way to make my application stand out in the stack of 100 résumés; need to leverage social networking tools and call friends or colleagues in professional associations for leads and referrals.

Stage 2

First Notes: Starting the Song with Gusto

Alex calls Juanita to see how her job search is going.

"Hey, Juanita, I heard that you've started to look for a new job. How's the hunt going?"

"Well, I did issue myself a hunting license, but I haven't exactly bagged the perfect job yet. I was encouraged by what you, Sally, and Omar suggested when we got together for lasagna. I have a good shopping list of must-haves and deal breakers. I'm polishing my sales pitch that covers what I want to convey in an interview. I'm pretty psyched about finding a better company and a moderately sane boss."

"Good start. How many applications have you filled out, and how many interviews have you had so far?"

"I've submitted ten applications in the last few weeks that have yielded one virtual interview and one in person. That's the good news. But I feel like I'm not doing well in those meetings. I'm so excited that I get nervous. I tend to stammer and forget what I want to say. When I was asked a few tough questions, my mind went blank. I don't even remember how I responded. But I'm pretty sure it wasn't good. I haven't heard back from either interviewer."

Alex sighs. "Looking for a new job can be a real roller coaster. Sometimes you're pumped, and other times you're either frozen in fear or totally discouraged."

Juanita jumps in. "Exactly! Any suggestions of how to get off that ride into a smoother vehicle?"

"You need to plan and practice. Anticipate what they might ask and consider how you want to respond. After checking the company's website and social media, prepare a few juicy opening questions that you can ask them. And mostly stay alert and in the moment. Stop going up into your head to critique your own performance. Focus intently on what they're saying, how they're saying it, and any other vibes or nonverbal cues that you notice—"

"But, Alex," Juanita interrupts again. "What about when they throw me a curveball question, or I say something stupid?"

"If they catch you off guard, or you screw up, rehearse a few key phrases that will help you recover and regroup. I can help you do a trial run if you want."

"Alex, you're the best! That'd be great. I'll call you next week when I'm ready. Thanks a bazillion!"

You Never Get a Second Chance to Make a First Impression

You've probably heard that expression. Different researchers claim it takes between seven and sixty seconds for people to form an initial impression of you when they meet you. One study suggests that we make that first impression in a tenth of a second—before we have time to shake hands or say hello. Empirical evidence suggests that it is both rare and difficult to change the first impression people have of us without a great deal of compelling evidence.

So once you've decided to look for a new song to sing, it helps to anticipate those situations in which you'll meet key people for the first time. These include interviews with recruiters, human resource staff, or the actual hiring manager. It may also apply to networking events, job fairs, or other settings in which you'll interact with people who can help you get your foot in the door. Like Juanita, you need to prepare for those encounters, craft questions you want to pose to them, and anticipate inquiries they'll make of you. Find someone like Alex to practice with, or practice by recording yourself on your phone or looking in the mirror. The more you plan and rehearse, the more confident you'll feel, and the better your first impression is likely to be.

Alex's other advice is also crucial: concentrate on what the other person says and does. Anytime you're in a high-stress environment where your actions and results matter, it's human nature to focus more on self-critique and analysis of your performance than on the actual conversation.

In general, we *speak and hear* about 125 words per minute. We *think* an average of 500 words per minute—maybe 350 if we're tired or 750 if we're overly caffeinated. So as we listen to someone's 125 words per minute coming into our brains, we have lots of room in what I call the "back forty acres" for distracting or critical thoughts. People with anxiety about public speaking struggle with this pattern frequently.

The Back Forty

Thoughts average 500 wpm

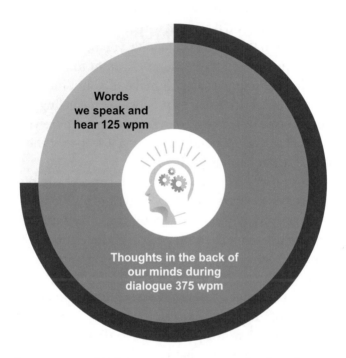

Words we speak and hear 125 wpm

Thoughts in the back of our minds during dialogue 375 wpm

Because we can think four times faster than we speak or hear, there is room in the "back forty" of our brain for many random thoughts. They may be not only disconnected from the conversation in the front of the brain, but may also reduce one's attention to the main conversation.

In that back forty, you may have thoughts like this:

- "I wonder if I turned off the coffee pot before I left home this morning."

- "I hope this is over soon and that I can find the bathroom nearby."

- "Darn, I wish I hadn't made that stupid response to what he said. He's going to think I'm totally inept."

- "She looks bored. I think I'm making a bad impression. There's no way I'll get hired here."

When you notice your attention has drifted to the back forty, gently bring it back to the person you're speaking with—to what they're saying and to the nonverbal cues they're giving you. The more you stay focused on the interaction versus the self-judgment, the better you'll present yourself.

Three Common Patterns at the Start of a New Song

When people are checking out the possibilities for singing new music with others, either as the candidate for a new position, a volunteer for a new project, or as the person seeking people to staff a new team, their approaches vary widely. Many fall into one of three categories that form a continuum from too strong to too weak.

Steamroller　　　　　**Skeptic**　　　　　**Shy Sheep**

⬅―――――――――――――――――――――――➡

When people approach a new relationship,
their behavior often falls into one of three categories.

When **Steamrollers** approach an interview, a new project, or a new team, they overwhelm everyone who's sitting in the same zip code with them. They talk too much, too loud, and too fast. Everything is described in superlatives: the best, the brightest, and the most innovative. They tell you how great their skills, ideas, and experience are. They suck all the oxygen out of the room. In short, they come on way too strong. It's like the idiom based on Shakespeare, "Methinks thou doth protest too much."

If someone is really that terrific, they usually just demonstrate their abilities with their performance and behavior, and thus reduce the need to brag. The demonstration is generally much more convincing than the sales pitch.

Shy Sheep are, in some ways, the opposite of Steamrollers. When they start a new song, you can hardly hear them singing. Their voice is often barely above a whisper. They apologize frequently and hesitate in their responses to questions. They may stutter or say "um" a lot. They might tremble, perspire, or get teary. They tend to fidget with clothes, hair, or objects in front of them. Sometimes they may overtly plead for a chance to engage with you. Their quiet, wavering presentation ironically telegraphs their anxiety quite loudly.

These are two extremes of how people typically show up for interviews, conversations about new projects, or efforts to assemble a new team. There is another common pattern that fits between these two ends of the continuum.

People who are **Skeptics** will clearly demonstrate how guarded and untrusting they are. They disclose as little as possible when asked direct questions or say things like, "I'm not at liberty to discuss that." Their eyes may nervously dart around the room. They might ask if the conversation is being recorded. They ask questions about who this information will be shared with and how it will be used. They're cynical and critical of the mistakes and failings of others. They complain about prior teams or bosses who treated them badly, often playing the victim role. They repeatedly discuss the half-empty part of the glass, rather than talking about the half-full portion, such as strengths, successes, and opportunities.

While it's common and sometimes easy to be too much of a Steamroller, too Shy, or too Skeptical, it is more of a challenge to start the song with a balance of confidence, humility, and harmony.

One candidate that I interviewed several years ago managed to move across the entire spectrum from Steamroller to Shy Sheep during the three hours he was in our building. Joe was interviewing for a position as a seminar trainer. Our protocol was to schedule each candidate for individual interviews with three or four of our team members, one after the other. Then the team would meet to debrief, share observations, and decide which candidate to hire.

Joe had his first interview with me. He bustled into my office loudly and squeezed my hand so hard that I expected to hear my fingers break. He pumped my hand up and down like he was jacking up a car to change a flat tire. He was clearly on the Steamroller track. Once he sat down, he never stopped talking. He just delivered the prepared "song" in his head. I never got a word in edgewise.

He was sweating profusely. He had a briefcase full of products that he had developed for all of the "fabulously successful" seminars he had created and "sold tons of."

He reminded me of those sleazy guys on street corners in some big cities who have six wristwatches pinned to the inside of each flap of their coat: as you walk by, they flip open their coat and ask, "Wanna buy a watch? Great price!" I wanted to ask Joe if he had such wonderful seminars and products that he'd "sold tons of," why he was applying to work for us. However, he never took a long enough breath to let me ask.

I was totally turned off by his anxious overselling of himself. In his effort to convince me of his skills and experience, he came across as a braggart. I couldn't wait to get him out of my office.

I passed him off to each of my colleagues. When he had left and we met to confer, I made a startling discovery. As he moved down the hall for each subsequent interview, he let a little more steam out of his own engine. He was less energized and confident with each meeting. By the time he got to my fourth teammate, the poor guy was totally out of bravado and started to cry. It turns out he had hardly sold any of his own programs and was desperate for a regular salary with benefits.

Joe discredited himself by downgrading from an overly confident Steamroller to a pleading puddle of Shyness and insecurity in the space of three hours. He was unable to find the sweet spot between arrogance and begging for the chance to start a new song. It is indeed a delicate balancing act to show interest and initiative without seeming too enthused or pompous on one end of the continuum, or too guarded, anxious, and apologetic in the other extreme. Needless to say, we never considered hiring him.

You Get What You're Looking for When You Stop Looking: The Delicate Balance between Apathy and Desperation

An interesting paradox faces you when you decide to look for a new job, a new role with a current employer, or even a new social relationship. On one hand, you need to have enough confidence and skills to take steps to

- Reach out to people,

- Complete applications,

- Make proposals,

- Set up interviews, or

- Extend invitations to talk.

If you're lucky, the world comes to you in the form of a recruiter, a posted job opening, a chance meeting at a party, or a friend reaching out to give you a lead. Most of the time, however, it's up to you to make the contacts and proposals. You don't want to convey anxiety like Joe. You also don't want fear or apathy to make you sit at home, waiting for the phone to ring or the texts and emails to pour in. You need to find the sweet spot, the perfect musical tone between apathy and desperation.

So how can you find that delicate balance without being too much of a Steamroller, too Skeptical, or too Shy? If people are on the Steamroller or Skeptic parts of the continuum, they tend to come on too strong at the start of a new song—either too positive and enthusiastic in the case of the Steamroller, or too negative in the case of the Skeptic. Their excessive positive or negative energy sounds out of tune. It can palpably hit people and push them away. Interviewers can sense that they are desperately clutching for the relationship or pessimistic about engaging in one.

When people are too Shy, they hold back too much as they try to begin a new song with someone. Their lack of energy fails to engage the people with whom they want to start singing. They make little or no impression on others. They may come across as weak, boring, or guarded. They are often too afraid to cue up the song and initiate contact.

I first noticed this paradox with a friend who had been single for a long time. She was so eager to be in a long-term relationship that her anxiety to connect with a potential boyfriend caused her to vacillate between being a Steamroller and a Shy Sheep like Joe did. The result was that she pushed away most of the eligible men that she dated. She ultimately found the man she's been successfully married to for decades when she found that sweet spot between being open but not grasping for a relationship.

The Excitement (and Anxiety) of Interviews, Courtships, and Other New Contacts

When you have decided to audition or look for a new work relationship, there can be a lot of energy involved. That energy can either manifest as tremendous **excitement**, where the new person, team or organization looks perfect, aka "just what you are looking for," or **anxiety**, leaving you to wonder if you can sell yourself effectively, and if you do, if you will succeed in the new role to meet or exceed others' expectations.

Too much of either type of energy can put you on the Steamroller-to-Shy-Sheep continuum. I once had a boss who liked to say, "Just because some of something is good doesn't mean that more of it is better."

The goal is to channel your energy, be it positive or negative, in a way that helps you focus and present yourself effectively in applications, proposals, formal interviews, or informal conversations. Train yourself to be realistic. This new job, project, or relationship prospect is not likely to be either "the best thing since sliced bread"—that is, the perfect company, boss, vendor, or team per the ideals that you drafted in your shopping list—or the most miserable company, boss, vendor, or team on the planet that contains all of the nonnegotiable items from your shopping list.

Seek to use the momentum that comes with the first notes of the song you hope to sing so that you are as observant and objective as possible. This helps you ask smart questions, share information appropriately, and analyze interactions accurately to help you make decisions about any future music.

If you find yourself feeling zero excitement or anxiety about the prospects of a new song, that can also be a problem. It's a bit like well-trained musicians. Even though they may have performed a given piece of music many times, most professionals report that they feel a good bit of excitement before a concert. Sometimes it's enthusiasm, but often it's heart-pounding angst as if they were a neophyte.[28]

One indication of their professionalism, however, is that they can channel that energy to make their delivery better. If you feel no energy, you have nothing to leverage. If you feel no buzz about the prospective new song, you need to ask yourself some serious questions:

- Am I really ready to start singing?

- Do I like the kind of music I'm considering? (If I hate country music and love heavy metal, why am I interviewing for country? Wrong place, wrong song.)

- What's holding me back? What's killing my energy? How do I address these barriers?

Nonverbal Cues: No, That's Not What I Meant!

When we are anxious for any reason, we tend to broadcast our nervousness with loud and clear signals. Those signs are easy to read if you pay attention. Decades ago, a professor of psychology at UCLA named Albert Mehrabian began studying and writing about the impact of nonverbal cues

---

28 It's interesting to note that a great many performers—actors, musicians, stand-up comics, and motivational speakers—are very introverted, shy, and lacking in confidence in spite of their public extroverted profession and demonstrated successes. I've had performers tell me they can screw up their confidence, walk onto the stage, and "do their thing" because there's distance between them and the audience. Often, they cannot see the audience with the house lights down. They say that's much easier than face-to-face conversations. And they don't like to go out to dinner or to the after-party: they go back to their hotel room and order room service.

on the messages we seek to convey. His research concluded that, on average, in a face-to-face conversation, the message is communicated

- Only 7 percent by the specific *words* we choose,

- About 38 percent by the *tone* of voice we use, and

- At least 55 percent by our *nonverbal cues* that we demonstrate, including facial expressions, amount of eye contact, speed of talking, absence of talking (silence), gestures, distance between us and the other person, and repetitive movements such as tapping fingers or playing with a pen.

Countless books and articles have been written about body language. They need to be considered carefully. One nonverbal cue does not always mean the same thing. For example, some authors say that if you sit with your arms crossed over your chest, it means you are closed to the other person's ideas. That is one possible interpretation. It also might mean that the room is cold, and you wish you'd worn warmer clothes.

I once interviewed a woman who had her arms crossed across her chest during the entire meeting. This gesture made her look stern or skeptical. It turns out that a button had popped on her blouse, and she was trying to conceal her wardrobe malfunction. After we hired her, she admitted her embarrassment and was actually a truly open and receptive person, not closed at all.[29]

---

29 When I was pregnant, I often sat with my arms crossed over my baby bump as it provided a comfortable shelf for my arms. It was not necessarily a sign of being closed to others' ideas.

Don't Think about Pink Elephants

You probably know the mental trick of saying to someone, "For the next sixty seconds, think about whatever you want, but don't think about pink elephants. Really, anything at all, just not pink elephants! Are you ready to think for sixty seconds about anything but not about *pink elephants*? Okay, go." There is now no way that those blushing pachyderms are not stomping through your brain. There's a simple explanation for this. When you say, "Don't do X," your brain typically hears only, "Do X," and filters out the "don't."

This ties back to Dr. Cooperrider's Appreciative Inquiry model. If you identify what works well and what motivates you, it is easier to shift your focus from past failures to the new music you seek. It applies to how you view individual relationships as well as team dynamics and fosters more positive results. The implications of using an appreciative eye to examine and improve work relationships are potent and far-reaching. Appreciative inquiry is a bit like the glass half-full, glass half-empty philosophy except on steroids. It makes a strong case for using the assets and resources of the half-full part of the glass to deal with what's missing, not working, or half-empty.

This is based on a basic psychological principle that you get more of what you focus on. One of Dr. Cooperrider's core principles of Appreciative Inquiry is the Anticipatory Principle: what we anticipate or pay attention to influences our actions. This means that we move toward whatever we pay attention to. If we focus on problems, we tend to get more problems. If we emphasize strengths and successes, we're more likely to leverage those attributes to help resolve the problems more effectively.

This concept of moving toward wherever your focus is ties directly to your efforts to sing a new song. The shopping lists that you drafted in Stage 1 with your must-haves and nonnegotiables provide important bookends or boundaries for your efforts to create and maintain harmonious relationships by focusing on what you most want and need.

But if you wear your skeptical spectacles, especially during the first notes of a song, you will unconsciously be drawn to what's wrong, what won't work, what's missing, or what's threatening. In other words, you'll only see the half-empty part of the glass and will miss what's in the half-full part of the glass. You'll have trouble filling the glass with more of the desirable sweet notes that you most want to sing. Again, it's a balancing act: you want to be realistic but keep your focus directed to the music you hope to create.

I remember a difficult conversation I needed to have with a former boss. He could be intimidating, especially if you were asking to do something he didn't like or value. I was feeling quite shaky and vulnerable. I told my colleague, Steve, that I was afraid I'd get teary once I got into the boss's office. I admitted to Steve that I'd been walking around all day muttering to myself, "Don't cry in there. Don't cry in there."

Steve wisely redirected me by suggesting a better mantra: "I will stay strong, calm, and confident." He told me to visualize myself in the boss's office staying strong, calm, and confident. I took the word *tears* out of the image. It worked. I stayed dry-eyed and had a productive conversation with my boss.

Rehearsals Are Not Just for Musicians: Plan, Prepare, and Practice

It is often said that practice makes perfect. While that may be true in some situations,[30] it's usually more accurate to say

---

30 Though I really have no idea what those situations would be. If normal is a theoretical concept, merely a point at the top of the bell curve, isn't perfect as well? Sometimes a meal or a latte or the fit of a shoe might cause you to exclaim, "Ah, that's perfect!" But otherwise, "perfect" strikes me as abstract, if not unattainable most of the time.

that practice makes *progress or improvement*. This is not only true for concert pianists and rock stars. If you were to ask an extraordinary singer-songwriter like David Wilcox how he's able to get his guitar licks to be so precise and his lyrics so powerful, he'd tell you he often spends hours if not days on one bass run or one line in a verse. He goes over and over it until it's just right, if not perfect. My father used to call it barn yarding, going over a difficult musical passage enough times until you could play it well—or at least better.

It's the same with skilled athletes. I'm sure that famous tennis players weren't born with a killer serve, and star basketball players couldn't dunk successfully the first time they held a ball. They take the move they want to perfect, visualize the result they want—the anticipatory principle again—focus on where they want the ball to go, and then do it over and over until they have the level of accuracy they seek.

Timothy Gallwey, renowned sports psychology expert, has applied this concept to tennis, golf, and skiing, as well as music, stress, and organizational productivity. He distinguishes the inner game, which plays out in your mind, from the outer game or the overt actions that everyone sees you take. He has developed numerous techniques that allow the inner game to include more positive messages to shift your focus, and hence your results toward what you want to achieve.

Several different studies talk about how it can take anywhere from 18 to 254 days to repeat a behavior enough to make it a new habit, with the average being 66 days. That research reinforces the importance of practice. Both athletes and musicians call it muscle memory. They repeat a specific musical phrase or make a specific move so many times that their muscles remember how to do it, making it more likely that they'll perform successfully.

It stands to reason, therefore, that when you want to start a new song by singing in tune with confidence and skill that you need some practice, just like professional musicians or athletes. You need to

- Focus on the goal or desired outcome that you seek (rather than on all the things that could go wrong),

- Analyze what behaviors, tools, and information you need to succeed, and then

- Prepare and rehearse in one of several ways.

How to plan, prepare, and practice?

- Do your homework. If you're interviewing with a new organization, look them up online. See what history, current data, and future direction you can find about them.

- Use social media to connect with people you may know who work there: contact them and gather more information.

- If it's appropriate and parts of the organization have open, unsecured areas, make a site visit. Sit in the lobby, eat in their cafeteria, and observe conversations, how people dress, what the vibe is. Notice if people seem relaxed or stressed, calm or rushed.

- If it's a promotion in your current organization or the prospect of working on a new project, do similar kinds of investigation. In this age of information, there is no excuse to sing the first notes without background data.

- Review your shopping lists. Consider what you must have, hope to have, and refuse to put up with in this new song.

- Think about how well your lists line up with what you find out about the new organization, boss, or team. While nothing is ever a perfect match, you want to be sure you're heading toward the right kind of music.

- Anticipate what you'll hear and what you'll be asked in any interviews or informal meetings. Think about how you might answer those expected questions. Consider examples and anecdotes that highlight your experience, skills, and qualifications for this new song without being a Steamroller or a Shy Sheep. Find ways to make your answers focused and concise so that you don't ramble and reduce the clarity of your message.

- Plan a few solid questions to pose to the people you're trying to sing with. You want to gather more information to help you evaluate this new potential song. Asking focused questions also shows that you are prepared for and are genuinely interested in the possibility of creating beautiful music together. It indicates you've done some vocal warm-ups and prepared for the conversation.

- As the saying goes, "How do you get to Carnegie Hall? Practice, practice, practice!" Get a friend or a coach to do a mock interview or conversation with you. Give them enough background so that they have context and will ask some of your anticipated questions. You can also practice in front of a mirror (where no one can hear you, so they're not concerned that you're talking to yourself in the bathroom), or record yourself, play it back, and see what you want to edit.

Improv Theater: Expect the Unexpected

One of the aspects of improvisational theater that makes it so fascinating yet challenging is the paradox that actors have woven through their training and preparation: expect the unexpected. Martial artists and boxers often operate from the same premise. They must anticipate that reactions from others may surprise them, and they need to be ready to respond to those surprises effectively. They have to watch and listen carefully, be flexible and engaged, and yet stay calm and grounded. It is essential that they trust their own instincts and ability to react well.

When people ask me what the job of a management consultant really involves when coaching an individual, leading a seminar, or facilitating a difficult meeting, I say, "It's really improv theater!" Improv actors do a lot to prepare for a performance and hone their skills. They create clear boundaries and desired outcomes. Then within those boundaries, they use their preparation and skills to expect the unexpected and feel confident in responding to whatever comes up.

According to the Myers-Briggs dimension of Extraversion and Introversion, Extroverts tend to improv more skillfully or at least more comfortably than Introverts do. Since Extroverts often think well on their feet, they're more prone to make up responses or new tunes on the spot, composing as they go. Introverts prefer to think about something first and sort the information in their own head before replying. That said,

- Introverts can learn good improv skills in order to expect (and react to) the unexpected with more finesse, and

- Extroverts can be caught off guard and rendered speechless as much as Introverts when confronted with surprising or uncomfortable questions.

One of the toughest interviews that I ever had also became one of my favorites. I had never met Dave, the CEO of an organization I'd been consulting with for six months. I asked his human resources manager for an introduction. The purpose was not to get a job but just to meet him and possibly involve him in my consulting projects. He started with fairly standard questions that were easy. Then he leaned back in his chair, put his hands behind his head and his feet up on his desk (a rude power play that he admitted later he did on purpose), and said, "So, Susan, tell me why you charge so much for your services."

I was blown away. In the fifteen years I'd had my company to that point, no one had ever asked me that in quite that way.

My reply: "Well, Dave, that's an interesting question (a good technique to stall, let you catch your breath, and plan a response) that no one's ever asked me before (subtle feedback that the question was unusual if not inappropriate). A few things occur to me. (This was pure improv theater: I was making up the points as I went.) First, our rates are average in the Denver area for the type of work we do. (While I was making point one, I was thinking up point two.) Second, the meter's not running every minute we're with clients. If someone calls us for a five- or ten-minute conversation, or a meeting runs a few minutes over, we don't charge for that time. (Still spinning my wheels like crazy and inventing as I went forward.) But, Dave, I guess the most important answer is that our clients say that we add value."

I was screaming inside my head, but apparently calm on the outside. Dave and I got to be pals and laughed about that for a long time after the interview. He admitted he was testing to see how I'd respond to a provocative question and cared more about my delivery than the content of my reply. The ability to stay calm under fire, not get rattled, and respond to challenges without taking it personally is usually hard, and always a good skill to develop.[31]

So how do you strengthen your improv skills and expect the unexpected when singing the first notes of a new song and trying to start the relationship off harmoniously?

- Consider what topics or questions might make you squirm and prepare some possible responses.

- If you practice with a colleague or a coach, suggest that they ask you some curveball questions that you weren't expecting. It will give you a chance to practice responding to tough or surprising questions without getting flustered. The *way* you answer those startling questions is almost more important than what you actually say in response.

- Develop some phrases that I call techniques to verbally run in place. Some of my favorites include

    ◦ That's an interesting question (or a great question).

    ◦ No one's ever asked me that before.

    ◦ Let me think about that for a moment, so that I can give you a clear answer.

    ◦ Tell me some more about that: what's behind your question (or your reason for asking it)? (Or if others are in the room, you might say) Before I respond, I'd like to give others a chance to weigh in. What do the rest of you think about that?

---

31 Truth be told, I am not always that calm. I can get rattled like anyone else. That, however, was one of my finer moments.

The purpose of these run-in-place techniques is to keep the conversation going while giving your brain a chance to process—or recover from the question and try to improv a good reply.

Ask for time to reflect. While it's not always appropriate, sometimes you can ask for more time—be it a minute, an hour, or a day. You could say something like:

- "That's a really good (or complex) question. I'd like to think about that for (a few minutes, an hour, etc.) or gather some information about it." or

- "Would it be okay if I get back to you with an answer in X amount of time?" (as long as you make sure that you get back to them, so that you don't appear to be avoiding) or

- "Let me take a moment to organize my thoughts before I respond."

When I prepared for the qualifying exams for my master's degree, it was intimidating to try to cram a whole year's worth of information into my head to access for the exam. What was scarier still was the fact that the exam was an oral exam with three professors staring me down for over an hour. I'd never had an oral exam before, and since I often take notes to sort my ideas, I couldn't imagine how I'd pass the exam with them firing questions at me. At that point in my life, I had not yet honed my improv skills.

I went into the exam room with a pen and a blank piece of white paper. Before they started, I screwed up my courage and asked this favor: "Gentlemen, I know this is an oral exam, but part of my preferred thinking style is to organize thoughts on paper first. When you ask me each question, would you give me thirty seconds to make some notes so that I can give you as cogent a reply as possible? You can see that this paper is blank and has no notes on it."

They were totally baffled by my request. I doubt anyone had asked for this before. One of them actually examined the paper, holding it up to the light, to make sure it was blank, and that I wasn't cheating. Finally, they agreed to my odd request. So each time they asked me a question, I took thirty seconds or less, made some notes, looked up at the professors, and started to spew out my newly acquired knowledge. The brief notetaking not only helped me plan my response but also gave me a chance to breathe and calm down, otherwise known as engaging brain before engaging mouth.

- Embellish the truth. This one is tricky and smacks of dishonesty, so use it carefully. It involves taking what's factual and putting it in different, maybe prettier packaging so that it accomplishes your goal. This presumes that your embellishment does no damage.

One time, I was home from college for winter break and driving my mom's car to a dental appointment. I was a few minutes late and driving ten miles over the speed limit. A cop pulled me over. He asked where I was going in such a hurry.

My reply: "I'm so sorry, Officer. I'm home from college. I haven't driven for four months. I'm not feeling well and on my way to a doctor appointment that's two miles from here. If you could just give me a warning this time, I won't be late to my appointment, and I'll promise to be more conscious of the speed limit from now on." Amazingly, he let me go with a warning, told me to be more careful, and said he hoped I felt better.[32]

So what was true? What was factual?

- Home from college, driving mom's car.

- Hadn't driven in four months.

---

32 It helps when the police officer is kind and compassionate. I'm not always that lucky!

- On my way to an appointment and late.

- I was sorry I was speeding, especially because I got caught.

What was related to the truth but stretching it a bit (aka a prettier package)?

- My dentist was named Dr. Binder, so he was a (dental) doctor.

- I wasn't feeling well because I'd been stopped for speeding and was not looking forward to a dental appointment or to a possible ticket.

Some would call this lying or, at best, fibbing. Others would say it was a creative way to package the truth. You obviously need to be careful to not misrepresent the truth about yourself, your skills, or experience when trying to start a new song with the right notes. But you can think about how to present or package any information that might be problematic.

Job seekers walk this tightrope with situations like a long lapse between jobs or when looking for a new job after being fired. You don't want to sound as if you've been sitting around binge-watching your favorite TV shows and eating candy bars during the ten months you've been unemployed. It might be fair to say you wanted some time off to reassess priorities and next steps.

Similarly, if you have been fired from your prior job, you have to plan carefully how to discuss this. Prospective employers may ask why you left your previous job. If they call for references, you never know if your former boss will give the minimum required information—that is, that you worked there from this date to that date and had the job title of X, or if they'll blackball you, say how terrible you were, and why you were fired.

A musical equivalent to adjusting the message is when a singer finds that some of the notes are too high or too low to sing. They will often transpose the song to a new key that fits better, or just change the melody line and sing different notes to accommodate their vocal range. Some purists might say this is not being accurate or true to the composition in its original key. I'd say it's a reasonable adaptation when there's no compelling reason to adhere to the original score.

The First Wrong Notes

Let's say you do a lot of things right for the audition: You

- Make a good first impression,

- Find the sweet spot between apathy and desperation,

- Manage your excitement and energy appropriately,

- Pay attention to nonverbal cues,

- Focus on your lists of what you want, hope to have, and won't tolerate, and

- Rehearse, research, and practice your improv skills.

You might still make a mistake by saying or doing something that's out of tune. How do you recover, apologize, and/or follow up?

We've all had the experience of having something halfway out of our mouth and thinking, "Wow! I shouldn't be saying that!" or "I wish I'd handled that differently." It's like the expression, "Our vision is 20/20 in hindsight." Unfortunately, we can't edit live conversations with the click of an undo or delete button.

There are sometimes options for a do-over.

- If someone says something that indicates they are confused by or critical of something you've just said or done,
  - Listen, breathe, and paraphrase their response;
  - Clarify or modify your answer or draw them out with open questions about what isn't sounding harmonious to them. You might say something like, "What about my comment causes you concern?"

- If someone gives you nonverbal cues, such as silence, furrowed brow, clenched teeth, sideways glances to others in the room or fidgeting, they might be indicating that you are singing out of tune. You need to check in:
  - Notice and breathe, and
  - Ask an open question, such as "What are your thoughts about that?" or "How does that fit with what you're looking for?"

- Sometimes, there's no overt or nonverbal cue from the person you're talking to, but you just have that uh-oh feeling in the pit of your stomach and wish you'd sung better. In that case, you can try a redirect:
  - "However, some people might see that differently," and then try your comment with improved content and/or delivery, or
  - "I'm not sure that was a clear response to your question. Let me try it another way."

This is much more transparent, as you're admitting to less-than-ideal music. This is sometimes very engaging and other times too revealing.

You don't always get the chance for a do-over, especially if you've said something that was embarrassing or hurtful to the other person or somehow too incriminating about you. Whether you do or do not have the option, the noticing, listening, and breathing are crucial.[33] They increase your awareness of when you need a do-over and give you a few split seconds to think about how and if to approach it.

Sometimes, it's better to retract and recompose your response later, after the initial conversation and after you've had time to reflect. Just remember that we have opportunities for do-overs more often than we might realize. The act of admitting and correcting a mistake demonstrates your self-awareness, humility, and courage. We are, after all, human and imperfect. Do you really want to have a relationship with someone who fails to value those attributes?

Final Notes

Once you've decided you want to start a new song, there are clearly many elements that contribute to making those first notes as clear, confident, and in tune as possible. It helps to keep these tools on your proverbial music rack. Plan, practice, redirect as needed, and then expect the unexpected. Many of the skills and mindsets that you utilize in Auditions and First Notes will also help you navigate this next stage, New Songs, more successfully. That is when the music starts to get quite interesting.

Rehearsals:

Application Exercises for First Notes

Use this section to prepare for an interview, promotion, or recruitment to a new project team.

Choose one of these exercises to help you apply the Stage 2 information to your current experience. Then decide if it would be helpful to try a second type of rehearsal.

1. **Think about the people you want to approach and how best to contact them in the organization or department where you want to interview**. Is it best to get a third-party introduction, contact a recruiter, email, text, or call? People involved with hiring are often so barraged with applications that they don't always respond in a timely manner, if at all. It's a tricky balancing act to decide the right contact to call and how often to reach out, so that you demonstrate your interest without being a pest.

2. **Do your homework**. Decide the best ways to gather data about the company or department from their website, people you know who work there, or others on social media, and possibly an anonymous site visit if possible.

3. **Rehearse for the start of this song using the suggestions in this chapter**. Look for ways to complete one or more of these tasks:

   • Review your shopping list including characteristics that you must have, hope to have, and are not willing to put up with (deal breakers).

- Anticipate what you'll hear and what you'll be asked in an interview. Prepare your responses, including a few short, relevant examples or anecdotes.

- Plan a few questions that you want to ask the leader or interviewers to signal your interest and preparation.

- Practice your comments and questions with a coach, a friend, a colleague, in the mirror, or by recording and reviewing yourself. Be conscious of how to convey your interest without seeming desperate or pushy.

- Map out and practice verbal running-in-place techniques in case you're asked something that catches you off guard. Phrases like, "That's an interesting question, Irving," or "No one's ever asked me that before—let me think about that for a minute" give you time to catch your breath and quickly think about how to respond.

4. **Use stress management techniques before the interview**. Find some calming or centering practices that work for you. Some people use aerobic exercise or yoga to help them relax and release tensions from the day. Others establish a regular practice of meditation. There are numerous varieties to choose from, and they range from one minute to an hour, once or twice a day. They may involve

- Rhythmic breathing,

- Repeating a mantra,

- Visualizing yourself in a beautiful, relaxing place, or

- Listening to soothing music.

You can read a book, take a class, watch a video online, or download an app on your phone to learn how to practice these techniques. The important point is to find an approach to test for several days in a row and then decide what works best for you. Most people can't tell what will be most useful to them until they practice it regularly for a while. The benefits tend to be cumulative, so starting days or weeks before the first interview will likely yield more benefits than starting the day before.

5. **Practice observing nonverbal cues**. Take any low-risk situation—in the line at the grocery store, on a train or bus during your daily commute, in a coffee shop, restaurant, or library where people are hanging out alone or with a few others. You can also try muting the sound on a TV program or video. Just notice someone's nonverbal cues: the expression on their face, gestures and posture, distance between them and others, eye contact or lack thereof, movement or lack thereof, and if they're in a conversation with others, who's doing most of the talking. If you can hear their conversation, consider volume as well.

   See how much information you can infer just by noticing these cues. You're just guessing, and it's probably not appropriate to approach them to check out your hunches. But it's a great way to strengthen your observational muscles. This will help you be more aware in higher risk situations where you do have to pay attention to these cues while listening to the content of the conversation at the same time.

6. **Consider some formal training to improve your skills and confidence in being articulate and responding clearly and calmly to unexpected questions that interviewers might ask you.**

   - Take an interactive public speaking seminar. Good programs give you suggestions of how to organize your content, opportunities to practice and get feedback from the instructor and fellow students, possibly record your presentation for later review, and respond to unanticipated questions from the group.

- Join a Toastmasters club near your home or work. They tend to have chapters that meet early morning, noontime, and late afternoon or evening. Their goal is to help people be more comfortable with public speaking. Most people who join a club find it to be a supportive, encouraging community and eventually have fun participating.

- Sign up for a class in improv theater. You will learn techniques to respond to unexpected comments and behaviors; it will build your confidence for interviews; and you're likely to have an entertaining experience.

7. **Build in time to relax and focus just before you go into an interview or challenging conversation**. Try to get a good night's sleep the night before and have a healthy meal so that your blood sugar's not low, and you can think clearly. Decide what will help you just before you enter the meeting. To dispel any anxiety, you might

- Take a walk,

- Do breathing exercises,

- Do a short meditation technique,

- Say a prayer,

- Listen to music that either revs you up or calms you down,

- Visualize your desired outcome,

- Knit, or

- Do a puzzle or play a short game on your phone.

Experiment with different routines to see what will help you be calm but energized and able to concentrate on observing, listening, and speaking effectively.

Musicians have a tradition for this called the Green Room. Most performance venues have a room in the back where the artists can relax before they go on stage. Some musicians and actors have specific requests of what they want in the room: peppermint tea, protein bars, double lattes, a salad, for example. A good friend of mine requests a couch in the room so that he can stretch out and possibly nap before show time. Some performers who live at sea level but perform in cities like Denver at elevation request an oxygen tank in the Green Room so that they can suck on some extra oxygen to compensate for the thin Colorado air that they're not used to.

Stage 3

New Songs: Making Beautiful Music Together

Juanita calls Sally to meet up for a walk one Saturday.

Sally greets her friend warmly. "Hey, Juanita. I hear you got a new job. Congrats! How's it going?" Juanita had gotten a new job a month earlier.

Juanita smiles. "Well, I'm pretty happy. As you and the guys know, I was ready for a change. I might not have been brave enough to make the move if the three of you hadn't been so encouraging.

"That's what friends are for, Juanita. Okay, so gimme the details. I want some vicarious excitement here."

"My boss is pretty chill: smart, well organized, but calm. She's a refreshing change from the person I worked with before. The team I'm on is okay, but I'm not totally comfortable with everyone yet."

"Patience, mon amie. You've only been there, what? Four weeks?"

"Right, I know, but I get nervous when I don't totally trust people. Two of them are fine—straightforward, cooperative, friendly. Gus is chronically grumpy. He never smiles, rarely initiates conversation, and kind of grunts when I say hi to him in the morning. BJ just wears me out. She's always moving and talking quickly, never sits still, and is always trying to shift projects from her desk to mine."

"Okay, let's play Sherlock Holmes," Sally suggests. "What's your guess about the agendas that Gus and BJ each have?"

"Well, I've heard that Gus was best buds with the person who had my position before me. The rumor is that he feels abandoned by his former pal and may be jealous that his friend got a promotion to another department. With BJ, I'm just not sure. Maybe she thinks I'm a wimp—somebody she can off-load tasks she doesn't like or have time for."

"Juanita, if BJ hasn't figured it out yet, she will. You're no wimp! So, what are your options to build better rapport with Gus and BJ?"

"Good question, Sal. With BJ, I want to come across as helpful and open to new assignments. But she's not my boss, and I need to find a way to tactfully set some boundaries with her. Maybe I should ask my boss for advice."

"Be careful. Don't make it sound like you're complaining about BJ. Just ask for help clarifying priorities. And what about Grumpy Gus?"

"Know where I can get him a personality transplant?" Sally laughs and shakes her head.

"No?" continues Juanita, feigning surprise. "Okay, well then maybe again asking for advice from my boss or the other teammates. It may take time. I'm not ready to ask him to go to lunch with me. It's hard to imagine what a real conversation with him would be like."

"You've got this, pal. Patience, courage, boundaries, and asking good questions. I bet in a few more weeks, you'll be singing a happier song."

"You're one of my favorite cheerleaders, Sally! Thanks. Stay tuned. Hey, how about coffee after our walk?"

Sally laughs again. "Twist my arm, but only if I can get whipped cream on top."

Make Commitments and Draw Up Contracts

Once you've been hired for the new job, gotten promoted into the new position, or chosen to work on a new project team, it's time to start singing in earnest. This phase is crucial, because the *way* you start singing can have a major impact on how the rest of the song plays out. People are most often excited and energized when a new song starts. The question is this: How can you best channel that enthusiasm to get you started on the right notes with the right people at the right tempo?

Just like the sweet spot between apathy and desperation in Stage 2, you need to balance your happiness about the new musical opportunity with some caution and craft in your new relationships.

The *caution* often takes the form of

- Asking lots of questions to gather information, context, and history,

- Reaching out to get to know people, their roles, and contributions,

- Clarifying what people are hoping or expecting from you in your new role, and possibly

- Detecting what some people might be resenting, afraid of, or confused by, given your new position.

It's a balancing act, because you want to share your interest and commitment without overwhelming people like an eager puppy who jumps all over everyone. You also want to avoid stepping on hidden land mines. In an effort to impress the rest of the chorus, some new singers come on too strong. They start making or suggesting changes on day one, often trampling on philosophies or projects that people greatly value and have worked on for a long time.

If any of your colleagues were hoping to get your new role for themselves or for a friend, they could be quite unhappy to see you show up. They might have no interest in singing harmoniously with you. So it's important to tread lightly, sing softly at first until you learn the prevailing music, and begin to build trust with the other singers.

To *craft* new relationships successfully, it often helps to surface others' expectations overtly and make clear agreements. I call this **negotiating a new relationship**. It takes the form of one-on-one conversations that include questions you prepare to ask your fellow musicians as well as information that you can share about your own style. This accelerates the process of getting acquainted. It is especially important to do with your immediate supervisor but is also important to discuss with peers and any direct reports you may have.

Some sample questions that you might ask include these:

- What are one or two of your greatest strengths as an employee/boss/team member?

- What can you tell me about your work style that would be helpful for me to know?

  - When someone asks you an important question, do you prefer to discuss it and think out loud, or would you rather have time to reflect and respond later?

  - Are you more of a big picture or detail person?

  - Do you tend to make decisions based more on facts and standards or values and relationships?

- ◦ Is your style one of structure and sequential order or more of flexibility and spontaneity?

- ◦ Do you prefer in-person conversations, phone calls, or emails and texts?

- ◦ Is your best time for creativity and problem solving first thing in the day or after two cups of coffee?

- Tell me about the best boss/peer/direct report that you ever worked with. What was it about that person that made it easy and enjoyable for you to interact with them?

- What, if any, pet peeves do you have so I know to avoid them?

- What, if any, requests do you have of me as we begin working together so that we can be as productive as possible?

Some examples of what you might share with the other person include insights like this:

- I really appreciate and thrive on direct feedback. I'd rather hear directly from you if there's a problem than hear it secondhand or not at all.

- I'm systematic and prefer to do things one at a time, rather than multitask several unfinished projects all at once.

- I get rattled and intimidated when someone interrupts me or cuts me off in a meeting. Even when you disagree, it helps when you can hear me out before sharing your own point of view.

- I have the most energy at [8:00 a.m. or right after lunch or on Mondays and Fridays].

- I'm a visual person, so I remember details better if they're written or if I can take notes.

You need to tailor the questions to the person, their role, and the situation. You may not want to ask them all at once. However, the very act of your asking questions like these and then sharing some factoids about your own style usually helps to start building trust. This interaction also helps you know what works and what might backfire with a given individual.

The way people respond to your efforts to overtly negotiate this new music will tell you as much about them as what their answers to specific questions reveal. If the person you're talking to seems guarded or uncomfortable that you're asking for this type of information, that suggests that trust may be low, or resentment may be high. You may need to explain why you're asking, proceed cautiously, and save some of the questions for later.

With some new relationships, it's important to draw up formal documents that spell out agreements, goals, timelines, and other expectations. Often, the acts of listening, asking questions, and cautiously making suggestions are all that is required at first.

It is like when two people decide to sing a duet. They need to choose the song, make sure it's the right song for the occasion, decide what key to sing it in, and agree who will sing which part. Then tempo, accompaniment, rehearsal schedules, and other style decisions need to be discussed and agreed upon. Regardless of whether it's a new boss, a new team, or a song to sing at someone's wedding, the more overt you make your expectations and commitments, the better are your chances of singing in tune.

Going Public about Decisions

Unless you like to sing only in the shower or alone in your car, you eventually have to sing for other people if you want to be a serious singer. Even if you only sing a lullaby to your child at bedtime, or a quiet, soothing song to your critically ill grandparent, music is meant to be shared.

Similarly, to make harmonious music with others at work, you need to go public about agreements and plans that you make with them. Sometimes that means only a one-on-one conversation about goals and roles. Other times, it could be a strategic planning retreat with a team that involves multiple meetings over several months. On some occasions, it entails a formal presentation to an entire division or organization.

You can come up with the most brilliant strategies and tactics, but if they are not communicated to the right people in the right way at the right time, they're generally not worth the paper they're printed on—or the space they take up on your hard drive.

Playing your piano in your own living room when no one is home involves a lot less risk and requires much less courage than performing a solo at a concert in front of a large audience. The analogy fits when considering the publicizing of decisions with others at work. One model that may help you decide what to share and how to share it comes from Interaction Associates, a consulting firm based in Boston. They call it Levels of Involvement.

Levels of Involvement

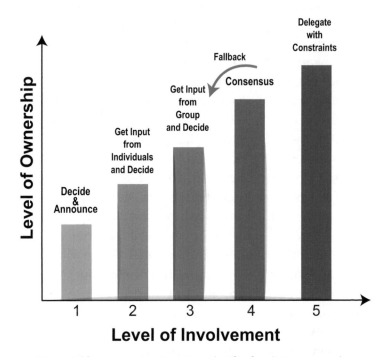

This model from Interaction Associates identifies five distinct approaches to decision-making. The more involvement people are offered, the more buy-in they have. Sometimes greater involvement is neither possible nor appropriate. Sometimes greater buy-in is not essential.

The beauty of this model is that it helps you decide how to make and share your decisions. It also is tied to how much involvement you want and need from others, based on how much they need to own or buy into the decisions.

1. **Decide & Announce** has the least amount of involvement or input, and hence often has the lowest amount of buy-in. There are times, especially as a leader, that you don't need people to *like* something; you just need them to *do* it. You can decide on your own and inform others.

New Songs: Making Beautiful Music Together | 117

This is true when conditions are mandated by laws, finances, your boss, or others with authority. It also applies for emergencies when there is no time for input, or when there is only one viable option. There may be less ownership, but this level takes less time and effort to use. Your decision is unilateral.

2. **Get 1:1 Input**, then decide and report back. This would be appropriate if the leader has the time and desire to hear from people individually, consolidate their feedback, make the decision, and let others know what was decided and why. This approach is helpful when people are either less confident or more likely to share opinions honestly outside of a group meeting. Coworkers may have more buy-in, but it's still your decision. It does, however, take additional time, depending on how many people are approached for comments.

3. **Get Group Input**, then decide and report back. This is similar to the second level described above. The leader is still drawing out the team's ideas and using that information to make the decision. The advantage is that it may be more efficient to hear from everyone together in a group meeting. That way, team members may get ideas and build enthusiasm from hearing their colleagues' opinions. Also, more opportunities for input often (but not always) yield more buy-in.

    These are the risks of soliciting group input:

    ◦   Stronger personalities may sway or silence less confident people by singing more loudly.

    ◦   It may take more time if individuals don't agree or have lots to say about the decision.

- ○ The group may split, where half want X and half want Y, so that half will be unhappy with whatever you ultimately decide.

- ○ The group could rally around one idea that you know is not feasible or desirable. If you then make a decision contrary to what the group lobbied for, they may be mad at you, and they may refuse to support or sing with you when it's time for implementation.

4. **Get Consensus** in which the team keeps discussing until they find a decision they can align around and solidly support. You strive to get everyone singing on the same page, where people thoroughly understand and buy into the decision. When they leave the meeting, they speak with one harmonious voice about roles and next steps.

   That's the good news: more involvement and more buy-in. An indicator of this level of ownership is that they sing or talk about the decision as if it were their own idea, even when it wasn't their first choice (versus "You won't believe what the boss is making us do now!"). Consensus decision-making also builds people's skills for effectively approaching subsequent decisions.

   Here are the downsides of seeking consensus:

   - ○ It may take a lot more time and patience to get everyone's input and, thus, may not be practical in all situations.

   - ○ It requires that team members see each other as allies, pulling toward the same goals, not as adversaries competing for power, attention, or resources.

- ○ Concerns must be surfaced and addressed directly if true support for final decisions is to be reached. So discussions may get contentious.

- ○ Consensus isn't always possible. Sometimes the leader, seeking consensus and reaching a stalemate, may need a fallback position: "Since we can't get to a decision that we all agree on, I'll take all of the ideas we've shared on this, summarize them, and then let you know how we'll proceed." The leader is basically defaulting to level three, getting group input and then deciding. In some situations, that's the best you can do.

For several years, I facilitated strategic planning efforts with the leadership team of one of our clients. It was a very coherent, productive team that collaborated well. One year, however, there was one major priority that the whole team wanted to include in the plan, and the CEO wanted something else. The team was basically ganging up on their boss and pressuring her to choose their approach. We ultimately came up with a third alternative that everyone could support and that restored harmony to the team. It also avoided the CEO's needing to fall back to level three (get group input and decide herself). It was, however, more tense, time consuming, and a definite test for everyone's antiperspirant.

5. **Delegate with Constraints**. This flavor of decision-making works well when you don't need everyone's involvement or ownership. You need to have an individual or a cohesive subgroup that can make the decision for everyone else, given the proper direction and parameters. This ties to the delegation steps defined later in Stage 5, Encores, in which the

person or people to whom the decision is delegated need clear objectives, time frames, budget, and other considerations, plus the authority and latitude that fit with their skills and experience.

I once worked with a manager who said to his team, "We have an extra $2,000 in our budget to spend before year-end. Which two or three people want to work on this and decide how to spend this money in a way that will improve morale in the department?" He let them self-select for the delegation, rather than considering and choosing the best people for the task. Also, while he stated the goal of improving morale, he was unclear about parameters such as what types of expenditures would be acceptable.

They came back to their boss and said they'd decided to buy a $2,000 espresso machine for the breakroom, since everyone liked good coffee. The boss went ballistic and said it was the dumbest idea he'd ever heard, that they didn't understand anything about morale building, "un-delegated" the decision, and chose to spend the money on a team-building seminar that did little to enhance morale. Because he didn't delegate with clear parameters, everyone was unhappy, morale got worse, and disharmony increased! That said, delegation with clear expectations and parameters can be a useful approach for certain decision-making.

These five Levels of Involvement help you structure the decision-making process and the communication that follows. They also help with the acceptance of any given decision and the management of the team's expectations. If your colleagues know that Decision A is yours to make and then share (Decide & Announce), and that there's no room for input, it manages their expectations and may reduce resistance to the plan. If they know that Decision B requires Consensus, they can prepare for more time and energy. They'll be primed to have to collectively slog through many options and permutations in the hope of coming up with something they can all solidly align with and execute successfully.

The value of this model is that it forces the leader to "decide how to decide" to clarify to themselves and then to others which type of decision this will be. Then people know what to expect regarding their amount of input (from zero to 100%), who's the ultimate decision maker, and how the decision will be communicated. Such an approach also helps the leader avoid being too rigid and authoritarian with all decisions or being too indecisive and waiting for total consensus for every issue.

One woman I have had the pleasure to work with had been a manager in a department that was saddled with unclear goals, lack of follow-through, and significant tensions among coworkers. She was promoted to be the vice president. After cautiously gathering data, asking questions, and clarifying expectations, she pulled her entire department together for a meeting in her second week. Using level one, Decide & Announce, she shared her vision for their department, what she'd been asked to do by the CEO, and what she knew needed to be done.

She exhibited what I call the perfect balance of backbone or courage and heart or compassion by saying this: "There are two things you need to know about me. One is that I refuse to put up with the CRAP that's gone on in this department for years. We will no longer be known as the department that is mired in anger, blame, gossip, chaos, and lack of follow-through. Instead, we will work toward developing a reputation of excellence, creativity, collaboration, and customer service. The second thing you need to know is that I have confidence that *every single one of you* can help me turn this department around. I will do whatever I can to support you in this united effort to make this a productive and enjoyable place to work."

She was using Decide & Announce. She was not, at this point, asking for their input. She was drawing a line in the sand (backbone) and simultaneously expressing her support and confidence in them individually and collectively (heart) to make the needed changes.

A month later, she began efforts with her managers to pull together as a stronger leadership team and craft a strategic plan for the department with them. This was a combination of levels three (Group Input to guide her decisions), four (Consensus), and five (Delegation with scope and time constraints). She needed higher levels of involvement in order to encourage higher levels of ownership or buy-in.

As the external consultant, I could see that, within four months of her promotion, the culture and relationships within the management team had begun to shift. There were still some clashing chords, but the disharmony was reduced. The team noticed it as well and realized that they needed to find ways to cascade these changes in procedures and working relationships down through all levels of the department. The VP began with a bold new song and used different Levels of Involvement to encourage everyone to sing with her.

The moral of this story is that you have to go public with your decisions at some point in your new musical relationships. You also have to make conscious choices about Levels of Involvement and, hence, what to share with whom, how, and when.

Enjoy the Honeymoon Period

People often describe the beginning of a new job or project as the honeymoon period, just like with a new dating relationship or a new marriage. In some situations, the honeymoon can last for weeks or even months. People are polite, generally happy you've joined their crew, and maybe eager for the help and new ideas you'll offer.

Conversely, you are also on your best behavior—cheerful but not too eager, doing your best to gather intel and build trust without being intrusive or presumptuous. Others may invite you out to lunch to get acquainted or accept your invitations to get together. The first parts of the song sound surprisingly good. Neither your calendar nor your email inbox is too full yet because coworkers are just finding out about your arrival, and you're figuring out where you fit in.[34]

In other scenarios, the honeymoon is over in the first few hours, when new hires feel they've been thrown into the proverbial fire with instructions like this: "Here's your desk. This is where the coffee pot and bathroom are.[35] This position has been vacant for three months. We're five months behind our deadlines and 40 percent over budget. We hired you to get us back on track with our timelines, resources, and quality results. Here are the materials that your predecessor left when he moved to Botswana. My office is down the hall. Let me know if you have questions. Oh, and by the way, I'm leaving on vacation Friday for two weeks and will be off the grid."

The suggestion here is to enjoy the honeymoon, however long it lasts. Also accept that whatever disharmony or awkwardness accompanies it will shift one way or the other. If your office mates are painfully polite, somewhat distant, and not totally honest, they will hopefully get more real with you once you start to develop rapport by showing them your competence and noble intentions.

---

34 I once started a job on April Fool's Day. My boss walked me around the department to introduce me. It was awkward, because they all thought it was an April Fool's joke. They didn't believe he had really hired someone new. It took a while for people to take me seriously.

35 These are two interrelated resources. It's helpful when your new boss tells you about both of them at the same time.

If people are sullen or hostile, it may be because

- They don't like change,

- They miss the person you're replacing,

- Your predecessor left hard feelings, incompetence, or other collateral damage upon departure,

- You got the job, the promotion, or the project team that they applied for and didn't get, and/or

- You remind them of one of their family members who scares or annoys them.

In this case, "Your mission, should you choose to accept it,"[36] is to figure out why people are infusing your honeymoon period with negativity. Then, in addition to all of your other new job duties and things to learn about your new music, you need to find some ways to reduce the resistance and start to build some harmony into the relationships.

Can You Believe What I'm Putting Up With—and Still Smiling?

A common pattern that's related to the honeymoon phenomenon is the tendency to sing all kinds of songs and put up with all sorts of challenges that you normally wouldn't tolerate. People in new positions or new teams are often willing to take on whatever tasks are delegated to them and work crazy hours at first in an effort to appear cooperative and enthused.

---

36 "Your mission, should you choose to accept it," was always included in the first few minutes of *Mission: Impossible*, a popular TV show in the 1970s. If you've never seen it, or haven't seen it in fifty years, check it out. It's a classic series from that era.

We all want to make a good first impression. Sometimes that happens because you are filling a long-standing void, the rest of the department is glad you've shown up, and they are desperate for your help. Some coworkers will take advantage of you as the newbie who's trying to make good music with everyone else and will jettison to you whatever they've wanted to unload for a long time.

This is yet another balancing act. You want to be helpful and collaborative. At the same time, you don't want to give the impression that you're a doormat that others can walk on, willing to gnaw on whatever bones people toss to you. While singing new songs in Stage 3, it's useful to be

- Clear about the key priorities given to you by your boss or your team,

- Open to opportunities connected to the tasks that people ask you to take on,

- Realistic about your own personal bandwidth regarding how much you can learn, take on, and juggle, given your own experience and energy levels, and

- Able to tactfully set boundaries with others about what you can, should, and want to put into your new music folder.

This balancing act is further supported by two additional ideas: *pacing yourself* and *building up your confidence.*

Pace Yourself

You likely know the expressions, "Rome wasn't built in a day," and "How do you eat an elephant? One bite at a time!" That applies to the need to pace yourself when singing new music. Two musical analogies fit here.

1. **Tempo:** If you sing a song too fast, you run out of breath, and others can't understand the lyrics. Usually, it sounds terrible. Similarly, if you sing too slowly, it drags, sounds boring, and lacks expression. You can also run out of breath if you draw phrases out too long. This sounds bad as well. Pacing ties to the balancing act just mentioned. Some people will have unrealistic expectations about how fast you can solve all the problems in front of you. I know of other situations where a new person is not yet trusted, so the boss or team leader has them sitting around, twiddling their thumbs or whistling *Dixie*, because they haven't been given any specific assignments or direction.

2. **Volume:** In a choir, when people are insecure or anxious, they may sing too loudly, as if to impress others with their voice. Conversely, they may sing too softly, because they are afraid of being off-key or singing the wrong notes. The analogy fits with people singing new songs in a work setting. Due to lack of confidence and familiarity, some new team members talk too much and too loudly in meetings. They're the first to jump into a conversation or offer an opinion. Others hold back when they are new to a role. Their volume is so low that people forget they have entered the room or joined the team.

Yes, you want to impress the new people you're working with. Yes, you want to be in tune when you start singing. Yes, you want to demonstrate your desire to contribute and achieve. You also don't want to step on others' toes or come on too strong at first. If you are aware of these two ends of the continuum of participation, it will be easier to pace yourself and find some middle ground. Be present, chime in, and participate, but don't sing at the top of your lungs. You will know when to raise your volume as you listen, observe, and hence develop credibility and trust with your fellow singers.

Build Your Confidence

One of the reasons that you need to pace yourself is that it takes time to build solid confidence when singing a new song. I don't mean bravado, when you go overboard, trying to convince others (and yourself) how great you are. Don't protest too much. Don't tell me how great you are. Just quietly demonstrate your competence. Building confidence takes time and work.

When I've needed to learn a new song to sing myself, or I have led a choir that's learning a new song, we start out tentatively:

- What's that pitch?

- How do I find my next note from the prior one?

- How do you pronounce that foreign word?

- How do I fit all the syllables into that measure?

- I'm not sure I can hit that high note and sing it softly.

- How do I sing that long phrase without running out of breath?

My choir would often look at a new piece of music and say to me, "No way. We'll never be able to sing this!" Then we'd work on it, learn it, and polish it. Once we'd performed it, they'd ask me, "How did we do that? We sounded rather good!" Answer: we worked on it, built our skills, and increased our confidence.

You can implement several strategies to increase your self-assurance as you begin a new song. Here are three suggestions:

1. **Stay calm and be patient**. Don't expect to know the whole song perfectly during the first run-through.[37] Be optimistic about your ability to learn the music, but also give yourself time to work through it. (Pacing again.) When you make a mistake or miss a cue, don't freak out. See it as an AFLE.[38] Ask yourself, "What can I learn from that gaff? How will it help me do better moving forward?"

2. **Ask for help when learning a new song**. It shows that you're open to input and humble enough to admit that you don't know everything. There is, again, an issue of balance: you don't want to pester fellow singers with too many questions. That might annoy others or make you seem insecure. You also need to be careful to ask smart questions versus superfluous questions that you could answer with a quick Google search or a check with the company's policy manual.

3. **Notice small gains**. It seems to be human nature that if we or others do nine things well and goof up on the tenth, we only focus on our mistake. Managers struggle with this pattern all the time. If most of their team is doing well but one is in trouble, it's the problem child who gets most of that manager's

---

37 Unless you're a great sight-reader like my husband. He can often sing through a piece of music he's never seen before and not miss a note. But that's a specific skill, and even he makes mistakes sometimes.

38 This is an acronym that I'm quite fond of. When faced with a challenging situation or an embarrassing mistake, consider it an AFLE: Another Flipping [or whatever F-word you choose here] Learning Experience! Then, to mitigate your stress or frustration, you can say to yourself, "Okay, this is an AFLE. Maybe a HUGE AFLE. What can I learn from this?" It is a much more positive reframe for a negative experience. It's like changing a song from a minor to a major key.

attention, while the rest of the team gets ignored. So notice your progress as you learn new music:

- ○ I still can't complete that task as fast as my colleagues, but at least I didn't make any mistakes, or

- ○ Even though the boss still wants me to do that faster, it's still twice as fast as the first time I did it.

Quietly pat yourself on the back for progress toward a goal or desired standard of performance.

Final Notes

Making beautiful music together in this third stage of new songs can be both exciting and exhausting. The challenges of surfacing underlying tensions, learning people's styles, negotiating clear boundaries and agreements, and hopefully building trust all require patience and courage.

There are lots of balancing acts involved: when to assert yourself and when to hold back, when to Decide & Announce and when to seek Consensus, when to agree to help out and when to refuse. The musical muscles you develop in this stage will serve you well in Stage 4: Clashing Chords when the first significant disagreements emerge. This next stage will have a profound impact on your ability to maintain and enjoy harmony in your relationships long term.

Rehearsals:

Application Exercises for New Songs

Choose one of these exercises to help you apply the Stage 3 information to your current experience. Then decide if it would be helpful to try a second type of rehearsal.

1. **Do a listening tour**. One of my clients was hired as the CEO of an organization with about 300 employees and multiple locations. She was new to the city as well, so she lacked a network of local professional colleagues as well as context and history about the company. So one of her first priorities was to take what she called her listening tour.

   - It took her a couple of months since she went to every location and talked to as many people as she could in each building. She asked a lot of open-ended questions and took notes. She also gave employees a chance to ask her questions. It was a terrific way for her to get to know the organization and vice versa. She successfully established more trust and open communication in a few months than her predecessor had built in his multiyear tenure. Then, when she had to make difficult decisions or share unpopular news, her messages were based on a solid foundation with her workforce.

   - Depending on your level in your new organization and your time available, consider scheduling a listening tour to get better acquainted with the people on your team and in other departments. Jot down at least three or four questions that you want to ask each individual or small group. Invite them to ask you their questions. If they ask you something that you need to look up or think about before answering, commit to get back to them by a certain date. Then be sure to follow up.

2. **Plan and schedule one-on-ones to "negotiate new relationships."** These differ from listening tours in their format and goal. They're nearly always with just one person, unless there's a compelling reason to talk to a small group together. Their purpose is to find out specifics about the work styles of your boss, peers, and any direct reports you may have. You might also want some one-on-ones with key customers or contacts in other departments with whom you will work closely.

   - You'll find a list of sample questions that you might ask as well as what kinds of information you might plan to share with them at the beginning of this chapter in a section called "Make Commitments and Draw Up Contracts." The list is intended to give you ideas. Amend it to fit your situation and the people you'll be working with. Usually, people appreciate your taking an interest in them and their preferences. The data you collect may help you identify pet peeves and prevent your stepping on hidden land mines with your colleagues.

   - Because most people don't have these kinds of overt conversations, some of your coworkers may find it odd or intrusive. Some may have trouble describing their style. And if trust is low or resentment about your new position is high, people may resist disclosing much. These are additional reasons to plan your negotiation conversations carefully, tailor them to the person and their role, and be ready to adjust if you sense hesitation or annoyance.

3. **Sort out agreements, expectations, and decisions**. This is especially important with your immediate supervisor. Effective leaders know to initiate this with new team members instead of expecting you to read minds and intuit what is needed. Hopefully you were given a job description. If it's not clear, ask for clarification. If it doesn't exist, plan some specific questions about the scope of your duties, tasks, and priorities. Take notes on what you hear. Then, to confirm what you hear, decide if you want to just paraphrase it back in the moment or send an email summarizing the key points.

   - Sometimes, agreements, goals, and priorities need to be formally written and recorded for future reference. Other times, a direct and honest conversation with confirmation of decisions made will suffice. It helps to clarify Levels of Agreement (introduced earlier in this stage), so that everyone understands who has what authority to take which actions. Concurrence on what information gets shared with whom, when, and how is another set of arrangements that is important to articulate. These types of boundary definitions help you avoid sour notes at the start of a new song.

4. **Find a mentor**. You don't have to sort out all of this music on your own. When you're learning new music in a new job or new role, it's often wise to enlist the help of a mentor or coach. That person can support your work on skills such as assertiveness, confidence-building, patient listening, exchanging feedback, setting limits with others, and work-life balance.

   - Some people find a mentor within their new organization who has a positive track record, demonstrated skills, and time to meet with you periodically. Their role may vary, but it frequently includes asking you reflective questions, giving you perspective on your current project or team, or building your skills and confidence in certain areas. It's important that there be the right chemistry or rapport between the mentor and mentee. You may need to check out two or three different people until you find the right match. (See Sniffing and Wagging in Stage 1.)

- Some organizations have formal mentoring programs in which they help new people connect with the right person who has more seniority and experience. Other times, people prefer to look outside of their current company for a mentor who can be more objective and anonymous. An external mentor might also be a paid relationship with someone who bills themself as an executive coach. Regardless of where and how you find a mentor, it can be a great use of your time and resources.

5. **Identify resistance and potential foes**. While you may still be enjoying the honeymoon period of this new music, your efforts to have a listening tour and negotiate relationships may have identified some people who are less than thrilled with the new harmonies you have started to sing. Rather than just writing them off as negative nellies, it is important to decide how to build trust, win them over, or at least reduce the tension between you. This is a tricky process. You don't want your efforts for establishing rapport to create more disharmony.

- There are several reasons that people may not be eager to make harmonious music with you yet, as I discussed earlier. Sometimes, the act of drawing them out, asking them a few nonthreatening questions, and being open to their ideas can begin the thawing process. This is always where I prefer to start; it's most direct and doesn't draw others into the potential drama needlessly.

- Other times, it may be appropriate to ask your boss or a new peer that you trust if they know how to help you build rapport with certain people. Be careful, however. You don't know who is that person's best buddy, or who will run to that person and say, "You'll never guess what our new recruit asked me about you." Nothing ever works 100 percent of the time. In spite of the risk, however, it's important to find a cautious way to improve the music and reduce the resistance before it solidifies into a negative pattern.

6. **Keep a progress log**. Recognize your successive approximations of steps taken toward achieving your goal. Let's say I'm learning to play the violin. My initial notes sound pretty painful, and my neck cramps from trying to hold the instrument properly. While I probably can't play a Bach cantata after two lessons, it's helpful to acknowledge this:

- At least I've learned to hold the violin for thirty minutes of practicing without needing pain meds when I'm done.

- After two lessons, I've got the bowing technique somewhat mastered and can play notes on the E string in tune.

- After a month of lessons and practicing, I've learned three songs in the first book.

- I'm getting more disciplined about practicing between lessons: I get in thirty minutes a day, four times a week versus ten minutes two times a week when I first started.

- These are successive approximations toward your goal of playing in your first recital. It's helpful to keep some kind of written or electronic record of your progress in learning new job duties and building stronger relationships at the beginning of this new song. Recording even small progress indicators helps to build your confidence and reduce your focus on mistakes and frustrations.

7. **Note errors or setbacks**. In addition to a progress log or some method of tracking your progress in the new songs you are singing, it is still important to track what is not working. When we don't pay attention to what needs improvement, we reduce our ability to grow our skills and hence increase the harmony in our relationships.

   - Remember that an AFLE is Another Frigging Learning Experience. Use your AFLEs as a signal of an opportunity to learn, rather than as a bat with which you beat yourself over the head. It might be a quiet little hint of a need for progress, like a very soft note sung delicately in a gentle song. It could also be a loud crash of cymbals and drums that you cannot ignore.

   - The more you can reframe any errors or setbacks as valuable feedback to move you forward, the more likely you are to create better music with the tasks and people in your new song. You might also feel better about the music.

Stage 4

Clashing Chords: Resolving Initial Dissonance

Juanita and Omar are working together on a volunteer project for a local nonprofit one evening. They are waiting for a meeting to start and have some time to chat.

"Juanita, I heard about the new job you started a few months ago. Sounds great. How's it going?"

"Well, Omar, the honeymoon period is definitely over. It was lovely for the two or three weeks that it lasted. Then things exploded: a VP of IT got fired, we lost a major customer, and I got to experience my first budgeting process in this organization. None of it was pretty."

Omar sighs. "Wow! Sounds like the proverbial perfect storm. The dark underbelly of people's personalities tends to come out at times like that. What were people doing that added to the stress?"

"The IT department went into total chaos mode. Since their functions impact everyone else, no one could get any tech problems solved or new programs set up. If you contacted someone in IT, you got a snippy response or no reply at all. This, of course, made everyone else cranky. The loss of the major account threw a wrench in our revenue projections, so we all had to figure out adjustments for the rest of the fiscal year.

"Yikes—and you were doing budgets in the middle of this mess?"

"Yeah. One of my teammates warned me that our boss always gets edgy when we're preparing the budget, so I tried to not take the harsh criticism or slow response time personally. It's been anything but warm and fuzzy of late."

"You've always been the calm one when others are freaking out, Juanita. What has worked for you in your prior jobs that would help you cope with the cacophony there?"

"Thanks for the vote of confidence, Omar. I guess I have to keep reminding myself to not get threatened by nasty comments. When someone says something harsh, I try to extract any useful feedback and ignore the snark. I need to see this as a phase we're going through and have some confidence that we'll come out stronger when we get through this rough period."

"Sounds good so far, but how do you keep yourself from getting snarky too?"

"I keep looking for the sweet spot between joining in their pity parties and panic attacks on one end of the continuum and acting blasé like nothing's wrong on the other end. I'm doing my best to ask smart questions and separate facts from fears and rumors. I'm also going to the gym more often to burn off the stress."

"Good job. Way to leverage your previous achievements for use in this new challenge. The way you respond to all the insanity around you now will help to create more positive, harmonious patterns going forward. Keep me posted on how it all rolls out." Omar pauses. "Oh, it looks like the meeting is finally starting. I hope this one's not too long."

The Honeymoon Period—a Distant Memory

For any first notes that you sing with a new boss, team, or project, the proverbial honeymoon that may have lasted an hour or month must come to an end. It is at that point that you have the start of your official disharmony with one or more people at work. It may be the first time that you or someone else loses their temper about either a big or small problem. It might be when you find out that colleagues are withdrawing, withholding information, or quietly working to sabotage your efforts. It could be the moment when you realize that you are totally overwhelmed with what has been delegated to you. Whether it's overt and in your face, or quiet and behind your back, the honeymoon is officially over.

This shift can be sudden or can creep up on you gradually. Either way, it can be a shock to realize that you were enjoying the beautiful music that you made together at first, and now the song sounds discordant and painful to your ears. The novelty of the new relationship has worn off. The song may start to become repetitive and boring. Whatever trust and excitement you had built up in the beginning is now being threatened.

This is when people's real personalities rise to the top with a gradual crescendo or a sudden fortissimo. I worked on a project once that demonstrated this phenomenon. At first, the company president presented himself as the quintessentially enlightened leader. He seemed to be values-driven and to care about his employees, contractors, and customers. I thought I had found consulting nirvana—the ideal company with the practices and priorities that completely aligned with my own.

That was until the company lost a major client, had a sudden drop in income, and started looking at whom to lay off. At this point, the president's underlying temperament started to come through loud and clear. Under the pressure of his financial challenges, he shifted from the way he *wanted* to be to how he had *learned* to act in tough environments. He got moody, stingy, and mean. He showed signs of strong prejudice against women, people of color, and people whose religion was different from his own. The progressive nice-guy mask was off, and the default setting underneath was not at all handsome or melodious.

This is not to say that he was a bad person. It's common that when we're under pressure—mad, frightened, or otherwise uncomfortable—many of the positive behaviors we aspire to demonstrate go right out the window. We start singing off-key. Think of a tame house cat or dog who shows you love and affection with loud purring or incessant tail wagging. But when they are cornered, injured, or upset in some way, they hiss and scratch or bark and bite. It's hard to recognize the savage beast that they have become.

Remember that the honeymoon period will end sometime, and when it does, you or others may not show up as your best self. It's the first speed bump on the road of your relationship, the first sour note in the song you've just started singing. What's important at this point is to not freak out, overreact, or assume that it's over and you have to leave. Instead, you need to

- Step back,

- Pause the song,

- Take a deep breath,

- Maybe count to ten like your mom told you to do when you were upset,

- Analyze what's going on and what you can learn from it, and then

- Restart the music more skillfully: decide which are the best actions for you to take.

More Speed Bumps—Common Responses to Conflict

The way you respond to the first speed bump may set the tone for how you respond to subsequent challenges later on in the music. When I talk with clients about resolving conflicts, I like to say that anytime you have two or more people in the same room (or on the same call or the same email/text chain), you have the potential for disagreements.

Interpersonal conflict is common, natural, and inevitable. Many people avoid it like the plague. Some people actually enjoy conflict and may have been brought up in families with lots of loud, overt arguing. As a result, they are not afraid of it and sometimes actively provoke it with others. When people are on either extreme of this continuum—let's say they might be intensely conflict-avoidant or frequently looking for a good fight—they tend to manage disagreements poorly.

One important aspect of conflict is how you choose to respond to it. When handled effectively, static between individuals can lead to new, creative ideas and stronger, healthier relationships. Unfortunately, many people have neither the skills nor the courage to create those positive results.

Kenneth Thomas and Ralph Kilmann developed a model that talks about five common responses to conflict that can be abbreviated: A-A-C-C-C.

- *Avoidance* is just what it sounds like: You don't address the conflict but instead, ignore it. It's like an ostrich putting its head in the sand, thinking, "If I don't look at it, it will go away." Avoidance might include withdrawing, postponing, or somehow sidestepping the problem. As a result, you don't meet your own needs and usually don't help the other person either. If you're lucky, the problem will go away on its own. Often, the problem gets worse. It is sometimes called lose-lose because the conflict is not addressed or resolved.

- *Accommodation* is often seen as weakness, extreme politeness, or generosity. You yield to someone else's demands but don't communicate your own thoughts and feelings honestly. You may meet others' needs by doing what they ask, but you tend to deny your own priorities and reactions. People who accommodate tend to feel imposed upon and resentful. You may be solving the conflict for others, but it remains or multiplies for you. People consider it lose-win: I lose because I don't stand up for myself; you win because I did what you wanted.

- *Competition* in a conflict scenario is not like healthy athletic competition. Instead, it is exerting your own will over others, ignoring their priorities or responses. It might mean defending your point of view and doing what you think is in everyone's best interests. It can be using formal authority or the power of your personality to force others to meet your needs. It may be seen as win-lose: I win because I got you to do what I wanted; you lose because I was insisting on my approach and ignoring your views and feelings.

- *Compromise* may be the best you can hope for to resolve a conflict. It amounts to splitting the difference or dividing the pie. The good news is that we each get some of what we wanted; we each had to make concessions; and we generally needed some productive discussion to identify a solution. The downside of Compromise is that it is often unstable and creates resentment later on. If I'm more focused on what I had to give up than on what I actually got in the exchange, I'm likely to be unhappy, trust you less, and maybe want revenge later on. Compromise can also lead to lower quality decisions if the two sides need to water things down in order to walk away with a small portion of what they wanted. It ends up being win-lose, because while we both won something, we both had to give up something as well.

- *Collaboration* is often considered to be the best possible response to conflict. Sometimes that's true. It means that we sit down, discuss the problem directly, share concerns and requests honestly, and seek a solution that we both completely buy into. We have to want to resolve the issue, have a modicum of trust, and see each other as allies who will solve the problem together. If we consider each other to be adversaries, our chances are slim or none that we'll find an agreement that works 100 percent for both of us. It is the most stable of the five responses because of the mindset and dialogue that it requires. The bad news about Collaboration is that it takes more time, more skills, and is not always possible or worth the effort. Avoidance, Accommodation, Competition, and Compromise can manage a conflict, but Collaboration is the only one that really *resolves* it. As a result, Collaboration is the only response that is labeled as win-win, since, by definition, we find and agree to a path forward that we both are satisfied with.

Each style has pros and cons, depending on the situation. Any one of these responses can be the best possible option, the most appropriate to use that creates beautiful music. In other scenarios, that same style can be a terrible choice that produces more disharmony and chaos.

	Good Choice	Bad (or Disastrous) Option
Avoidance	When you are indifferent	When it's important or recurring
	When it's a minor issue	When repercussions are far-reaching
	When there's physical threat	When you have to protect others
Accommodation	When it's safer to give in	When it makes you look weak
	When you feel generous	When you'll resent giving in
	When you have no authority	When others depend on you
	When it's not important to you	When it's important to you or others
Competition/ Power	When it's a crisis	When you'll make a small issue bigger or more volatile
	When you have the authority to decide	When others challenge your authority or outrank you
	When you only need compliance	When you need buy-in, support
	When trust is high	When trust is low

	Good Choice	Bad (or Disastrous) Option
Compromise	When something is better than nothing	When something is not sufficient
	When people are happy with half the pie	When people are dissatisfied with the half they got
	When the decision is solid	When the decision is too watered down or low-quality
	When people feel good about the decisions long term	When people have buyer's remorse and want to renegotiate ASAP
Collaboration	When you need full buy-in and commitment	When compliance is all you need
	When the issue is important	When it's minor or short term
	When you have energy/time	When you're stressed, tired, rushed
	When you're patient and want to build trust	When you're angry, scared, or don't care about the relationship

People who handle speed bumps and sour notes well have two important assets:

1. They have all five of these tools in their interpersonal toolboxes. They understand them, know how to use each one, and have the courage and willingness to use the right one when the song calls for it.

2. They have the emotional intelligence and awareness to know when to use which one with which people for which situations.

Some people have an instinctive ability to know how to use these five tools skillfully in the right way at the right time. It's not unlike the rare individuals who have perfect pitch or can play an instrument by ear at the age of four.

- The bad news: the rest of us need to learn how to apply them effectively.

- The good news: they are learnable skills, just like learning to sing or play a musical instrument.

Initial Attractions Become Annoyances

You may have heard the expression "opposites attract." It's definitely true when people are dating and contemplating marriage. If I'm an introvert and have trouble initiating conversation with others, but you're a clear extrovert who is comfortable chatting affably with everyone, I might initially admire that and wish I had your skills. But let's say you and I get married. It may drive me to distraction that you always want us to go to parties and invite lots of people over to our house, while I'd prefer that the two of us spend more quiet evenings at home together.

An example at work would be if I were flexible but disorganized, and my boss was more structured and precise. At first, I might think, "Wow! My boss is so prepared and on time. She never misses deadlines, and her reports are spot on. Now that I'm working with her, I hope to learn from her and emulate her behaviors. I want my song to be like hers." It is common, however, that as the song plays on, your boss's exacting behaviors might begin to grate on you. You might feel like she is nit-picky, overly critical of errors, and resistant to new approaches.

When you work with or for someone whose music is quite different from your own, the challenge is to find the middle ground. How do you find the sweet spot between the extremes of "Oh, I LOVE that characteristic" and "If they do that one more time, I'll scream"? On a good day, you recognize how the two of you are different. You talk about it and look for ways to meet in the middle. Ideally, you can also learn from each other.

Let's say I like structured meetings with agendas and firm start and stop times. Your preference is for meetings to start when everyone is ready, go till we're done, and not be limited by rigid agendas that restrict brainstorming and open dialogue. How can we incorporate enough structure and timeliness so that I'm not squirming, while still building into the agenda enough room for the free flow of ideas that you value?

Another common type of discord would be between the detail person and the big-picture thinker. I once worked with a wonderful man named Kevin. He was smart, kind, and hard-working. He was also very precise and concrete in his thinking. He always wanted to see the facts first and take things one step at a time.

By contrast, my tendency is to start by looking at the whole situation and where we want to end up, and then fill in the details within that framework. I am prone to trust my instincts first and then consider the data. So he and I had interesting meetings. We had to figure out how to speak each other's language or sing in each other's key. We learned that

- If Kevin had information to share with me, he needed to tell me, "I have some facts about the XYZ project. I want to give them to you, so we'll know how to budget for this." Voilà! He gave me the context first, a picture frame within which to put his facts before he started his data dump. I knew what song we'd sing before he started the music.

- If I had information to share with Kevin, I realized that I needed to have my specifics in hand, preferably on paper or in an email document, and organized in a sequential way that would lead him from the first to the last notes of the song in a logical progression.

I have often sung with other people whose vocal ranges are higher or lower than my own. If their range is much higher than mine, they'll pitch the song so high that I'm squeaking out the top notes and sound like a wounded animal. If I pitch it too low for them, they struggle to hit the low notes and often sound like they're growling rather than singing.[39] When you find a key that works for both of you, instead of being the key of C or G or B flat, I call it the key of compromise. We often need to look for the key of compromise at work as well.

Peel Subsequent Layers Off the Onion— Personality Types and Emotional Intelligence

A common pattern is characteristic of this fourth stage of confronting initial dissonance and finding ways to resolve differences. It's a bit like peeling back layers of an onion to get better acquainted with the core. With onions, it's easy: as you peel back layers, you find . . . more onion.

With people the music is more complicated.[40] When you work with someone over time and get to know them better, their true personality traits emerge more clearly. Unless

---

39 My youngest son and I have this musical battle frequently. His voice has become more tenor, and mine is most comfortable in the alto range. Because we know about this difference, we smile when one of us pitches a song too high or low for the other. Then we adjust to a different key—the key of compromise.

40 And like with onions, our human layers and shortcomings sometimes make us cry.

they have high levels of emotional intelligence, they tend to be less aware of how they're impacting others, less able to control their own feelings, and less skilled at managing others' emotions in stressful situations.

When you and the people you work with have peeled back some onion layers, you at least have a better idea of who and what you're dealing with. If you're paying attention, you're familiar with people's behavior patterns. You know who you can count on in a crisis, because they stay calm, clear, and strong. You are aware of others' hot buttons that make people angry, scared, or hypercritical. With healthier, more melodic relationships, you can talk about some of these inner layers and negotiate ways to better support each other.

For example, you know that your boss gets short-tempered and dissonant when you have to develop the next year's budget. This awareness can help you preempt a conflict by talking about how stressful the next few weeks may be while you are working on the budget. You can ask how to help the process go more smoothly. You may also be able to avoid taking the boss's cranky comments personally, knowing they're more related to the budget than to you.

If you know a colleague gets intimidated in certain meetings and clams up, refusing to sing and share his good ideas, you could make a point of inviting him into the music and ask, "What do you think about this proposal?" You could also prepare for better music from him by suggesting before the meeting that you'll overtly encourage him to chime in and help him to prepare for that participation.

Personality Types

The Myers-Briggs Type Inventory (MBTI) and Kolbe Indexes described in the Overture and Stage 1 are two of many assessments available to help you analyze your own personal styles and preferences. They also give you a framework with which to view others' behaviors and make educated guesses about their profiles. The advantages to using these measurements include the ability to increase two key emotional intelligence tools—self-awareness and awareness of others:

- If you understand more about yourself and how you move through the world, you can make some decisions about which tactics work well and which behaviors might yield impacts that differ from what you intend. You can then work to shift your approach in the hope of better results.

- The frameworks also provide a lens through which to observe others' actions and patterns. Those observations then help you to make some predictions about how people may interact with you and how they may influence the music. When you consider that someone's behavior may be a function of their personality type or how they're hardwired, it may also help you hear the current disharmony objectively, rather than to take it as a personal attack on you.

Emotional Intelligence

The six emotional intelligence skills described in Stage 1 represent additional onion layers that may become apparent during initial dissonance that occurs in your relationship. When you or others tend to misuse or underutilize any of these skills, the deficiencies may contribute to the conflicts.

1. **Emotional self-awareness** is defined in the Genos model as your ability to notice the pros and cons of

the behaviors you demonstrate with others and what impact you have on them.

2. **Emotional awareness of others** is about your capacity to pay attention to others' needs and reactions, validate their feelings, and modify your own style to interact more effectively with them when needed.

3. **Authenticity** has to do with how well you express yourself honestly and openly, keep commitments, and inspire others to do the same with you.

4. **Emotional reasoning** involves your willingness to consider your and others' feelings and values in addition to the fact-based data that you use to make decisions.

5. **Emotional self-management** relates to your ability to recognize and improve how to handle your own moods and emotions as they impact your activities and interactions with others.

6. **Inspiring performance** entails how you encourage optimal performance in others when you and they are addressing challenges, working toward goals, and encouraging each other.

Team Clashes

The only thing worse than someone singing off-key is a whole bunch of people who are not in tune with each other. During the coronavirus pandemic of 2020 when people were quarantined, video conference calls became popular for meetings, happy hours, and also choirs.

I was on several unfortunate calls where people all had their microphones on, not muted, and they were trying to sing "Happy

Birthday" or songs for a religious service or some other songs they all knew. The result was a painful cacophony! People can't always hear accurately in an online conference call. There can be slight delays and pitches can be distorted. So people would start the song at different times, in different keys, and proceed at different tempos. At times, team interactions in the workplace resemble several people singing badly on a video conference call.

In 1965, Bruce Tuckman first proposed the model of group development known as Forming-Storming-Norming-Performing-Adjourning.[41] In many ways, his model parallels the six stages of relationship evolution I describe in this book. When you put a group of individuals together into any sort of team, they also go through predictable phases.

The Forming stage is similar to the Auditions, First Notes and New Songs I have outlined so far. People are polite, checking each other out, and they avoid conflict. Tuckman's Storming stage relates to the Clashing Chords between individuals. Both are uncomfortable yet necessary for the team or individual relationships to progress. The Norming stage resembles the Encores (Stage 5 in this book), where there is more collaboration and fine-tuning of dynamics.

Finally, Performing and Adjourning parallel my Finales (Stage 6), where relationships either hum along smoothly or finish a project and move on. Once you increase your competence in conducting the stages of individual relationship evolution, it is easier to understand and lead these elements of team development as well.

Many other theories of team development support Tuckman's model. One that has been wildly popular in the last two decades is based on Patrick Lencioni's *Five Dysfunctions of a Team* and his subsequent books. His interconnected dysfunctions of stumbling blocks include

---

41   His original model had only the first four stages. He added Adjourning in 1977.

1. Absence of Trust

2. Fear of Conflict

3. Lack of Commitment

4. Avoidance of Accountability

5. Inattention to Results

Any one of these factors, much less a combination of two or more, can feed into the static among team members. Because the dysfunctions are interlocking and build on each other, there is usually more than one in play at a time. The language in the model can be helpful in first analyzing what's missing in the team dynamics and then deciding what steps to take to address the deficiencies that are causing the team's cacophony.

Leslie's Double Bind Theory

My good friend Leslie taught me something about marriage relationships that perfectly applies to this stage of relationship development at work. She said that if you're dating someone or know them casually and have an argument, you may tell yourself,

- "Well, we clearly don't agree on that," or

- "S/he is really being a jerk about this and is definitely confused about the facts," or

- "If that's how s/he thinks and feels about this issue, we'll have to just agree to disagree," or

- "I'm not sure I want to be around someone with that perspective or values."

But if you're married to that person when the argument occurs, you risk a double bind by telling yourself,

- "Oh no, I'm MARRIED to this conflict! I'm stuck with it! It will never change," or

- "You'll always do this to me," or

- "This is awful. We'll *never* resolve this. What will I do?" or

- "I can't live with this disharmony. We'll have to get a divorce!"

The double bind is that instead of just focusing on the event causing the clash, you "awfulize" and assume that you will never resolve it or restore harmony. You make the discord into a bigger, louder issue than it needs to be by either (1) linking it to past conflicts ("This is just like when you yelled at me, forgot to follow through, lied to me and so on, last month.") or (2) projecting continued sour notes in the future ("It'll never change. It will always be like this.").

I remember exactly where I was sitting one month after our wedding when I had my first major argument with my wonderful husband, to whom I've been married for over four decades. I don't recall the content of the conflict. I just remember that I felt totally overwhelmed and panicked. I was certain that I had just married this problem and convinced that it would never get resolved—that I was stuck with it. I had fallen into Leslie's Double Bind.[42]

Leslie's Double Bind Theory applies to work relationships as well, especially in this fourth stage of Clashing Chords. Now

---

42 Once I calmed down, I was able to remember Leslie's Double Bind Theory. That allowed me to start breathing again and ultimately find a time to approach my husband and look for a solution that worked for both of us.

that the honeymoon is over and people may not be all sweet and melodic with each other, it is very tempting to think,

- "Oh no, I'm *stuck with* this cranky boss, nit-picking colleague, or nonresponsive customer. I'll have to live with his or her nasty patterns forever," or

- "I thought this was the dream job, perfect boss, or best possible project team, but now I know it'll just be a recurring nightmare until I can take my vacation time," or

- "That's it. S/he's sung this badly before. It'll never improve. I need to quit and find something better!"

Howard Markman, a well-known psychologist who specializes in marriage and family therapy, advises people to separate the *event* from the *issue*. His suggestion has important implications for work relationships. Here are some ways that people often jump from a specific event to a larger, more global issue:

Event: You didn't finish your part of our report on time, so now we've missed the deadline, and our boss is breathing down my neck.

Issue: You seem disorganized and don't manage your time well. As a result, you have trouble keeping commitments for deadlines that you agree to. This causes me to not trust you and frequently pester you about time frames and responsibility.

Event: You didn't tell me the truth about how much the customer disliked my presentation. So I kept calling the customer, assuming they wanted to close the deal. I felt like a fool when I found out they weren't the least bit interested and had hired another company.

Issue: You seem to struggle with being assertive and sharing honest feedback. Maybe you worry that I'll be mad and not hear you out. I'd much rather hear negative feedback and know where I stand with you than be left in the dark. What do I need to do to encourage you to be more straightforward and honest with me?

Markman recommends that, especially when one or more people are upset in the moment, you only talk about that event at first. Exchange feedback using the feedback model outlined in the next chapter and find a way to resolve this specific disagreement or out-of-tune song.

Then set a time later, when you've both calmed down, to talk about the larger issue and find ways to address it together and avoid future events. The way you approach initial dissonance in your work relationships may set a pattern for how you respond to subsequent challenges. Learning to separate the event from the issue is an essential tool to help the new relationship develop more harmoniously.

Emergence of Scar Tissue

In Stage 1 of relationship development, Auditions, when you are deciding if you even want to join the choir, part of your process is to unpack your emotional baggage. One item that is often packed into that suitcase is emotional scar tissue from painful or frustrating songs that you've sung in the past.

When Clashing Chords first appear in a relationship at work, at least two types of reactions may occur. One is the possibility that this initial disagreement ties back to some of your earlier emotional scars. It can also be related to your colleagues' old wounds or personal triggers you may not be aware of. The result is that you and/or your peers may overreact to what is a relatively minor problem.

It's like a message that goes off in your head or theirs, saying, "Oh no! Here we go again!" We tend to have less patience with issues that remind us of emotional scars from the past.

Another common occurrence is the risk of developing new scar tissue as a result of this initial clash. You may step on an interpersonal land mine by annoying or disappointing a colleague, because you weren't aware of the policy, protocol, or other people's expectations. You may be overwhelmed by new duties, new processes, or the need to learn new skills. Regardless of what causes the first disharmony, it's crucial to address it early and appropriately so that a small event does not become a larger, more dissonant issue that creates new emotional scars.

When you develop emotionally intelligent skills, you become more aware of how you and others react when chords do clash. That, in turn, helps you to build your confidence in addressing initial disagreements constructively. By using the two styles that Thomas and Kilmann define as Compromise and Collaboration, your chances are much better of resolving initial differences and avoiding emotional scars than the people who typically Avoid and Accommodate on one end of the scale, hoping the problems will go away or resolve themselves (which they often don't), or the folks who frequently use their construct of Competition, trying to impose their views on others, often making the disagreements louder and more discordant, while creating additional scar tissue in the new relationship.

Some people believe that when we are born, we are pure and innocent. However, all of us have some emotional scar tissue by the time we reach adulthood. So the goal is not to remain unscathed. It is important to acknowledge we all have our defenses and pet peeves, and we bring them to work with us every day uninvited. People who create harmony at work develop the skills to recognize and navigate those emotional scars.

Build Trust and Patience

Trust is one of those words that gets tossed around frequently when describing relationships of any kind. People have written numerous books, delivered plenty of seminars, and posted many podcasts on the subject. Trust can be slow to build, difficult to maintain over time, and, sadly, can be destroyed in a minute. Sometimes it only takes one inappropriate comment, one betrayal of a confidence, or one unethical action to undo the trust that you have worked hard to create and support for years.

There are so many stories of what gets discovered when an employee resigns, is fired, takes vacation, goes out on medical leave, or dies suddenly. Sometimes coworkers have had a sense that something is amiss, and other times they are completely blindsided.

For example, when the executive director of a small nonprofit took a job in another city, the board members and remaining staff were appalled to find that the executive director had hidden in her desk months of notices about unpaid payroll taxes. The backlog of taxes due, plus the resulting penalties and interest payments, left the organization with such a huge debt that they were forced to close their doors. Since the executive director had resigned, there was no way to repair the damage and rebuild trust. The board may not have even wanted to make that effort, had she still been in town.

In another company, a manager was investigating the high rate of turnover among women in his department. He discovered that one of the men who worked there had been sexually harassing several women and had had affairs with some of them. The abused women had all chosen to resign, rather than report it and confront their accuser. After consulting with their legal and human resources departments, the manager had to make a difficult decision. Should they fire this man outright? Or might discipline and counseling realistically help him behave better and rebuild trust with his manager and peers?

Sometimes the breach of trust is less egregious. It might be that you and I frequently work together on projects. I might need you to provide information or do your part of the task before I can complete my responsibilities and meet our deadlines. Let's say you repeatedly tell me you'll bring me your contributions by X date, and you usually miss the deadlines. Or maybe you always arrive five to ten minutes late for a meeting, often seeming frazzled and unprepared. When that's your pattern, it becomes difficult, if not impossible, for me to trust that you'll honor deadlines or show up on time and be prepared.

When this is the pattern, I may start telling you I need your materials by Wednesday when I really need them by Friday. Or I might tell you the meeting starts at 1:45, when the true start time is 2:00. You then think, "She doesn't really need it by Wednesday—I have more time," or "They never start meetings on time. I can show up later." The net result is a loss of trust on both sides: neither of us believes the other anymore, and we start adjusting our behavior accordingly.

Vulnerability-Based Trust

In Patrick Lencioni's *Five Dysfunctions of a Team* and one of his sequels, *The Advantage*, he creates a second pyramid to show the building blocks needed to overcome team dysfunctions and create productive work relationships:

- Vulnerability-based Trust

- Productive Conflict

- Commitment

- Accountability

- Results

He shows how solid interactions start with trust that then link to vulnerability. He describes it as being more than just predictability: I trust you'll meet your deadlines or show up on time. While that's important, it's not sufficient. There also needs to be a willingness to be vulnerable, so that people feel safe enough that they can be honest and transparent with each other. It's the kind of trust that allows you to say things like this:

- "I messed up, it's my fault, and I'm really sorry."

- "I'm totally overwhelmed and need your help."

- "I feel discounted. I'm frustrated that you often ignore my input."

That level of vulnerability-based trust gives people the confidence to share their mistakes and concerns, give honest feedback and, thus, ask for help without fear of reprisals. It's a deeper, more difficult type of trust to build and maintain than trusting others to keep commitments and do good work. It takes time and hard work to develop. This deeper kind of trust is the building block that is required for productive conflict. These two elements make way for stronger commitment and accountability, which lead to better results.

Trust also can evaporate instantly with one experience of a loud, clashing chord when someone feels attacked, embarrassed, or undermined. Much of the disharmony in the workplace happens when trust is somehow broken, either all at once or gradually eroded over time.

Emotional Bank Accounts

In Stephen Covey's multi-decade best seller, *The 7 Habits of Highly Effective People*, he created a wonderful metaphor that he calls the Emotional Bank Account. It's the ideal vehicle to explore levels of trust and how to increase them. He says that "it describes the amount of trust that's been built up in a relationship," in the same way that savings can be built up or depleted in a financial bank account.

"If I make deposits into an Emotional Bank Account with you through courtesy, kindness, honesty, and keeping my commitments to you, I build up a reserve," according to Covey, and hence more trust. If I make a small mistake and do something that you dislike, that negative action makes a small emotional withdrawal and depletes the reserve in the account a little bit. You may be angry with me, but you still fundamentally like and respect me as a person. We still have a positive balance in our Emotional Bank Accounts with each other.

Conversely, if I am often rude, inconsiderate, inattentive, manipulative, or unreliable, I'm making larger withdrawals in my Emotional Bank Account with you. If we make more withdrawals than deposits and the balance in the account gets too low, we run the risk of being overdrawn with each other. It's just like with your financial bank account: if you put in $100 and try to withdraw $200, your checks will bounce, and your credit score will go down.

When you are addressing initial dissonance in this new song that you are singing at work, you probably still have a positive balance with your colleagues. Assuming they were happy that you were hired, promoted, or assigned to a project team, your Emotional Bank Accounts are still likely in the black. You're more able to cut each other some slack and write off the first few withdrawals as your being new to the team, not having the right information, or not being clear about protocols.

There are, however, many ways that people in new relationships start out with fairly low balances in their Emotional Bank Accounts with others. If, for example, your colleagues

- Wanted another candidate to be hired rather than you,

- Didn't want someone new brought onto the team at all,

- Are at all threatened by you, your competence, and your experience, or

- Have any kind of emotional baggage about you and your presence on the team,

it may only take a few small withdrawals for you to be overdrawn with each other.

I had one client where two vice presidents in the organization, Carl and Bob, had a strong working relationship and a positive Emotional Bank Account balance with each other. There was good chemistry between them, and they naturally liked each other. When Bob left to take a job in another city, his replacement, Dean, was hired. There were clashing chords between Carl and Dean within a week or so of Dean's arrival. Carl missed Bob and was certain Dean would never measure up.

Dean was basically starting this new important relationship with Carl overdrawn. With lots of coaching, Carl and Dean would sometimes get to a slightly positive balance in their Emotional Bank Accounts. But there were more withdrawals than deposits, leaving them often overdrawn, angry, and mistrustful of each other. Each minor mistake that either guy made was taken personally because trust was so chronically low. They'll never be best friends or go to dinner together. They learned, however, that if they wanted to get their jobs done effectively and keep from driving each other nuts, they had to make conscious efforts to make more deposits than withdrawals to keep their Emotional Bank Account reserves up and seek to rebuild trust.

Patience

Patience is definitely a first cousin to trust. It's easier to be patient with others if you are well rested, calm, and feel safe with someone. It also helps if you generally like and agree with the other person. Patience plays a key role in every stage of relationship development, but it's especially important during initial clashes.

Our ability to be patient with others is tied to at least four factors: stress, personality, new behaviors, and self-acceptance.

- If I am **stressed** to the hilt, I'm like a rubber band that has been stretched to its limit, often for a long period of time. I have no elasticity left, and so I become brittle and likely to snap. If I am that overstretched rubber band, it's difficult, if not impossible, for me to be patient with others. As you're getting to know new coworkers and confronting initial clashes, you can often recognize the uber-stressed people. They often radiate tension wherever they go.

- Some people are just inherently less patient than others. That's how they're hardwired. They may be the smart, Type-A, hard-charging **personality** whose mind moves quickly and whose mouth moves even faster. They see a task or a problem, look for a solution, and are eager to get it handled. They finish others' sentences. Some of these speed demons also thrive on caffeine, while others just run on natural adrenaline. They may accomplish a lot, but often at a cost in their relationships. They tend to have a reputation for getting irritated with others who move at a slower pace than they do. Again, these intense colleagues will often show a predictable pattern of impatience, so recognizing that will help you navigate initial and subsequent clashes.

- Often, when we try something for the first time, we perform badly or fail completely. It takes time and multiple repetitions of the desired action to build our competence and confidence. So when you and others are trying out new ways to interact, be patient with yourself and others. Know that with practice and sometimes clear feedback, the **new behavior** may get easier, or at least feel less awkward.

- The most difficult factor to identify can be when we are impatient with ourselves. **Self-acceptance** is challenging, because you may be your own harshest critic. Awareness of your shortcomings is clearly an important asset in creating harmony at work. However, the downside of knowing yourself well is that you are all too familiar with your faults, even when others don't see them. So when you acknowledge a mistake that you have made repeatedly, you tend to get impatient that you're singing that note *wrong again*. Some people can be forgiving of others but have a hard time cutting themselves any slack. For others, because they are hypercritical of themselves, they project that negativity and impatience onto others as well. Brené Brown has written and spoken extensively about the powerful impacts of shame and guilt. They're directly tied to our ability to be patient with ourselves and others.

Final Notes

Trust and patience are two characteristics that people talk about extensively but often have no idea how to build and maintain. As soon as someone says to you, "It's okay, you can trust me," it tends to make people nervous and even less trusting. It's similar when you feel agitated: it generally will not help you to calm down if someone tells you that "you just need to be patient and calm down!" It's easy to say, "Let's have positive Emotional Bank Account balances and vulnerability-based trust," but they're both difficult to create and sustain over time.

Your good intentions to trust and be patient are necessary but rarely sufficient. Even though they are often in short supply, both behaviors can be developed with conscious and consistent effort. They require time, skill, and motivation. Ironically, it takes trust and patience to develop trust and patience:

- We have to trust and believe that we can create more confidence and honesty with each other, and

- We need patience to learn the music and make better harmony together moving forward.

The people who most effectively navigate this fourth stage of relationship harmony are the ones with the most willingness to observe patterns, exchange feedback, avoid double binds, foster trust, and exercise patience. They have also developed the healthy relationship skills that will help to propel them into Stage 5: Encores. Next, we will look at what additional tools and perspectives are essential for increasing the relationship harmony and further improving the music over time.

Rehearsals:

Application Exercises for Clashing Chords

Choose one of these exercises to help you apply the Stage 4 information to your current experience. Then decide if it would be helpful to try a second type of rehearsal.

1. **Plan how to react to your first speed bump.** It's important to know that the honeymoon period will eventually end, sooner or later. The tendency is to freak out, assume the sky is falling, and believe that it's the beginning of the end. (See Leslie's Double Bind.) So remind yourself to

   - Step back and pause the song,

   - Take a deep breath and maybe count to ten like your mom told you to do when you were upset,

   - Analyze what's going on and what you can learn from it, and then

   - Restart the music more skillfully: decide which are the best actions for you to take.

   Use your insights and awareness from this first discordant note to help you either avoid or prepare for the next challenge. Make some notes about this first experience. You might want to get some advice from a trusted colleague, friend, or family member. All of these efforts to reflect and record will help you leverage this important AFLE (aka learning opportunity).

2. **Consider taking the Thomas-Kilmann Conflict Mode Instrument** referenced earlier. It will provide useful information about how you believe you most often respond to conflict. There are positive and negative attributes for each style and both good and bad times to use each one. The inventory may give you ideas of what to use more often and which styles to rely on less frequently. It will also provide a framework within which to observe and analyze others' responses to conflict. This, in turn, might help you predict how people might act in conflict situations and give you ideas about how best to respond to them.

   Please remember that your scores on this instrument only reflect what I like to call your own warped view of yourself. Sometimes people believe that they collaborate and compromise often and score themselves accordingly. But their impact on others does not always match their intention. Others may see them as using Avoidance, Accommodation, or Competition. The Thomas-Kilmann Instrument is not appropriate to use to get 360 feedback from your colleagues. There are other ways to request opinions about your impact on others. That said, it is still a valuable tool to help you think about and possibly adjust your responses to conflict more intentionally.

3. **Think about a relationship that started out strong but has become increasingly annoying.** Answer these questions:

   - What did I initially like or respect about this person? Why was I excited to work with them? What were the behaviors or expressed values that were a draw for me?

   - At what point did the music between us begin to shift from a major to minor key? What were the first aggravations—either small or large?

- What other events, actions, or conversations have occurred since that first minor chord that have increased my negative feelings toward this person?

- What are my options for improving the music with this person and transposing it back to a major key? How might I leverage the initial positives to rebuild rapport now?

One approach that might help with this analysis is to recognize style and priority differences between you. Sometimes, when we meet a person who is our polar opposite, it's very appealing at first. This happens in personal relationships all the time: it is said that opposites attract. Review the MBTI and Thomas-Kilmann models, as well as the styles outlined in other assessments. If you and the other person are opposites, ask yourself these questions:

- How can we leverage those differences, so that we learn from and complement each other rather than annoy the daylights out of each other?

- How can I predict different responses and perspectives from them and not let their approach annoy, threaten, or discourage me?

- What can I learn about myself and the other person, based on the way their initial appeal has become challenging? How can I find the key of compromise between us?

4. **Review Lencioni's *Five Dysfunctions of a Team*.** Whether the disharmony that you've begun to experience is with an individual or a team, ask yourself which dysfunction is creating the most cacophony now. Think about what options you have that will help you address the dysfunction(s) and begin to repair or improve the music.

Decide if your best approach is to read, study, and journal. Conversely, it might be to get coaching from a boss, peer, or someone outside of work. The most challenging, sometimes riskiest, and possibly the most productive route is to approach the person with whom you're clashing. Plan how to share your concerns directly but calmly, without anger, accusation, or apology. Use I-statements, such as "I'm frustrated/disappointed/confused by the sense that we are often not on the same page regarding priorities or approach," rather than "You're really annoying. You argue or discount whatever I say. Why can't you just support me once in a while like a normal person?"

Find a way to plan and possibly rehearse this conversation so that you have more confidence and composure when you initiate it. Anticipate challenging responses or questions you might get from the other person and plan how to respond honestly yet rationally.

5. **Notice and avoid falling into Leslie's Double Bind.** The first time you hit a clashing chord in a relationship that had been going well, it's tempting to say something like, "Oh my goodness! Game over! It's never going to get better. I can never fix this. It's sour notes from this point forward. I either have to learn to cope with this bad music or look for another job."

Don't awfulize. Stay focused on the specific *event* that is currently causing disharmony. Remember that the first clashing chord does not mean that the song is over. It's just one chord. Calm yourself down enough to figure out how to approach the other person using the feedback model. Be prepared to listen to and digest whatever feedback they may have for you. It will ideally be a conversation, not a solo aria.

Once you've dealt successfully with the event, then consider how to discuss the larger issue with the other person to find a longer-term path to better music with them. Also think about what triggers you might trip in each other. Do either of you have a pet peeve that relates to scar tissue from prior relationships? If so, those triggers might draw you into a double bind. When you step back and reflect, it may be easier to defuse those triggers, find ways to avoid them, and hence build a stronger, more positive relationship.

6. **Take stock of the Emotional Bank Accounts you have** with any of the people involved in your initial dissonance. Ask yourself honestly if you each make more deposits or withdrawals with each other. If you identify many small withdrawals, or a few large ones, consider what you and the other people can do to start making sincere deposits. It doesn't work as well if it's just lip service, such as, "Gee, your new hairstyle looks really nice." Although some folks need to start small with tiny deposits like that, just to get into a new habit of noticing and sharing positives with the other person.

    If you realize that you're making withdrawals with the other person by being too critical, interrupting them in meetings, not keeping commitments, or coming on too strong, make a concerted effort to deposit something positive in their Emotional Bank Account several times a week, if not daily, by being respectful, keeping commitments, and being supportive when you can. Seek to keep withdrawals to a minimum.

    If you feel as if others are making too many withdrawals from your Emotional Bank Account, plan and practice how to give them feedback about what they're doing, how it affects you, and what you'd request they do differently. Sometimes people are unaware of what a negative impact they have on others. Until you and the other people are all making more deposits than withdrawals, it will be difficult, if not impossible, to build more trust and hence reduce the dissonance in the music.

Also consider your levels of vulnerability-based trust. Keeping commitments and doing your part is only the first level of trust. Ask yourself if you're building or eroding vulnerability-based trust with others by considering the degree to which you are honest and transparent with each other.

- Can we admit mistakes and ask each other for help?

- Are we comfortable giving each other direct yet constructive feedback?

If vulnerability-based trust is low or nonexistent, consider ways to build it. Get coaching from colleagues at work or people you know well outside of the office. You don't have to figure this out all by yourself; asking for help on this is a way to practice building vulnerability-based trust.

7. **Pay attention to your level of impatience** with the person or people with whom you're experiencing your first clashing chords. Make an educated guess about the source of your impatience. Is it a function of

- Your stress level in this new company, new team, or new position?

- Your personality style and natural tendency to want to solve problems too quickly?

- Your own impatience with yourself and the music that you still haven't mastered, which then causes you to project that impatience onto others?

It may be that the act of stopping, reflecting, and noticing possible impatience with yourself and others will be what you need to start reducing it. If the pause and introspection are not enough, it's a good idea to ask for help, either within your new organization or externally.

Stage 5

Encores: Fine-tuning the Evolving Song

Juanita hadn't talked to Alex for a while and decided to give him a call to say hello.

When he answers, Juanita says, "Hey, Alex, long time, no chat. How's life treating you?"

"Not too bad, Juanita. I could complain, but it'd be stupid. Nice to hear from you. What's new?"

"Actually I'm pretty good. Sometimes I pinch myself, because I don't believe how well this job is going. Sure, we have speed bumps at times, but I feel like I'm definitely hitting my stride with my boss and my team. Most of the time, we're really on the same page with each other. I feel very supported by them, and it's easy to return the favor."

"Great to hear, my friend. I'm not sure I can say the same for my current situation. What are you doing right? What brilliant advice can you offer me?"

"The company offers lots of training, so I'm taking advantage of this. Several of the seminars are about specific communication and leadership skills. They've increased my awareness of what behaviors create harmony within a work team, and I'm trying to consciously practice the tools as much as possible."

"Sounds terrific, Juanita," Alex says. "What about your boss? What's she like?"

"I've never worked for someone so open and grounded as she is. She's clear about her priorities and how they support our collective goals. She knows when to be directive and when to step back so that we can figure things out ourselves. She delegates in a way that lets us know who's supposed to do what. And when there's a problem, she encourages honest feedback and listens to it without getting defensive. She trusts us, and that keeps us all very motivated."

"I'm impressed, Juanita. You've come a long way from that lunch conversation months ago with Sally, Omar, and me when you couldn't decide what to do next. Do you have any openings at your company? Maybe I should apply!"

Juanita laughs. "You'll be the first on your block to know if I hear of an opening, Alex. Hope to see you before too long. Gotta run. Ciao."

Singing as a Duo or Choir

Once you work through the initial Clashing Chords in Stage 4, you and others hopefully emerge with stronger rapport and insight. Whether you're looking at a relationship with one other person at work, or if you're considering the interactions of a team, Stage 5 now requires that you incorporate certain tools and practices that will keep your relationships harmonious and healthy.

It may seem easier to sing as a duo with just one other person. You're juggling just your own personality traits, priorities, and values along with theirs. You need to consider only two voices, maybe singing in unison at times, maybe holding a melody line with a simple harmony line added on. Assuming that you and the other person are equally motivated to make your duet succeed, it can be more straightforward to make agreements, sort out disagreements, and resolve style clashes. You're dealing with only two Emotional Bank Accounts, a concept introduced in the previous stage.

Conversely, a duet can be more challenging than singing with a whole team. It's just you two, so anyone's sour notes are more noticeable. It can feel scary to try to strengthen your duo when it's just your perspective versus the other person's. Unless you get help from a supervisor, peer, or coach, it may be hard to get a reality check and can feel like a tug-of-war.

Depending on each person's background, skills, and defenses, it is sometimes difficult to get both people on equal ground, both reading from the same sheet of music. In many one-on-one relationships, one person feels like they have more power, influence, and assets than their colleague. As a result, the evolution of harmonious music between the two coworkers becomes more difficult.

The choral arrangements of a team with three or more people can be quite interesting and fun. You have so many different approaches, preferences, patterns, and moods at any given moment that it can be hard to track all that's going on. If you've ever tried to graphically track a conversation in a meeting, in which you literally draw a line from one person to the next to track who speaks in which order, it becomes a lot of crisscrossed lines as the comments bounce back and forth across the room.

Occasionally there's a structured agenda in which the leader says, "Let's go around the table and hear a report from each of you." More often, the discussion is like a ball that bounces back and forth among different people. If someone is shy or disengaged and says nothing, the ball passes repeatedly over their head. If two individuals are engaged in a verbal tug-of-war, they toss that verbal ball back and forth with such force that no one else can participate.

By contrast when a team is singing together well with high levels of motivation, trust, and respect, they can create some beautiful and exciting music together. They build on each other's ideas, raise concerns constructively, and generate energy synergistically where the whole is greater than the sum of the parts.

Miles Kierson, a successful organizational consultant, has done extensive work with senior team alignment. He differentiates true alignment from agreement, majority rule, or just giving in. He defines alignment as "a specific type of relationship to decisions and decision-making. It's the most powerful type of relationship you can have to a decision." It's stronger than agreement as in, "Okay, we'll do it your way (grumble grumble)." It's a commitment to own or buy into a decision and make that course of action succeed, whether you love it or not, even when it's not your first choice.

Kierson emphasizes that team members must first be *willing* to be aligned. They must accept that they are not always right and won't always get their way. They also need to recognize that this type of alignment is neither easy, fast, nor a one-and-done. We could be aligned on the first three issues facing us but then hit a roadblock on the fourth.

The team needs to be willing to wrestle with themselves and each other about decisions that are uncomfortable, confusing, or in conflict with their values. The team leader also has to create a culture of trust, so that members will come to them to discuss those roadblocks. Without a mutual agreement to listen deeply, debate, and sometimes be influenced by others, alignment is difficult if not impossible.

When the members of a team are aligned, they have a shared understanding and commitment to fully support the vision or plan. They can sustain the focus, momentum, and enthusiasm that are needed to follow through and achieve goals. The result is greater productivity and satisfaction that in turn creates more harmonious music for the duo or the choir.

In order to be aligned, individuals on the team need to be able and willing to agree to these behaviors:

- **Speak directly and honestly** with each other so that you raise questions and concerns. These obstacles must be discussed and resolved before true alignment can be achieved. In other words, you sometimes have to be willing to not be aligned at first to make way for true alignment later.

- **Let go of their own position** when it is time to be aligned or agree to explore further options and defer the decision so you can achieve alignment later.

- **Make it each team member's job to own the decision**, to support it, to speak about it with one voice, and to make it successful once the decision has been made.

- **Coach each other** with direct, honest feedback when someone's behavior does not support or demonstrate team alignment.

Musicians need to practice their craft continuously. They do scales and warm-up exercises. They rehearse individually and collectively until they learn and polish the music. When teams do the requisite skill practice to build honest dialogue and raise concerns constructively, they're much more likely to compose solid, sustainable decisions and cultures that continue to enhance the music long term and create more harmony at work. Their rehearsals help them achieve true alignment.

A professional musician that I know was coaching two high school soloists who wanted to sing a particularly challenging duet together. She said that when you learn the notes, pitches, and timing, it's like you're renting a home and staying there for a while. But once you really know the music and absorb it into your bones, then it's as if you have bought the house and moved in to really live there for the long term.

Teams that get good at true alignment don't just rent or go through the motions. They buy the tools and skills, so that the harmonies are "in their bones" and woven into the fabric of their team's culture. That allows them to instinctively fine-tune and evolve the song, encore after encore.

Often, leaders hire consultants to facilitate a retreat when their team is producing more clashing chords than harmony. Successful leaders don't wait for conflicts. They know they need to schedule a retreat where the main goal is preventive, to reinforce the skills that will build on their strengths and bolster alignment.

Vision, Values, Goals and Priorities

To be able to make good music with another person or a whole team in this stage, you need to be both clear about and aligned around three key elements.

Vision

To move the music forward, everyone involved needs to understand and be excited about where they want to go with the overall composition. Leaders in all types of organizations struggle with a clear and compelling vision, often as part of their strategic planning process. If the mission of a team or company is why they exist, the vision is where they want to go. When they finish their project, meet their goals, or finish the year, what do they want to have achieved?

It's similar to when musicians plan a concert. They first consider

- What is the theme or message that we want to convey?

- What kind of mood can we create, or what feelings can we evoke during the concert?

- What pieces should we include in the program?

- What do we want the audience to walk away with when we're done?

- How do we build a strong rapport with the audience for this performance and subsequent events?

People who create and maintain harmony at work ask similar questions in order to have a clear vision that everyone aligns around and buys into with enthusiasm.

- Where do we want to be in a year or three years?

- What success measures will let us know we're making progress?

- How will we feel about our team and organization when we achieve this vision?

- How will others see us and evaluate our efforts?

- How will we maintain our energy and commitment when we face challenges?

It's called being on the same page of music.

Values

It really helps people work harmoniously together when they are operating with a common set of values. Organizational or team values can be defined as a list of terms that indicates what you stand for and serves as a moral or philosophical guide.

Ideally those values *permeate* all you do; are evident in your activities, not just written on a wall plaque; *serve as guides for your decisions and align with your mission, vision, and goals;* cause individual and collective *concern when they are violated* or ignored; and are one of the *last things you give up.*

Examples of values that a team or a corporation might adopt include these:

- Innovation and creativity

- Profitability and financial sustainability

- Excellent customer service

- Individual competition

- Employee satisfaction and learning

- Diversity and inclusion

- Tradition, structure, and stability

- Collaboration and integrity

When values are clearly articulated and agreed upon, it is more likely that everyone will consistently use them to guide their actions, which leads to better harmony. There are, however, at least two types of situations that undermine those values and hence create discord.

Let's say that I'm your peer and that I value collaboration and integrity. But my actions demonstrate that I'm focused on individual competition and advancing my own career path at the expense of yours. As a result, I'm less likely to be honest or share ideas with you, as I'm looking out for my own agenda and reputation. When there is a disconnect between what I say is important and how I demonstrate what I value, my actions will speak louder than my words. It's difficult, if not impossible, to build trust and respect. We're unlikely to align and sing from the same sheet of music. We will struggle to create a harmonious working relationship.

A similar gap can occur when values are either not clearly articulated and agreed to, or when we each admit that we're pulling in different directions. It is unlikely, for example, that you and I will work well together if one of us values tradition, structure, and stability, while the other considers it vital to be innovative and creative.

Similarly, excellent customer service might or might not fit well with cutting costs in an effort to increase profitability. These scenarios demonstrate why the values of a team or an organization play such a central role in Stage 5 when you are trying to fine-tune the evolving song.

Goals and Priorities

If a team or organization aligns around a clear vision and values, they're well on their way to enhancing the music. They also need S.M.A.R.T. goals and priorities that they all understand and support. Goals need to be

- **S**pecific: that is, targeted rather than vague,

- **M**easurable or quantifiable,

- **A**chievable: possibly aspirational but still realistic,

- **R**elevant to the nature and current state of the group trying to achieve them, and

- **T**ime-bound, having deadlines and possible milestones along the way.

There are lots of misconceptions about goal setting. Sometimes, people resist the establishment of specific, measurable goals, especially for one- to three-year time frames.

The pushback usually includes comments like, "How can we set a goal for twelve months from now? We aren't even sure where the market will be in *two* months!" or "If we set these goals now, they'll be rigid and box us in. They won't allow for creativity and flexibility." or "If we set these goals and fail, we'll all feel bad, and morale will be in the dumps."

Setting goals does not mean they're cast in stone. As a client of mine once said, they can be "cast in Jell-O!"[43]

Once you set the goals, they may need to be modified when employees, customers, and other factors change. When you need to pivot, it's important to have a vision and goals that you can change *from*. They are your road map from which you may need to detour. Without them, it would be like getting in your car with no map, no desired destination, and saying, "I'm not sure where we're going. We'll just drive till we get somewhere."[44]

Setting S.M.A.R.T. goals fosters the clarity and buy-in that create harmonious alignment. They also allow people to set *priorities* regarding what has to come first in terms of time, energy, and budget. Without defined priorities, everything is seen as equally urgent, causing people to feel paralyzed and overwhelmed. If everything is a number-one priority, then nothing is a priority.

I was once called in to work with a senior team that had literally been working on their five-year plan for *three* years. Their boss told me to take them to a hotel, "lock them in a conference room for as many days as it takes, bring in as much pizza, coffee, and chocolate as you need, and don't let them return to work without a solid, finished five-year plan!"[45]

---

43 I'm not at all fond of Jell-O, but I like the metaphor.

44 Some people actually like to travel like this. While it can work well for free spirits on vacation, it is a difficult approach to pull off at work and rarely leads to success.

45 I do not advocate this style of management. The boss was part of the problem and contributed to the team's inability to complete a reasonable plan. By the way, I did let them sleep, take bathroom breaks, and ordered in more than pizza, coffee, and chocolate.

When I first reviewed what they had labored over for three years, I was aghast. They had twenty top priorities. Under each of those twenty goals, there were several subgoals and lots of action steps. It made my head hurt. My first question was, "How likely is it that you can achieve all twenty of these goals in the *next* five years?" Their unanimous reply[46] was, "Not the least bit likely, no way, over our dead bodies!"

So our first task was to pare those twenty items down to three or four that could realistically drive the organization forward and possibly be achieved in the next five years. From there, we could craft S.M.A.R.T. goals with action steps, timelines, budgets, and accountabilities (who was responsible for what). We ultimately turned those goals into a clear, realistic five-year plan that they all agreed on and were excited to implement.

They were astounded that they had accomplished more in three days than in the prior three years. More importantly, the process, the way we approached the task, had allowed for honest dialogue and the rebuilding of trust that supported the alignment they needed to implement the plan. They were also pleased that they were starting to like each other again. The music had improved considerably: new key, new tune, new tempo, new parts to sing.

Roles, Routines, and Boundaries

As a duo or team evolves and strengthens, they're better able to answer the questions from that old Abbott and Costello routine, "Who's on First?"

---

46   Which was one of the first things they all agreed on and was something positive to build on.

Roles

The longer you work with someone, the easier it is to sort out: this is my part, that's your responsibility, and this third area is something we need to work on together. Limits of authority and responsibility are well defined. When roles are clear, things are less likely to fall through the cracks ("I thought YOU were doing that!" "No, that was clearly on YOUR list."). This also reduces the risk of double dipping,[47] when two or more people both work on the same thing at the same time, unaware that others are also completing the same task or project. When they discover the overlap, there is usually frustration about time wasted, lack of shared information, and disagreement about whose version of the work is best to use.

In the same way that goals are often modified as they play out, roles may sometimes need adjustment. Just because you've been leading X and I've been overseeing Y doesn't mean that the division of labor will always be the same. I might need to delegate X to you because I've taken on new responsibilities with Z. You might want me to cross-train you to do X, so that you can expand your skills. You and I might want to switch out X and Y because we're both getting bored and need some new challenges. As long as there is clear agreement about authority and responsibility, people are empowered to rotate and shift to meet the changing needs of employees and the organization they are running.

Routines

Established schedules and procedures are one of the tools that help people fine-tune and develop their work tasks and relationships. Routines provide people with predictability,

---

47   Double dipping is great for ice cream cones but is generally disastrous and annoying for work projects.

the ability to plan, and hence some degree of comfort so they have a better idea of what to expect on a daily basis. Much neuroscience data suggest that when we can make certain tasks routinized or automatic, they become second nature and therefore use less brain power and energy.

Most people have a routine for getting ready for work each day. They get up, often at the same time, do their regular hygiene activities, maybe exercise, maybe fix breakfast and pack a lunch, maybe do things for family members, and head out the door. Often people drive the same way to and from work or take the same bus at the same time every day.

The neurological benefit to this is that you don't have to think: now I'll brush my teeth; now I'll get dressed; now I'll make breakfast. You do it by rote, thereby freeing up your mind to focus on other things, conserving energy and reducing stress. Routines usually help us increase efficiency and accuracy, as key steps are less likely to be forgotten or done incorrectly. When people like and are used to routines, they can get extremely uncomfortable and distracted when those patterns are interrupted by life events—personal, professional, or global.

Certain personality types rail against routines. They consider them to be boring and confining. They've learned that taking a different way to work each day or brushing your teeth with your nondominant hand keeps your brain active and healthy. They have a higher need for variety and challenge and refuse to eat the same food for breakfast every day. This type of person is less likely to be upset when routines are interrupted, as they have a greater tolerance for ambiguity and change. They often savor the excitement that can be created by the chaos of disrupted routines and unexpected events.

In Stage 5 of Encores, as you seek to strengthen relationships and build on past successes, it is helpful to consider your own and others' appetite for routines versus variety. If you and others value and rely on structure, then develop some coping strategies to use when routines are altered or destroyed. If you or your colleagues strive to avoid repetitive patterns whenever possible, consider how to honor and support those who depend on routines and who are more likely to freak out when that consistency disappears.

Boundaries

Once you have worked your way through the enthusiastic first notes, the excitement of the beautiful new songs you are singing together, and the predictable end of the honeymoon period and initial clashing chords, you have learned a fair amount about the people you are working with and hopefully have increased your own self-awareness as you interact with your colleagues.

Another element that helps to fine-tune your song is the establishment of clear boundaries. Some of the borders that people establish at work involve roles and routines:

- I know what's in my work area, and what's in yours.

- We all acknowledge that you're the pro at this, and I'm better with that.

- It's obvious that we need goals set by July 1 and budgets established by October 1.

There are, however, behavioral boundaries that you learn about or develop once you're no longer the new kid who has just joined the choir. Some have to do with people's

- Style: Are they a big-picture visionary or a data-driven facts person?

- Energy: Is their most creative thinking in the first hour of the day, or do they hit their stride after several cups of coffee and a few hours in the office?

- Communication mode: Do they prefer in-person conversations, or do they respond better to phone calls, texts, and emails?

- Privacy levels: Are they an open book, willing to tell you about their feelings and personal life, or are they more guarded, preferring to not share much about their internal thoughts, emotions, or their life outside of work?

These are only four possible examples of how you and your colleagues draw invisible lines around yourselves, some of which should never be crossed. The higher the levels of stress, disagreement, and mistrust that exist, the more crucial it is to recognize and respect these boundaries. Let's say I need to present something to you that I suspect you won't like or don't have the time to sort through. It behooves me to think about the best possible way to package my idea to increase the likelihood that you'll at least consider it.

If, for example, you are an intuitive, creative person who always looks at the strategic view and the most innovative directions, I need to start my presentation with the punchline: "I'd like to tell you about an approach that will blow the socks off our customers, make our competitors jealous, and really help our bottom line."

If you are a structured, well-organized person who does not appreciate impromptu meetings and likes to see drafts in writing before discussing them, I would be crossing an invisible line by dropping into your office with the comment, "I have a great idea that I want to run by you." It would be important to schedule a time to talk and send an email that outlines the proposal and what you hope to accomplish in the meeting.

Another common boundary issue that emerges involves over- and under-sharing. If I'm an open book, comfortable telling you how I feel about your comments or how things are progressing with my new love interest, that might either

- Draw you to me, build trust, and encourage you to share more easily with me, or

- Make you squirm when I seem to "emote" all over the place and waste your time, telling you about my social life, in which you have no interest, thus encouraging you to avoid me, so that you can get your work done and not have to listen to me prattle on.

Conversely, if I'm more guarded, disinclined to share my honest reactions to you, and not wishing to disclose anything about my personal life at work, that might

- Make you respect my reserve and my tendency to focus on work while at work, or

- Cause you to distrust my apparent lack of honesty and self-disclosure, wonder about my reactions and what I'm up to, and hence cause you to either pull away from me or pester me to reveal more.

Whatever the nature of the boundaries and how permeable or rigid they are, people who manage Stage 5 well pay attention to these often-invisible lines. They understand who needs what in their relationship with you, and who won't tolerate what types of behaviors when you interact.

Once you get to know and acknowledge this subtle music playing between you and your colleagues, you can make conscious choices about what to avoid and which lines need to be stepped over, even if you know it will create some disharmony with others. When people lack this awareness, they're crossing over boundaries unintentionally and are then surprised when the song sounds terrible or grinds to a screeching halt.

Improvisational Singing—a Leap of Faith

Printed music and rehearsals can be valuable, but goals and schedules are essential in the workplace. That said, sometimes you must improvise when unexpected events, conversations, or emotional reactions occur. When situations mandate that you sing without a written score or preparation, it's a bit like jumping off a cliff, not knowing how high the cliff is, how soft the ground is below, if you're wearing a parachute, and if so, if it will open. Depending on the perceived risk and your level of confidence, your actions can feel like a giant leap of faith.

Personality styles and experience can strongly influence how people respond to the need to improvise. In Stage 1, there's a brief description of MBTI preferences and Kolbe Scales. The Perceiver preference in the MBTI model describes people who "go with the flow," like to keep their options open, and often resist rigid structures. Kolbe's Quick Start Scale references how much or how little people are comfortable with ambiguity, risk, and surprises.

Some people who have a clear Perceiver preference on the MBTI or a high number on the Kolbe Quick Start Scale may actually enjoy and look forward to improvisation. It can be an adrenaline rush. They like the challenge of being on their toes and staying open to possibilities. The risk-taking triggers their creativity and motivation. They're excited to see how the music will turn out. If they hit a sour note or two, they just redirect and adjust. They usually find it fun and interesting. They are like jazz musicians who are skilled at improvisation. The more they improvise, the more they increase their confidence and skill in uncertain situations.

People trained in improv theater learn specific skills that they must hone if they are to succeed. They do a lot of preparation, even though their delivery seems random and spontaneous to the audience. They have a structure within which they function and a goal they hope to achieve. Then, within those parameters, they are free to ad lib and see where the conversation goes. Without the skill practice and structure, their improvisation would wander aimlessly and likely fall flat.

Anyone who facilitates meetings knows all about improvisational singing, just like improv actors do. Strong facilitators also do a great deal of preparation, especially if they are a new leader or an external consultant who isn't well-acquainted with the people in the room. They need to know the personalities, patterns, and history of the team. They establish boundaries by creating clear objectives, an agenda, and time frames for the meeting. They consider the room setup, handouts, audiovisual aids, and other logistics that could support or interfere with the meeting's goals.

They consider which techniques to use when, how much time to allot for each portion of the agenda, and what to do if one section runs long. All of this prework and structure allows them to flex or ad lib within those limits, based on the needs of the group, and still reach the goals of the meeting. If, in some meetings, the goals cannot be met and the agenda cannot be completed, the facilitator and team have a clear musical score from which to deviate. They know how to rearrange the music or amend the agenda.

By contrast, people who have a Judging preference on the MBTI or a low number on the Kolbe Quick Start Scale may be uncomfortable when they need to improvise. They rely on the certitude of music that is written out, rehearsed, and expected. They value structure and predictability. They don't like surprises.[48] They think that the people who do enjoy improv and ad lib are a bit wacko.

People who innately prefer consistency and certainty can learn to facilitate meetings well. They can practice ways of responding to unexpected comments or reactions that reduce the chance of putting their foot in their mouth and singing off-key. It just requires more energy and skill development than it does for people who gravitate toward improvisational music and relish it.

Motivation—an Internal Process

One of the ways to continue enhancing the music of your work relationships is to consider what motivates you and others to cooperate. Human motivation is a topic that has been studied extensively for decades. Hundreds of books and articles describe a variety of different theories on this subject. Many of them share this theme: no one can truly motivate someone else. I can't *make* you be motivated. That is because motivation is fundamentally an internal process that you must trigger within yourself. If I'm imposing something on you, it's not motivation, it's an external mandate or threat. So if

---

48   Early in our marriage, having not yet learned the MBTI model, I gave my husband, who has a clear Judging preference on the MBTI, a surprise party. Bad choice! He walked into our house, everyone jumped out and yelled, "Surprise!" His response: "What are you all doing here?" Their reply: "We wanted to surprise you on your birthday and help you celebrate!" Baffled, he looked at me and asked, "Why didn't you tell me they were coming?" Moral of the story: don't throw surprise parties for people who rely on predictability and who hate improv. Years later, he asked me if I'd ever want a surprise party for my birthday. Given that I'm someone who enjoys surprises and improv more than he does, I said, "Sure. That would be fun." His response: "Well then, you'd have to help me plan it." Never mind, my dear husband!

this is true, how can you ever get anyone else to act or agree according to your requests and proposals?

If I'm your manager or even your peer or direct report, I can't *do* motivation *to* you. But with some insight and planning, I can create an environment in which you're more likely to motivate yourself. There's an old expression that says, "You can lead a horse to water, but you can't make it drink."[49] My addition to this proverb is: If you run the horse around for an hour on a hot day, take it by the salt lick and then by the water trough, there's a better chance it will drink enthusiastically.

If you want someone to support your idea or help you with a task, you need to create an environment that increases the likelihood that they'll want to buy in. The late, illustrious Supreme Court Justice Ruth Bader Ginsburg has been quoted as saying, "Fight for the things that you care about, but do it in a way that will lead others to join you."[50] That's a very different approach from what some people do, which is to either badger you until you cave in and comply, or beg, plead, and guilt-trip you into agreement.

In 1943, Abraham Maslow proposed a well-known theory of motivation that is called the Hierarchy of Human Needs. It has five levels or tiers:

Maslow's Hierarchy of Needs

Maslow's classic Hierarchy of Human Needs depicts the importance of meeting basic needs at the lower levels first before attempting to increase your sense of self-worth or meet your highest potential.

His main premise is that you need to satisfy the lower-level needs before you are even interested in, much less motivated by the higher-level needs. In other words, if I am homeless, or don't have heat or food in my house (Level 1) or I don't feel safe from attack, tornadoes, or financial risk (Level 2), I'm not likely to focus on

- Level 3: Who loves or appreciates me? Am I accepted on this team or in this family? Am I trusted by friends and colleagues?

- Level 4: Do I feel good about myself? Do I have confidence and a sense of pride? Do I have a sense of dignity, accomplishment, independence and feel respected by others?

- Level 5: Am I achieving my highest potential and my most important life goals? Do I feel personally fulfilled?

So when you want to encourage someone to be motivated, it's helpful to know at what level someone is functioning in their life at that moment. If they are worried about exposure to a pandemic or an imminent risk of losing their job, it will be difficult if not impossible to engage them to focus on pride in their work or setting ambitious goals to stretch toward their highest potential.

In the middle of the twentieth century, Frederick Herzberg established a theory of motivation that has stood the test of time. He called it the two-factor theory of job satisfaction. He identified two factors:

- *Hygiene Factors* include things like clean bathrooms, comfortable air temperature, functioning equipment, decent food in the cafeteria, fair pay, and job security. These factors are extrinsic or external to the employees and often out of their control. These factors will not trigger motivation in and of themselves. But if they are absent (in other words, "It's too hot or cold in here." "My computer is always breaking down." "I'm not earning enough to make ends meet and need a second job."), they are likely to reduce job satisfaction.

- *Motivational Factors* include achievement, recognition, interesting duties or projects, responsibility, and the opportunity for growth and advancement. These factors spark intrinsic or internal reactions within each person. They are the elements of work life that are more likely to create true motivation, excitement, and commitment to the work tasks and the rest of the team.

It is true that the main reason that some people get out of bed and show up to work is that they need to feed and house their family. In that sense, you could argue that their paycheck motivates them. But Herzberg and others have found that even when people are well paid, well fed, and have an ergonomic desk chair in a lovely office, it is often not enough to excite and engage them so that they truly enjoy their job.

When their internal motivation is not triggered, it is difficult if not impossible to fine-tune any evolving relationships with them. Similarly, if you are just going through the motions, bored, or feeling unappreciated in your current role, it is not likely that you will continue to have harmonious relationships with others over time.

When it's your colleagues who are unhappy and apathetic, you need to think about where they are per Maslow's hierarchy, what hygiene and motivational factors might be missing, and what options you have to help them better meet their needs. Your hope is to reduce barriers to better engagement and hence promote better relationships. Sometimes, it's appropriate to ask open questions and offer assistance. Other times, that would be seen as intrusive. It depends on the other person's personality, whether they're your boss, peer, or direct report, and several other factors.

When you are the one who is not satisfied and inspired, you have more options for moving yourself forward. First, you need to analyze what has depleted your energy. Sometimes you can do that on your own. At times, it is helpful to enlist a colleague, friend, counselor, or coach to help you sort things out. Then you need to articulate what it would look like if things were better by asking questions like

- What would cause me to bound out of bed each day?[51]

- What would help me reach those higher tiers on Maslow's hierarchy?

- What would put a smile on my face when I think about my job or career?

Some of the exercises at the end of this stage will give you suggestions for how to focus this self-reflection in an effort to fine-tune your own personal music at work. Stage 6, Finales: Knowing If, When, and How to End the Song, addresses what to consider if you've decided that there's no way to improve this particular song, and it's time to move on to new music.

Influencing Others

Influence is a loaded word with many negative connotations. People often associate it with politics, government, cults, and manipulation. In reality, it is a neutral word that can be used either positively or negatively. It is like a hammer: you can use a hammer to build furniture or to destroy a valuable piece of sculpture.

Many of our interactions at work involve our efforts to convince others to support our positions, to help us with a task, or even just to listen to us. Much of the dissonant music that we hear is a result of ineffective influence efforts.

Many years ago, a colleague taught me that attempts to get others to cooperate and agree should be like the Hippocratic

---

51 A client once told me he had the habit of taking the stairs two at a time when he went up to his home office each morning. His young son asked him, "Dad, why do you take the stairs two at a time?" His reply, "I can't wait to see what's waiting in my inbox and what I'll get to do today!" That's a clear indication of tremendous enthusiasm and motivation.

oath that physicians take, which includes, "First, do no harm." Whatever I am trying to get you to do, my efforts should not create more damage to our relationship. In other words, even if you ultimately don't agree to help me, and I don't win this battle, hopefully my efforts won't prevent my working successfully with you on other issues in the future. Even if I win this battle, your refusing to work with me going forward would equate to losing the war.

Influence is closely tied to the topic of motivation, and it also has a great deal of research and theories that seek to explain it. It is sometimes easier to get cooperation if I have authority or positional power over you. If I'm your boss, a government agency, or your parent, I can say to you, "You have to do this, because I said so!" This is not, however, a tactic that will build trust, enthusiasm, or relationship harmony.

One way of considering how we influence each other more constructively is to consider two main approaches: Promote and Align.

Influence Styles

Promote

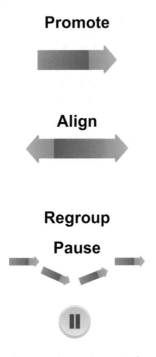

Align

Regroup
Pause

Promote uses persuasion, logic, and incentives. It is often a one-way sales pitch.

Align uses open questions, listening, emotion, and inspiration. It needs to be a dialogue and seeks to achieve buy-in.

Regroup is used to pause a conversation that needs a break, different information, time to reflect, or conflict resolution.

When I **Promote**, it's as if I'm trying to drive or push you in a certain direction. It often sounds like persuasion, logic, bartering, and selling. I might use phrases like

- "I need you to do X by Friday because—" and give you reasons.

- "The data show X, indicating that Y is the best course of action," providing a rationale.

- "Experience or industry standards have shown that we need to—" relying on credibility or authority.

- "I want you to do X. If you'll do that, I can do Y or Z for you in exchange," signaling a willingness to trade favors.

You state your goal or request clearly and directly, using facts and logic. Promote is appropriate and effective to use when all you need is compliance: when you have the authority, when it's an emergency or with people who want you to be brief: just tell me what you want, and I'll do it. It is strong, assertive, and avoids tentative or qualifying language. You may also anticipate objections and respond to them before they are even expressed. Its impact is often a hard sell.

When I **Align**, it is almost the opposite of Promote. It is important to use when I need more than compliance: I need you to commit or buy in. When used effectively, Align has none of the driving energy of Promote. Instead, I try to gently encourage you to follow me to a certain position without ever leaning on you with demands, facts, or positional power. I would use language like

- "Tell me about your thoughts on or concerns about—" to encourage them to say more.

- "How are you feeling about—" to surface emotions they haven't expressed yet.

- "So you're saying that—" to summarize or check your understanding of their comments and let them know they've been heard.

- "You say it's fine, but you look apprehensive—" to sort out mixed messages and surface their objections.

- "I'm worried/excited/confused about your comments that—" to disclose your own reactions to what they're saying.

- "We both want X to succeed. I see us moving forward in this way—" to create a picture of the desired result that includes both of you.

The Align style looks and sounds more indirect, even though you need to know where you want to end up. You do more listening than telling. You ask open questions and paraphrase responses to draw the other person out. You sometimes share your own feelings, as long as it's not a veiled Promote, such as "I think or feel like you *should*—" You may look for common ground and create an image of where you hope you can go together. It comes across as a soft sell.

Besides the compliance versus commitment distinction, Align requires one other key characteristic. In order to Align successfully, you, as the influencer, need to be open to influence from the other person. If a decision has been set or mandated by your boss, a board of directors, or government regulations, it doesn't work to use Align. The reason is that you would be asking for an opinion, and then telling the other person, "It doesn't matter what you think. It's already been decided."

A perfect example of the wrong way to use the Align style was when a CEO sent out a survey to all 200 of his employees. He said that they'd run out of space in their downtown office. They had three options: (1) get space on another floor in the same building, so that they were on two different levels, (2) move to another building nearby where they could all be on the same floor, or (3) move to a suburban office park twenty miles away.

Eighty percent of the employees said, "Let's stay in this building and get a second suite on another floor." The boss replied, "Too bad. I already rented the suburban office park space." The employees were livid and wondered why he had bothered to ask their opinion at all. Because the decision had been made, it would have been better for him to just Promote and say, "We need to move to the office park for these reasons."

In addition to these two approaches to influencing others, it is helpful to consider an additional tool. That is to back up and **Regroup**. When your initial attempts to Promote or Align don't go well, you sometimes need to stop the music temporarily. You might use language such as this:

- "I can see we're all getting a bit tired. How about if we think about this and resume the conversation tomorrow at nine a.m., when we've had time to consider everyone's comments?" (fatigue, low energy—need a longer break)

- "We've been talking about this for two hours. Let's take a break and resume in ten minutes with a new pitcher of water and a fresh pot of coffee." (need a short break)

- "It's clear that we've hit an impasse. I think Joe's input would be helpful with this. Let's wait till he's back in the office on Thursday and pull him into the discussion then." (need more information or participation from others)

- "I understand why you're upset about this, and why we're having trouble finding a solution that we can all buy into. Let me consider your feedback and think about how else we might approach this more effectively. I'll put it back on the agenda for next week's team meeting, bring in some additional data, and see if we can create a better plan then." (acknowledging disharmony and promising to reflect and reengage later)

- "Before we go on with this conversation, I want to share an observation. It seems like our discussion is going around in circles. We're back where we started an hour ago. What will it take to get us unstuck so that we can move this forward and reach a decision we all support?" (process or dynamics observation).

This last example is the most challenging and riskiest. You've stopped the content of the topic to talk about the relationships and communication. You're exploring how to decrease discord or stagnation and increase the interpersonal harmony before returning to the content.

You need to include three essential elements when Regrouping:

1. Give a clear and compelling reason for hitting the pause button.

2. Set a specific time and place when you'll come back to the topic.

3. Make sure that you do come back to your influence effort as promised. Otherwise, your efforts to Regroup look like you're avoiding, which is neither influential nor harmonious.

Regardless of the style used, all effective influence efforts need to have

- *A clear goal*: What are you trying to influence someone to do? Where are you hoping to lead them?

- *A clear strategy*: Which approach should you use—Promote or Align? Do you just need compliance (in which case, Promote works well), or do you need commitment (in which case you should start with Align)?

- *A **rationale*** for that strategy: What is it about the situation and the nature of your relationship with the person or team you seek to influence that suggests one approach over the other?

- *A **back-up plan***: If your first approach doesn't work, what behaviors, comments, or events would indicate that you need to shift to another style or Regroup? What red flags or sour notes should you watch and listen for?

Communication Tools to Enhance the Music

Musicians need several tools to help them communicate and perform their music successfully. They need a decent *score* that appeals to people. They need the *skills* to sing or play that score accurately and in tune. They need an understanding and appreciation of the *meaning or intent* of the music, so they can decide what interpretation to give the piece. And if they are performing as a duo or a chorus, they need to *practice and be in sync* with their fellow musicians to make sure that the volume, balance, harmonies, and tempos all line up.

It is the same story with the music of our relationships at work. It helps to have certain communication tools in your interpersonal tool kit so that you know which ones to use when and are skilled and confident utilizing each one. Most of these tools are ones that you've likely heard of, read about in a book or magazine, or learned about in a seminar.

When I'm coaching people on their use, I usually ask these questions and often get these answers:

- Do you know this tool? Have you read about it or gotten training in it? (Yes!)

- So then you know all about it, you're good at using it, and know how to use it, right? (No!)

- Why not? If you've read the book, seen the movie, and heard this song before, how come you're not a pro yet? (Because it's hard to do well. Because in the heat of the moment, I forget to use it. Because no one else on my team uses it, and I'd sound weird if I do. Because I worry that it'll make me look silly, weak, bossy, or rude.)

These tools and the ability to use them successfully are like any other skill you've developed in your life. Do you remember the first time you drove a car? Someone was telling you to keep your eyes on the road, "aim high with your vision," "keep your eyes moving from straight ahead, to the mirrors," and "keep your hands at ten and two on the steering wheel." If you are young enough to have had a cell phone at the time, there's no way you could concentrate on all of that and also make or receive a call.[52]

Now, after driving for years, you may drive down the road in autopilot, possibly eating lunch, having a deep conversation with a passenger or someone via Bluetooth on your phone. Sometimes, you're in such a distracted state that you might drive right past the street or highway exit where you need to turn.

The good news is that the mechanics of driving or shooting a basketball or baking bread get easier with practice. The other news is that if you are too much in autopilot mode, you may not be paying enough attention. With communication tools, you want to be comfortable and confident but still conscious of what you're doing.

With any skill or behavior, there are generally four levels from which you might operate:

1. *Unconscious competence*: It's second nature for me to do X. I can do it instinctively and successfully without having to concentrate much. X often feels effortless

---

52 Cell phone use while driving is generally agreed to be a bad idea, even for experienced drivers.

to me, doesn't require a lot of my energy, and I seem very natural to others when I do X. I make X look and sound good.

2. ***Conscious competence***: I know how to do X if I focus and practice, even though it may wear me out. I may have moderate degrees of confidence and harmony with X. Sometimes I make X look easy, even when I'm sweating bullets and working hard to do it well.[53]

3. ***Conscious incompetence***: I know that I'm not good at X and probably have some anxiety, embarrassment, or lack of confidence when confronted with X. I may avoid it whenever possible or get someone to help me with it.

4. ***Unconscious incompetence***: I don't do X well and don't realize what mistakes I'm making. Ignorance may feel like bliss at this level but doesn't produce relationship harmony or productivity long term. I may seem out of touch or lacking in self-awareness.

It might seem like the top level, unconscious competence, is best. The reality is that, like driving a car, it's comfortable to be innately good at something, but sometimes we're more successful if we are consciously competent, focused, and intentional. Then when we hit a patch of interpersonal "ice," we don't skid as badly and can recover faster when we're consciously competent.

Here are seven tools that are frequently taught in seminars and described in leadership books and articles. Like most people, you may say, "Oh yeah, I know that one," but may have lots of reasons for not using the technique or not feeling

---

53   It's like ducks swimming across the surface of a pond. They look like they're gliding effortlessly. They are, however, paddling like crazy under the surface of the water.

proficient with it. Ultimately, it will be helpful to have all of them in your music library and continue to increase your comfort and ability with each one.

Feedback

Feedback is what Ken Blanchard calls the Breakfast of Champions. Even when you know the theory and structure of exchanging feedback, it can still be a difficult tool to use. And it's not optional if you want harmony in your relationships at work. You need to be willing to tell people what's working well, what makes good music, and what you want them to do more of. You also need to have the skill and courage to tell your direct reports, your peers, and even your boss what is *not* working, what sounds out of tune, and what you'd request that they do differently.

The biggest problems with feedback are these:

- Most often, feedback is **not given** or it's **vague**. People assume you can read their mind and know what they think and feel about you. If you tell me I'm a great person, that's nice, but what am I doing well, and what should I do more of? If you say I'm a terrible human being, I only know that you're not happy with me. You haven't told me what's out of tune and what I need to change.[54]

---

54 I once had a boss who was a nice guy but had no clue about how to give clear feedback. I'd had several years of good performance reviews with comments like, "You're doing a great job, Susan! Keep up the good work." Reassuring but not really useful. Then I had a difficult year when I knew my performance had slipped. Here was the feedback he gave me: "You know, Susan, you've really not been up to snuff these last few months. I really need you to ratchet it up a bit and give it more umph." Snuff? What's that, relative to my job duties? Ratchet what up to where? And what is umph? I left the review meeting feeling confused, frustrated, and disheartened. I had no idea how to improve. I just knew my boss was unhappy with me.

- It's often **not timely**. If you tell me that a year ago I did something that didn't work for you, it's not useful, and I may not remember the incident. You've given me no opportunity in the last twelve months to correct the problem and improve the music.

- Feedback is inherently **subjective**. It's your opinion of what I'm doing or not doing and of the impact I'm having on you and others. Your view may be considerably different from my view of the music that we're trying to sing together.

- Most people are **uncomfortable** giving and receiving feedback. It's understandable that people don't like to exchange negative feedback. It may be a surprise, however, that people may not like to exchange positive feedback either.

  ◦ Some folks think, "I shouldn't have to tell you you're doing well: you should know. I don't have time to slather you with praise!" It's sort of the "no news is good news" philosophy.

  ◦ When people are on the receiving end of positive feedback, they may squirm. This could be because they don't believe your compliment is sincere, they lack the confidence that they can continue to succeed, or they're worried that the commendation is attached to a new assignment, such as, "You did great on that last project. So I've made you chair of the committee to tackle the next one."

The best way I know to give clear, direct feedback that is more likely to be understood is to boil it down to **three sentences**:

1. **Behavior:** Tell the person in specific terms what they did, didn't do, or are doing now. Seek to make this statement more factual than judgmental: describe what you saw or heard.

2. **Impact:** Tell them how their actions landed on you, how you felt about them, or what effects they had on you and your work.

3. **Request:** Suggest what they could do more of, less of, or differently that would help you and possibly help others to work better with them and be more productive.

An example of positive feedback might sound like this:

1. **Behavior**: "When you shared your honest concerns about our project timeline in our team meeting today—"

2. **Impact**: "I was so relieved. I'd been feeling the same way but hadn't figured out how to articulate the problems I saw. Your comments helped to perfectly redirect our meeting."

3. **Request**: "I'd suggest that you speak up more often with the same level of assertiveness. You're really smart, you have accurate data, and it would help to hear more of your ideas."

Negative feedback might sound like this:

1. **Behavior**: "When we are in meetings together, you often interrupt me. I might be halfway through my proposal, and you jump in with objections to what I'm saying."

2. **Impact**: "When you do that, I feel discounted, like you think that my contributions are of no value. When you cut me off, I get frustrated and lose confidence."

3. **Request**: "I'd ask that when we're in meetings together, you hear me out. First listen to my complete thought and seek to understand it. Then, if you disagree, please say, 'I see it another way.' That would feel much more supportive and less combative to me."

A few other suggestions to make *giving feedback* more effective include:

- **Prepare**: Plan what to say and how to say it, especially if you anticipate anger, tears, or denial from the receiver.

- **Be timely**: Share your feedback as close to the triggering event as possible. If you or the receiver need time to calm down, allow an hour or a day for that to be as clear and rational as possible, but no more.

- **Focus it**: Be specific about what the person has done or said, or failed to do or say, and what you are requesting. Avoid vague descriptors. Choose no more than two or three behaviors to share, so that you don't overwhelm the receiver.

- **Simplify**: (KISS—Keep it short and simple.) The benefit of three sentences is that it keeps the message concise and direct. When people have uncomfortable feedback to deliver, they often pad the message with extra words, thus diluting the impact.

- **Own it**: It's tempting to blame your feedback on others, with phrases like

- ○ "You know, everyone on the team is really annoyed with you!" or

- ○ "Harold and Sadie don't trust you."

Even if your feedback is based on what you're hearing from others, own it as your own observations and reactions with comments like

- ○ "When you do X, I feel Y, and I'd request that you do Z in the future," or

- ○ "When I hear from your teammates that they don't want to work with you, I get worried about tension within the team. I'd request that you and I look for ways to work together better."

- **Discuss it**: While you start with three sentences, feedback is more effective as a conversation rather than a lecture. If the receiver isn't using the five steps discussed next, draw them out. Ask how they'd summarize what you're telling them and elicit their reactions. Ultimately, you're hoping for their commitment to help you shift the music.

- **Follow up**: It's not enough to tell someone what you've observed, how it landed on you, and what you want them to start, stop, or change. Part of the conversation must include agreements to work on the new music together and some specific dates and times to talk later about progress. If you can't get that commitment to change, or you get lip service and no real change, you may need to seek help from your manager, human resources, or a peer.

When it comes to generosity, there is a biblical quote that says it is better to give than to receive. When it comes to

feedback, both the giving and receiving are equally important—
and sometimes both are challenging. In the same way that there
are specific considerations that make the giving of feedback
more successful, there are five steps you can take when *receiving
feedback* that will increase your understanding of the message
and also encourage more feedback in the future:

1. **Accept the feedback as a gift**, even if you don't agree
   with it, didn't ask for it, or don't like how it's delivered.
   Listen to the music. Try to understand and really
   hear it.[55]

2. **Paraphrase or summarize** what you're hearing. That
   helps you confirm what you heard, and it lets the giver
   know that you understood them. If you have misheard
   the feedback, it allows the giver to clarify.

3. Optional: If the giver is using vague statements like,
   "You *always* do X," or "You *never* do Y," **ask an open,
   clarifying question**, like "Tell me some more about
   what you mean by—" or "What would be an example
   of when I had too much X or not enough Y?"

4. Optional: Empathize with what the speaker says if
   you can do so honestly. If not, skip this step: your
   insincerity will likely show through.

---

55 My grandma, may she rest in peace, used to give us gifts that she
    thought we should have, not necessarily what we wanted. I remember
    as a kid getting bathrobes from Grandma from a department store
    that she liked. They were often ugly, with itchy lace at the collar, and
    far from the toys I would have preferred. I'd see the big rectangular box
    from her favorite store, thinking, "Oh no, it's a robe from Grandma!"
    I didn't even want to take it out of the box. Same thing with feedback:
    take it out of the box, try it on, even if it's ugly and itchy, and then
    decide if you want to return it for credit later—that is, *not* use all or
    part of the feedback.

5. Whether you like or agree with the feedback, whether you plan to act on it or not, whether it was delivered well or not, **thank the person** for taking the time and risk to share it with you.

Listening Deeply

Listening deeply is another term that is discussed and written about a great deal. That's the easy part—to read and talk about it. The challenge is to actually *do* it well, especially under pressure. It's a close relative of feedback that is also essential, not optional, to create and maintain strong, harmonious relationships at work.

Why is listening so hard? Unless we have a hearing loss, it is something we do automatically from the day we are born. So what gets in the way when we have two ears and good hearing?

- **Fatigue and stress**, leaving the listener with insufficient energy to listen deeply.

- **Lack of time and patience**, causing the listener to focus on how they plan to respond as soon as the speaker takes a breath, rather than truly attending to what the speaker says.

- **Lack of trust or respect for the speaker**, which makes it harder to believe or empathize with the speaker.

- **Conflicting priorities, values, or viewpoints** that reduce the listener's receptivity.

- **Fear, anger, and other strong emotions** that make it difficult to hear the message neutrally due to the listener's mental filters.

You could probably list other barriers, as if these five weren't enough to impede everyone's listening at some point. Like any other skill, some people innately listen well, even in high-tension situations. The rest of us need to learn how. The good news is that it is a learnable skill. The other news is that even when you know how to listen deeply and you've practiced often, it can still be difficult to pull off in some situations.

Deep listening, often called active listening, means that you give 100 percent of your attention to what someone is saying and how they're saying it. You're also reading between the lines, paying attention to what they may imply without saying it directly. You're not checking texts and emails, making coffee or cleaning off your desk while claiming to listen. Your eyes, ears, mind, and often heart are completely focused on the speaker. You're going way beyond just hearing their words so you can really comprehend and validate the speaker's message.

Here are three main reasons to pull this tool out of your interpersonal tool kit:

1. To encourage communication, to draw someone out: especially valuable if they are reticent to speak up or hot under the collar and need to vent.

2. To let the speaker feel completely heard and accepted: helpful when someone is upset, confused, or feeling ignored. This doesn't necessarily mean that you agree with what they're saying, only that you have heard and grasped their message.

3. To help both speaker and listener better understand the message and its impact: sometimes you are doing more than just encouraging and confirming a message. You're clarifying the meaning for the speaker as well as for yourself, especially when the speaker rambles or is very emotional.

The three main techniques that comprise deep listening are

1. **Asking open questions** to draw the speaker out and allow them to say more,

2. **Paraphrasing or summarizing** their message in your own words to highlight the main points of the message, and

3. Noticing and sometimes **responding to what they don't say**—what is inferred by their tone of voice, facial expression, other nonverbals. Sometimes you just silently notice this indirect message, and other times you might ask the speaker if it's accurate.

The method for integrating these three main tools often starts with an open question. When the speaker responds, you paraphrase or summarize what they've said. Then you either

- Ask another open question to follow up and get more information, and paraphrase again, or

- Share a reaction to the comment to check out your perception of the meta-message. For example, you might say, "I'm surprised/concerned/relieved to hear you say that," or "I get the impression that you're frustrated/overwhelmed/ecstatic about what happened in that meeting." By stating it tentatively, they have room to confirm or correct your reaction to their comments.

There are several common pitfalls to using deep listening. The first is to keep repeating the same words when you paraphrase. If your response to everything I say is, "What I think I hear you saying is—," people will think you just came from a seminar.[56] In the Additional Tools at the back of this

---

56 Or just finished reading this book.

book, you'll find suggestions for a variety of phrases to use as part of your active listening efforts.

If you ask open questions and draw the speaker out, you imply that you are willing to hear their ideas and possibly be influenced by them. So a second trap is to use these deep listening techniques about a decision that's already been made. It will create all kinds of cacophony and backlash if you ask, "What do you think we should do about X," paraphrase their ideas, and then say, "Well too bad, the CEO has already decided to do Y!" The speaker will wonder why you wasted time asking and will be reticent to share ideas with you in the future.

Third, when you are listening deeply, avoid giving advice and sharing your own stories early on. You may think of a brilliant way to help the speaker, once you hear what they're describing. You may have had a similar experience and want to demonstrate your empathy for their situation. They may even request your advice. The main reasons to hear them out first and save your own advice or personal sharing for later are these:

- Your advice effectively shuts up the speaker; you stop listening to them and start doing more of the talking;

- You may be giving them excellent advice for the wrong problem. Sometimes, the real underlying issue doesn't surface until you've asked a lot of open questions and summarized their comments; and

- By saying, "Your situation reminds me of a time when I was in the same bind," you may give them the impression that you think their problem is not as important or challenging as your own.

A big mistake that people make with this type of listening is to use it when they are in a hurry, impatient, tired, or upset. It only works well when you are feeling calm, grounded, and receptive. None of us feels that way all of the time. So, if you have four minutes until your next meeting starts, or it's 5:30 p.m. and your brain is setting in the western portion of your head, or you're really fuming or feeling threatened by the speaker, it's probably not the right time to access this tool. Renegotiate a different time when you're less pressured, less tired, or when you've had time to calm down.

If you've decided that deep listening would help to improve the music in a certain situation, try to have a neutral mindset. Go into the conversation pretending that you are a researcher or news reporter who wants to objectively gather information from the speaker. Act as if you have no investment in this conversation or in the relationship with the speaker. This is a tremendous challenge if the speaker is upset and lobbing attacks at you. You need to be able to say in a completely dispassionate voice, "So you were insulted by what I said and feel that I want to discredit your work. What specific comments did I make that made you feel that way?" Staying impartial while engaged in deep listening is probably the biggest challenge of all.

Assertiveness

Assertiveness can be defined as meeting your own needs while inviting collaboration with others. You express your own priorities clearly and firmly but still calmly and rationally. You also consider others' needs at the same time.

When people use assertive behaviors successfully, they can often promote what they want without creating discomfort for others. They may increase their own feelings of self-respect, confidence, and satisfaction. They often build mutual trust and respect with the other person. Hopefully, the decision or actions feel like a win-win for both parties.

Submission ◄────── Assertiveness ──────► Aggression

Submission is giving in to others' needs and demands while sacrificing your own wishes. **Aggression** is getting your own needs met without regard to others' needs or reactions. **Assertiveness** is the variable middle ground whose goal is to meet your own needs without damage to others while considering their views and priorities.

I think of assertiveness as being in the middle of a continuum. One end of that continuum is *aggression*. When someone is being aggressive, their attitude is generally, "I will get my needs met, no matter what it takes, no matter who I have to step on, and no matter how much disharmony my efforts produce." Aggressive people are often seen as mean, harsh, and uncaring. They get a given task accomplished, but at a large interpersonal cost. They tend to trigger resentment, fear, and sabotage in others. They rarely create harmony at work.

At the other end of this scale is *submission*. A submissive person is typically seen as weak, indecisive, and timid. They accommodate others too readily, rarely promote their own ideas, and usually do not get their own needs met: they're too busy taking care of everyone else's priorities. When you are submissive too often, it is difficult to earn others' respect. Due to the avoidance and capitulation required, being submissive often leaves you feeling defeated, ignored, frustrated, and lacking in confidence.

Submissive people may repeatedly take what feels like abuse until they are so fed up that they explode, lash out, get aggressive, or just quit. Their colleagues are usually surprised by the outburst or the sudden exit, as the passive person had never expressed that they were a simmering pot about to boil over.

By contrast, being assertive is a delicate balancing act. It can be a challenge to find the sweet spot between the extremes of aggression and submission. You need to consider how to meet your own needs and share your own views without trampling others (aggression) and without being too reticent or apologetic (submission). In the Additional Tools at the back of this book, there is a chart that distinguishes the behavioral cues of these three different types of behavior.

Assertiveness is an interesting relationship tool. If you ask four people what they think it means, you're likely to get at least six definitions. That is partly because many factors influence assertiveness. It's like a song that you play in different keys, at different tempos, depending on where you are and who you're talking to.

Situations: You might be comfortable being assertive and direct with family members but have trouble standing up for your opinions at work or vice versa. You might have been assertive at work before, but now that your boss is considering who to lay off, you might feel the need to hold back. You might have been quiet and accommodating as a new employee, but now that you've developed more confidence and credibility in your new role, you might be more willing to speak up.

Organizations: Each company and each team within that organization develops its own internal communication patterns. Some offices or shops establish a direct, cut-to-the-chase tone that might include colorful language. Other workplaces are much more reserved, where people are encouraged to drop indirect hints about their opinions. In those more restrained environments, swear words and loud voices are probably never used, and someone being blunt about what they want or think would stick out like a very sour note in the song. It usually takes a while for new team members to get an accurate read on the tempo and tone of conversations and relationships. If they are adaptable and paying attention, they can often fit into the music they hear around them.

Cultures: In addition to the situational and organizational patterns in each workplace, there are local and national influences that affect what assertiveness looks and sounds like in different cultures. While it's usually dangerous to generalize, many people would say that the pace and manner of speech in New York City is faster and stronger than in Denver. So acceptable assertiveness in New York might be too intense for a smaller city in the West.

Similarly, an American's levels of comfortable assertiveness might be too strong in London. Instead of saying, "I want you to do this by Tuesday," a Brit might soften the request by saying, "I was wondering if you could consider finishing this up by next Tuesday. How would that work for you?"

I once led a seminar for a multinational corporation based in the US. There were ten different nationalities in the room. We were practicing a model of assertiveness with extremely specific language that the company wanted everyone to use. A bright woman from their Tokyo office objected, saying, "I can use this assertive model when I speak to Americans who are used to it. But as a woman, I would *never* talk that way to a Japanese person, especially a Japanese man. It would be totally alien in our culture that values politeness, formality, and avoiding embarrassment."

As a result of these situational, organizational, and cultural overlays, there is no single formula for assertiveness. It is a range of responses on a continuum between submission and aggression. What works in one place in one time would look and sound either too strong or too weak with others. It is therefore paramount that you use your emotional intelligence skills to observe and listen to the musical cues around you. This awareness helps you to determine where on that continuum to place your song of seeking to meet your own needs without damage to others.

Collaboration

Collaboration can be generically defined as working with others to produce or create something. It is often called cooperation, partnership, or teamwork. That makes it sound easy. It is, however, rarely that simple or straightforward. The Thomas-Kilmann model in the prior chapter describes Collaboration as the best of the five approaches to conflict. As the old Gershwin song says, "Nice work if you can get it."

Collaboration is characterized by

- **Partnership mindsets** in which participants see each other as allies working toward mutual goals, rather than as competitors or adversaries,

- **Extensive conversation** to share information and perspectives, rather than quick overviews or absence of discussion,

- **Honest, direct articulation of conflicts and concerns**, rather than avoidance, vague conversation, or saying only what you think others want to hear,

- The **search for common ground** about priorities and values, rather than a competing approach and efforts to grab power or influence, and

- Most importantly, **commitment to solutions** that everyone completely buys into and supports, not just lip service, angry resignation, or silent resistance.

One indication that you've reached a collaborative decision is that, when everyone leaves the meeting, they all have the same understanding of what was agreed to. They communicate decisions to others with a uniform message, and they all implement decisions with equal, consistent enthusiasm. This needs to happen, even if the outcome was not everyone's first choice.

This ties directly to Kierson's definition of team alignment described early in this chapter. If I walk out of a meeting with my boss and peers, and subsequently report to my own team, "Well, we decided X in the leadership team meeting. I'm not a big fan of that approach, but the boss says we have to do X and do it well," then I am undermining the work that the leadership team has just done. We do not have true alignment, and the decision did not produce collaboration. My actions are sowing seeds for apathy, complaining, or outright opposition, thus killing any potential harmony that might have developed.

The two main downsides to Collaboration as a tool for promoting relationship harmony are that it is not always possible to achieve and not always worth the extra time and energy to develop it. Everyone involved in a given situation has to want to collaborate. They need to see the value and commit to put in the work to create it.

When there are tensions, conflicting priorities, or opposing views, people must *want* to work together to make solid decisions that they will *all* sing with enthusiasm. If people see each other as adversaries who compete for resources or authority, their chances of reaching a collaborative result are slim and none.

If it's a crisis situation or a time crunch, Collaboration is usually not an option. When the building is on fire, you don't sit around asking open-ended questions and summarizing ideas on a flip chart. Someone takes charge and says, "Melvin, close the windows! Henrietta, move those chairs, so people can get out quickly. Pat, go pull the fire alarm in the hall."[57]

---

57 I was once at a workshop that was held in the music room of a church. It was being recorded, so the videographer had bright lights on tall poles near the ceiling. The spotlights got so hot that they set off the sprinkler system in the room. While I'm usually good in a crisis, I froze. I'd never before been in a room where the sprinklers went off. The room was quickly filling with water, and people were scrambling. My colleague, Lisa Marie, got her wits about her faster than I did and said, "Mike, find someone to help you move that piano into the hall. Susan, grab that guitar and put it somewhere safe. Cindy, help them move the cameras out." Taking charge, not collaborative discussion, was exactly what was needed in the moment.

Sometimes, to use the Thomas-Kilmann language, it's easier and wiser to just Avoid, Accommodate, or Compromise. Other times, when it's a safety, legal, policy, or budget issue, you may have to use the Compete style and mandate an outcome. Each of these four styles is appropriate in some situations. That said, any of these four styles, when overused, can become a liability that creates significant disharmony in your relationships. Even Collaboration, as wonderful as it can be, can create barriers if you think that every situation requires it.

So how do you decide when it's a practical, smart investment of time and effort to collaborate? There are three main sets of questions I ask myself as part of my assessment about whether I should seek Collaboration:

1. **Perceptions**: How do I think we each contribute to the problem? What assumptions or biases may be acting as our respective filters? What other context or history might also color our effort to get on the same page?

2. **Risk-benefit analysis**: What do I see as the motivations or benefits for each of us to change and meet in the middle? What risks would we each be taking? What would be the pros and cons of taking *no* action?

3. **Predictions**: What communication styles or patterns have we used with each other before, and what results did those yield in the past? What do I expect will happen this time? How do I need to prepare in order to keep things rational and professional if we try to collaborate?

When you take time to reflect on your answers to these questions, you are more likely to make a better decision about whether collaboration is an appropriate tool to use in a given situation. If, after some reflection, you and others choose to work toward a collaborative decision, the next question is: How do we get from here to there? You need to have clear **objectives** for the conversation[s] you plan to have, a defined **strategy**, and some **confidence** in the use of the five key techniques that follow.

For most efforts at Collaboration, the objectives boil down to

- Discussing the issues or disagreements directly and honestly,

- Ensuring that everyone's viewpoints are heard and understood, and

- Finding solutions that everyone will buy into and support long term.

The strategy, especially for whoever facilitates the discussion, needs to include these steps:

- First defuse any anger or resentment that people may be feeling,

- Keep yourself and others off the defensive and avoid attacking each other, and most importantly,

- Strive to keep yourself and others calm, objective, and honest.

If you lead the collaboration efforts, you need to work through your own emotions before the meeting starts so you can achieve these objectives and use this strategy with others.

Psychologists say that it is difficult, if not impossible, to operate from your head and your heart at the same time. If you are ripping mad, insulted, threatened, or jumping up and down with enthusiasm, it is hard to think and communicate clearly. Whether you have strong positive or negative emotions, you have to calm yourself first. Then you are better able to help lead others through a solid, rational musical score that will get everyone singing on the same page, in tune, and at the same tempo.

The five main steps that are most likely to lead you to a successful outcome are these:

1. **Plan how to start the conversation**. The way you initiate the meeting will likely set the tone for what follows. Clarify goals, why they're important, and the value that each person in the room brings to the process.

2. **Defuse emotions**. Presuming that you've done your own prework to calm yourself first, give others the opportunity to do the same. It's like letting some of the air out of everyone's tires: you don't want others so overinflated that they might burst. You also don't want them totally deflated because then they can't move forward, and there's no energy to resolve conflicts. Build in structured but limited time for venting to avoid it becoming a gripe session. Deep or active listening behaviors are crucial for this step, so that others feel heard and acknowledged. It's also useful to help people clarify what they want to change or improve.

3. **Share perspectives—theirs, then yours**. Plan some open questions that will let people share their views. You may want someone to record key points on a flip chart, a note pad, or an electronic screen. Empathize with others' comments when you can do so sincerely. Summarize their comments, even when you disagree, so that they feel heard. Look for common ground with comments like, "I agree with your comment that it's been nerve-racking to do XYZ." Be as concise but specific as possible, attacking issues and not people.

   Once you've drawn others out, it may be appropriate for you to express what you believe needs to change or improve, comparing or contrasting that to others' views. When the other people have a view that differs greatly from your own, you can use phrases like, "I understand that you thought that meeting was ABC. I saw it differently." This avoids a tug-of-war that sounds like, "No, you're WRONG! It wasn't ABC. It was XYZ!" You're merely acknowledging different perceptions.[58]

4. **Create consensus if possible**. Review and record the problem definitions, the motivations for change, and the potential barriers to progress. Seek to get each person's overt commitment to the decisions you create together. Asking, "Are we all good with this plan?" is not sufficient. Silence doesn't necessarily mean agreement. It is important to use a specific technique to confirm buy-in from each participant to the collective decision and verify their willingness to be held accountable to implement it. That could include asking each person directly, asking for a show of hands, or signing a document.

5. **Decide, implement, and follow up**. It is important to review decisions, specify what steps will be taken, how, by whom, by when, and how you will measure progress or determine success. Reconfirm that everyone has bought into this plan and will support it moving forward, even if it's not their first choice. Discuss how this decision or plan will be communicated to others: who will say what, when, and get the next steps scheduled and assigned. Set times and dates to check on progress and amend plans as needed. This last step is often omitted. With no measures or follow up, the agreement is unlikely to be sustainable.

---

58 This is in lieu of saying, "Are you out of your mind? Are we talking about the same meeting? I was there too and didn't hear any of what you're referencing!" The hostile approach can be more fun and cathartic but rarely if ever produces harmony.

Delegation

The topic of delegation often comes up when gauging the level of harmony or discord among coworkers. It is also a tool that many leaders struggle to use effectively and need to master to help them survive and thrive. A common definition of delegation is pushing down tasks to the lowest appropriate level. The downsides of this definition include the

- Assumption of a clear chain of authority with a traditional, hierarchical structure, which no longer exists in many twenty-first-century organizations, and

- Somewhat condescending implication that if a task is delegated to you, you are somehow less skilled or intelligent than the person who assigned the task to you.

A more useful explanation might be to say that delegation means identifying who is the best person to complete this task or project now, given experience, skills, interest, and time available. In some situations, a team leader might define a project and say, "Kelly, I'd like you to take the lead to map out a timeline. Sadie, please figure out the budget and materials needed to complete this. Morris, I'd like you to draft the steps you think we should take to get the best results. Then, the three of you can coordinate your initial efforts to create the work plan."

In other settings, the team leader might outline the project and the roles needed to complete it and then say, "Who would feel most comfortable doing Part A? Which of you would be most interested and available to do Part B? I'm not sure we have the capacity for Part C within our team. Let's brainstorm who we might recruit to help with this."

A frequent source of conflict between leaders and their staff is how much oversight the leader should give an employee when delegating tasks. When leaders provide too much supervision, they're seen as overbearing and controlling. Their team often feels constrained, micromanaged, and not trusted. When leaders give too little supervision, they're seen as distant and non-supportive.

Ken Blanchard, leadership expert and coauthor with Spencer Johnson of the mega-best seller *The One Minute Manager*®, has a great term for uninvolved leaders: *seagull managers*. These leaders wait until someone does something wrong and then they fly in, dump (negative feedback) all over people, and fly away. This leaves their team feeling confused, resentful, and unmotivated.

It is a constant challenge for leaders to find the right combination of direction and support to meet the needs of each of their people on each task or goal. But when a leader uses a situational approach to correctly assess the development level of an employee on a task and match it with the appropriate leadership style, the employee is more likely to get the amount of direction and support they need to succeed, which creates harmony between the leader and the team member.

The degree to which leaders delegate tasks to their team, and their ability to use delegation in the right way with the right people, both have a big impact on the amount of harmony or conflict in the team's music. Some leaders refuse to delegate anything to anyone. They believe that they must do it all themselves to be efficient and accurate. They are seen as controlling and not collaborative. Others over-delegate (a la Blanchard's seagull manager theory) and are seen as not carrying their own fair share, asking the team to do all of the work. They also may try to take all the credit for successes but none of the blame for problems.

Effective delegation provides several benefits for both the leader and the team members:

- It **shares the load**: delegating some tasks to the team frees the leader to complete more strategic, bigger-picture responsibilities that might not be appropriate for others to carry out.

- It provides **cross-training and back-up**: if more than one person on a team is experienced in a task or process, it's easier for people to cover for each other during busy times and when people are on leave.

- It **develops skills and confidence**: if I delegate to you something that I'm good at but you've never done, it's a chance for you to learn and be challenged, especially if I used the Situational Leadership styles appropriately.

- It **leverages talent**: it may allow someone who is more qualified performing a task than the leader to complete it better and faster.

- It **increases harmony**: it typically builds trust and improves communication within the team.

Two key paradoxes are embedded into the process of delegation. The first is the trust paradox: I need to trust you so I can be comfortable delegating to you. But if I've never delegated a certain task to you before, it's hard to trust you. It's as if the leader who's delegating needs to make a leap of faith when it's a first-time delegation. The process looks like this:

Successful Delegation

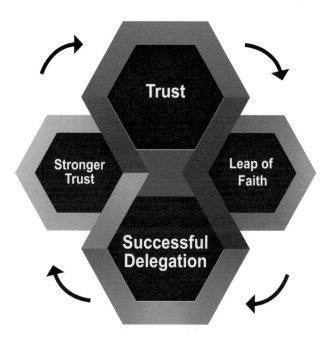

The first time you delegate to someone, before trust is built, you need to make a leap of faith. Hopefully the person does the task well, which strengthens trust, thus making the second delegation easier with a smaller risk or leap of faith.

Let's say this is the first time I've asked you to create a PowerPoint deck of slides for our presentation to the senior team. It's hard to trust you because you've never done this for me. But I know you have some skills with PowerPoint, you have a good eye for graphics, and you're committed to making finished products look great.

So I make a leap of faith, I give you clear instructions, check for understanding, and encourage you to ask for help as needed. I delegate, you do a great job, and it strengthens my trust in you for the next time I assign you a similar task.

But what if I make that leap of faith, delegate, and you do poorly? Have you and I just leaped off a cliff together? No. Now I have a coaching opportunity.

Delegation with Problems

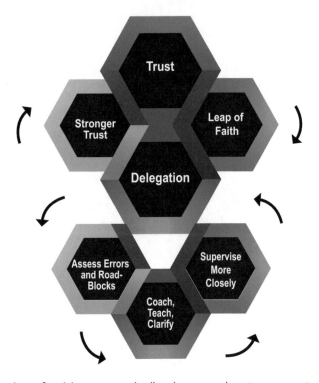

When a first delegation goes badly, it becomes a learning opportunity. You need to stop, assess what went wrong, exchange feedback, coach, encourage, and provide more resources. The hope is that the second attempt will go better, thus building trust and promoting subsequent successes.

We talk about what went wrong the first time and how to tune it up better on the next try. Then I give you more specific direction and support by supervising more closely in hopes that the second delegation succeeds. This would put us both on the path to strengthening trust and chances of success in the future.

The second paradox involves authority and responsibility, which are often defined as follows:

- *Authority*: the right to complete a task, take action, and/or access resources.

- *Responsibility*: being held accountable for the results of the work or actions taken.

When I'm coaching leaders in delegation, I often ask, "Which should you delegate, authority or responsibility?" Common answers include

- Authority—someone needs approval to proceed and use the resources required.

- Responsibility—if I delegate to you, I have to hold you responsible for getting it done correctly, on time, and within budget.

It's a trick question. The real answer is, "Some of each." I must delegate enough authority to you so that you have the time, materials, and ability to complete the task. If I tell you to clean the conference room but don't give you the key to the closet with the vacuum and supplies, I'm not giving you enough authority to successfully complete the delegated task. I also don't want to give you too much authority, so that you might go off in the wrong direction and get yourself in trouble. I want to give you enough rope so that you can do the job, but not enough rope to hang yourself.

With responsibility, I want to hold you responsible for the results you produce. But as your supervisor who delegates the task to you, I can never delegate away *all* of the responsibility. If you mess up, I can't say to my own boss, "Sorry, they messed up. Not my fault!" My boss will hold me responsible for what my team does. My boss's boss will hold him or her responsible if my team and I fail. That delegated responsibility floats all the way up to the CEO or the board.

People expect the top person in the organization to accept responsibility, even for actions they're not aware of. You can delegate some of the responsibility for delegated tasks, but as the delegator, you can never delegate it all away to the person you've asked to do the work.

Consider these six key steps to take that increase the likelihood of successful delegation:

- **Choose the right people** to whom you delegate a task. This is either the easiest or hardest step. It often ties back to developmental levels in Blanchard's Situational Leadership model. Have a solid rationale for delegating—to share the workload, to develop new skills, to acknowledge what motivates people, to free up your time for other priorities—and share that justification with the "delegatee(s)."

- **Set clear expectations** about desired results, timelines, methods, and resources. Just because something is clear in your mind doesn't mean others will know what you're thinking. Be sure that the goals you set are S.M.A.R.T.: Specific, Measurable, Attainable (realistic), Relevant (important), and Time-sensitive (with deadlines).

- **Decide how much authority** to grant with the delegation, and how you will hold others at least partly accountable, given that you must share some of the responsibility yourself. The amount of authority granted should be tied to their skills, experience, confidence, and commitment.

- **Allow appropriate latitude** for others to do the task or project in a different manner than you might do it. As long as they are clear about parameters for the task—complete it by Friday, don't spend more than $500, be sure it follows our policy—acknowledge that they may follow a different route, which may be faster, better, and more innovative than your own approach. Resist the temptation to be threatened or unsettled when a delegated task is done well but not done "the way we've always done it here."

- Remember to **follow up** no matter how competent and committed the employees are. Just because it's delegated doesn't mean you can forget about it, a la Blanchard's seagull management metaphor. At the beginning of the delegated task or project, it helps to clarify who will follow up, how, and how often.

- While it seems obvious, be sure to **give credit** where credit is due. It's often motivating to give someone sincere kudos, publicly or privately, but it's nearly always de-motivating to ignore their good work or take the credit for yourself. Giving credit, like following up, is one of the two steps most often overlooked in delegation.

Decision-making

Decision-making seems like it should be a slam-dunk and not in need of explanation. Yet it is another tool that challenges many leaders and team members. Some people tend to err on the side of being too rigid and abrupt, while others are too hesitant to fish or cut bait. Certain folks will vacillate for hours or days, rehashing the same discussion points to avoid leading the music to a clear conclusion with a decision.

Several factors impact the effectiveness of decision-making, and hence the degree of harmony or dissonance within the team. The most important are these three questions:

1. Who has the authority to make this decision?

2. What type of decision does it need to be (unilateral, gather input, consensus, or something else)?

3. How does it need to be communicated to whom, when, and by whom?

The Interaction Associates model described in Stage 3 regarding "Levels of Involvement" provides a great way to answer these three questions. It is easy to say that the more input people have into a decision, the more likely they are to accept and support it. It is more difficult to assess which is the appropriate level of input for each specific decision and situation.

Consider two additional factors when looking at how to make decisions effectively. The first is impact: who will be affected by this decision, and how will it land on them?

- Which individuals or subgroups will be impacted by this decision (customers, staff, board, departments, vendors, others)?

- How are they most likely to respond (enthusiastic acceptance, resistance, ambivalence, confusion, mixed reviews, other)?

- How will this decision impact our long-term goals, priorities, and strategic plan?

- What other issues do we need to consider, long and short term?

One other consideration is the quality-acceptance paradox. Sometimes the highest quality decision will not be accepted by the people who must approve or support it. Sometimes the most popular decision will not be a wise one. It is important to think about how to wrestle with this dilemma to help you develop the best possible decision that will have the greatest degree of buy-in.

Intention versus Impact

Intention and impact play an important role in how well people communicate and hence create harmony with others. It's not as much a tool as an awareness. In a perfect world, the intention of my words and actions matches my impact or how I "land" on others. For example, I strive to be helpful, and you see me as helpful. I try to be funny, and you find me funny. I step back in hopes of letting you be more independent and sing on your own, and you feel more empowered and confident.

Unfortunately, there is often a mismatch between what I intend and how I affect others. I strive to be helpful, and you see me as interfering or micromanaging. I try to be funny, and you find me sarcastic or disrespectful. I step back in hopes of letting you be more independent, and you feel unsupported or ignored by me.

The only thing worse than this discrepancy between intention and impact is when I don't recognize the gap. This is sometimes a lack of emotional intelligence on my part, not reading others' cues. Sometimes it's a result of others' poker faces—in other words, not displaying any cues that I might read. Also, when trust is low, people may be dishonest with you and say, "Great idea! Can't wait to get started on that." Then they bad-mouth you or undermine your efforts behind your back.

Many years ago, I worked with Tony, whose reactions were extremely hard to read. I sensed friction between us but couldn't pinpoint the cause of the disharmony. One day, he shocked me by saying, "You know, Susan, eighteen months ago, you did something that really annoyed me. It was in a meeting with Rhoda."

I asked, "What meeting, what did I do and by the way, who is Rhoda?" I had no idea what he was talking about.

He never answered my questions but added, "And then seventeen months ago, you did it again."

I was furious. Not only had he waited a year and a half to give me feedback, but his annoyance had been creating a subtle tension between us all that time. Once I calmed down, I was able to tell him that if he'd been willing to tell me about my impact seventeen and a half months ago, I would have remembered the meeting, remembered Rhoda, and had the chance to correct my missteps.

Another luckier situation where I did not land well was during the oral exam for my master's degree. I was incredibly nervous, as I'd never had an oral exam before. At that point in my life, I had not had much experience in improvisational thinking on my feet. I had been studying hard for months and wondered if I had crammed enough of the right information into my stressed cranium.

I sat facing three very stern professors who were senior faculty in the department. Naturally, their first question was about the topic I knew the least about. I started to answer the question, but I noticed that the man who had asked it started to shift from leaning forward in his chair with his elbows on the table and his chin in his hand. He began to lean way back, fold his arms across his chest, and furrow his brow. I remember thinking, "Oh no! I'm way off! He doesn't like what I'm saying."

So I finished the sentence and said, "However, some people see it differently." I then did a 180 and took my answer in the opposite direction. The professor shifted again, raising his eyebrows, unfolding his arms, and resuming his forward lean, chin in hand. I used his overt cues to shift what I said and how

I said it. I passed the exam. Had it been a written exam without those cues, I probably would have failed that question.

The punchline here is that to be able to build and maintain harmony at work, it's important to pay attention to verbal and nonverbal cues that can tell you if there's a disconnect between what you're intending and how you're being received by others. Sometimes it's obvious: you say something, and the other person furrows their brow, gasps or leans back in their chair and crosses their arms across their chest. Then you have options. You can say:

- "It looks like you're not happy with what I'm proposing. What are your concerns?" or

- "I'm not sure how to read your reaction. What are your thoughts?" or

- "I suspect that from the look on your face, you're confused by what I just said. Let me try it a different way and hopefully make it clearer." (basically, a do-over)

With people and situations where it's not clear what impact you've had, you need to ask them:

- "What's your reaction to my suggestion?" or

- "How do you feel about what I've just said?" or

- "I'd appreciate some feedback on my comments, so I know where I stand."

When we ignore these cues, don't draw people out to encourage feedback, or assume that our message is accurately received, we may be asking for trouble—and conflict. People who communicate well remember to check for alignment or disconnects between intention and impact and know how to revise the message when there's a disparity.

Final Notes

This fifth stage of Encores can be a satisfying time in the evolution of a relationship. Having moved through Auditions, First Notes, New Songs, and Clashing Chords, you may be tempted to feel like you can coast. You feel like saying, "Whew, I got this!" The song in your head might be Bobby McFerrin's "Don't Worry, Be Happy."

I hope the collection of tools and considerations presented in this stage have convinced you that you need to continuously work to maintain the harmony you have developed with others. When people don't have clarity about where they're headed (vision, values, goals, priorities) and how best to get there (roles, routines, boundaries), the music may revert to clashing chords. Likewise, things may slide into boredom and low energy.

The motivation, influence, and numerous communication tools are vital in maintaining the vibrancy and momentum of the song. These resources will also assist you with the decisions you will need to make in the sixth stage, Finales. Before we bring the curtain down, let's examine how to end the song. These resources will help you determine the lifespan of the music, as well as how to sustain it or bring it to a graceful conclusion.

Rehearsals:

Application Exercises for Encores

Choose one of these exercises to help you apply the Stage 5 information to your current experience. Then decide if it would be helpful to try a second type of rehearsal.

1. **Acknowledge the awkwardness of new behaviors**. Try this quick experiment. Fold your hands together with your fingers interlaced. Notice which thumb is on top of the other. Notice that this may feel comfortable.

   Now unlace your fingers and re-lace your fingers with the opposite thumb on top: if your right thumb was on top, re-lace them so that the left thumb is now on top or vice versa. It's cheating to just switch your thumbs: you need to completely re-lace all of your fingers. Notice that this configuration may feel awkward, weird, or uncomfortable, as if your shoes were on the wrong feet.

   Next, go back to the first configuration. Aahhh, better. Then back to the wrong way. Ugh. Finally, go back and forth between the first way and the wrong way, lacing and re-lacing eight times, and stop in the wrong position. How does it feel now, compared to the first time you laced them the unnatural way? It probably feels less uncomfortable but still not as normal as the first way.

   If you practiced this lacing and unlacing for thirty minutes, you'd likely be bored, and your hands would be tired. But the practice would probably cause the wrong way to feel much less awkward and nearly as comfortable as the first way. It may never be as comfortable as your default setting.

Use this exercise as a metaphor for how you could feel when you try out the new behaviors and responses suggested in this book. They may feel awkward at first. You might have to really concentrate to use them, just as you did the first time you re-laced your fingers the wrong way. But rest assured that with practice, they will get easier and feel more natural, even if they never become as comfortable as patterns you've adopted for years up to this point.

When a tool or strategy feels challenging, remember that you're re-lacing your fingers in a new way. Congratulate yourself for stretching yourself and experimenting. Ask for help or coaching if needed but have patience with yourself while you practice and gain more proficiency.

2. **Strengthen your listening muscles**. Many people struggle to listen deeply, especially when they feel challenged or even threatened by the speaker. Try this experiment with someone you know and trust well. It may be entertaining, and it will demonstrate how difficult it can be to deeply listen to someone else when you feel attacked or insulted.

    You are the listener, and your partner is the antagonist. Use a timer and take one minute to tell the antagonist about a value or belief you have that you feel strongly about. As an example, it might be your views on religion, politics, exercise, diet, education, or money.

    After sixty seconds, reset the timer. The antagonist now has two minutes to aggressively rip apart your ideas and feelings. S/he should also vehemently criticize you for having that position. While the antagonist is going after you and your views, all you get to do is listen deeply, paraphrase, and ask for clarification. You can't defend yourself, argue, or counterattack. You have to stay in a calm, neutral, receptive mode.

Do your best to stay in the role without laughing (often difficult) or stopping for commentary. It helps to do this exercise with someone who can role play a really obnoxious, hostile person. It doesn't work as well if the antagonist is too nice, or if you stay in the role for less than two whole minutes. (It may feel like an hour.)

When the two long minutes are up, stop and reflect with your partner. Talk about

- What was hard about staying in the neutral listener role and why,

- What felt natural or easy, and

- What insights you can apply from this exercise to real situations where you have to listen to someone who is antagonistic and strongly disagrees with you.

Then ask your partner if they want to switch roles to try staying in the listener role while you attack their position.[59]

3. **Set up a rehearsal for a difficult conversation you need to have.** It could be some feedback that you tried to share before, but it went badly, and you want to try again. It might be for a decision for which you need true alignment and buy-in. Perhaps it is a delegation situation that needs clarification, whether you are the delegator or delegatee. There are several steps that will help you prepare and practice.

---

59 It's more fun and cathartic to be the antagonist, albeit socially unacceptable and emotionally unintelligent outside of this practice exercise.

- Start by outlining your goals for the content of the discussion.

- Make note of which specific tools listed in this stage will be most helpful in creating the outcomes you seek.

- Anticipate perspectives and reactions that you and each of the other people involved might have.

- Reflect on how this type of conversation has gone with them in the past and consider what steps you can take to avoid possible sour notes that might emerge.

- Have a back-up plan of what you'll do and say if the dialogue starts to get out of tune.

Then decide your best options to rehearse.

- Is there someone at work whom you trust and who knows both you and the other people involved?

- Would it be better to practice with someone outside of work who is totally objective?

- Have you worked with a coach, mentor, or counselor who would give you honest, specific feedback?

- Would practicing alone in the mirror at home or recording your rehearsal and playing it back be most productive?

Whichever method you choose, make it a real, out-loud rehearsal. Don't just think about it silently in your own head or obsess about it at 2:00 a.m. when you're awake, worrying about things like this. There is power in verbally testing it out and, if possible, getting reactions to your nonverbals as well as your words. Then, based on what suggestions you receive, edit your plan, maybe do a second dress rehearsal, and consider what else you need to do to be calm and confident when you initiate the real conversation.

4. **Fill out a delegation assessment chart** if you are deciding what to delegate to whom.

Leader's Tasks	Check One of These		List of Names of Employees Who	
	Leader Must Complete Task	Task Could Be Delegated to Others	Can Do This Task Now	Could Be Trained to Do This Task

List out the leader's tasks in the first column. Sort each task as either being one that the leader must do [second column] or one that could be delegated [third column]. For any tasks that can be delegated, identify who is able to complete this task now [fourth column] or who could be trained to complete it later [fifth column].

In the first column, list all of the tasks or duties that are currently on your own plate. In the next two columns, sort each task by either checking the second column if you need to complete it yourself, or the third column if you believe it could be delegated with varying degrees of autonomy. In the last two columns, identify people who either have the skills and availability to complete a certain task now, or others who could be trained to complete it.

This will help you assess what you are able to delegate and to whom you could delegate tasks now or in the near future. Refer to Blanchard's Situational Leadership model to consider at which developmental level each employee listed is currently operating for that task. It will help you consider which leadership style you should use. That way, you can provide the right amount of direction and support and avoid over- or under-supervising.

Stage 6

Finales: Knowing If, When, and How to End the Song

Juanita arranges a lunch back at Sammy's Sandwich Shop, their hangout, to get together with her friends Alex, Sally, and Omar for the first time since she'd started her new job.

Omar greets everyone and says, "Juanita, thanks for setting up this lunch date. It's been ages since the four of us have gotten together. My how time flies when you're having fun. I'm not always sure I'm having fun though. What about the rest of you?"

"I'm doing fine," says Alex. "I've been in my same role with the same company for five years now. I know that sounds boring, but I appreciate the routine. I have enough going on at home with our kids, as well as managing health issues for my parents. So it's a relief to go to work, know what's going to happen, and be clear about what I'm supposed to do. I feel like I can hunker down there for several more years before looking for a promotion or new company."

Sally laughs. "Glad that works for you, Alex. I'm bored out of my gourd! My boss has me doing the same kinds of projects over and over. I can do them in my sleep. I keep looking for a promotion or even a change to another department, so that I can expand my skills. I need some new challenges to recharge my battery. I just want to get enthused about going to work again. My motivation has pretty much flat-lined, because I keep singing the same song day after day."

Omar looks straight at Sally and says, "Consider what your options are to help revive your enthusiasm while you search for a new position. Six months ago, I was feeling like you are now. I had to drag myself out of bed in the morning and found myself counting the hours till Friday at five o'clock."

Sally furrows her brow. "So what did you do, Omar?"

"My boss, who's very observant, noticed that I was running out of steam and had three suggestions. He recommended that I use our education benefits to take some classes in-house and also some at the university. He also told me about our EAP, Employee Assistance Program, that I could access for free if I wanted to talk to a counselor about any specific concerns. Finally, he reminded me that he'd always make time to chat with me any time I wanted a sounding board. So I've started taking some classes to finish my degree. I don't feel like I need the EAP now, but it's nice to know it's there. And the fact that he made these offers tuned up my mood right away. So I'm in much better spirits now."

Sally laughs again. "Omar, do you have any openings in your department? Or does your boss have a twin somewhere else that I might work for? Sounds like he's a terrific leader. Juanita, how about you? How's your new job going?"

Juanita pauses, looks around the table, and finally announces, "Well, I don't want to gloat, especially since you're having a rough time, Sally. But this may be the best job I've had so far. My team is rock solid. The chemistry between us is really good, probably because people know how to communicate honestly and resolve problems directly. My boss promoted me to a lead position, so I now have three staff reporting to me. I'm doing my best to notice what she does well and try to emulate her behaviors. She models how to listen well and give feedback effectively, both the kudos and the critiques. I always know where I stand with her, and I know what I need to focus on."

Sally interrupts with, "Yeah, but it can't be all sweetness and light. Doesn't anyone ever make any mistakes or lose their cool?"

Juanita nods. "Sure. When someone does have a problem or gets bent out of shape, it's expected that we put the issue on the table and talk it out. That way, we can look for a solution that we either all buy into or that at least is a compromise we can live with without pouting. I hope I can create the same levels of trust, clear direction, and openness with my direct reports."

Alex slaps Juanita on the back. "That's awesome. If I were wearing a hat right now, I'd take it off to you. You've come a long way from our last lunch together. At that point, you were whining and lacking in confidence. Look at you now: enthused, learning, and in a new leadership position. Sounds like you're going to be happy with this team for a long time."

"Thanks, Alex. I couldn't have done it without you three, my back-up band. If you hadn't encouraged me back then, I might have never looked for a new job and would have missed out on all these opportunities to grow. It takes a village. Don't move out of town, any of you!"

They finish their lunch with lighter conversation and promises to help Sally find more harmony at work.

Vary the Music—Growth, Change, Boredom, and Trauma

Once you've worked through Auditions, First Notes, New Songs, Clashing Chords, and Encores, you've probably logged a good amount of time with the person or people in those relationships. You've likely experienced a range of emotions, seen varying levels of trust and satisfaction, and increased your awareness of what skills you've mastered and which ones still need work. Maybe you've reached a state of knowing the song, knowing the singers, and knowing how they sing. That can be a wonderfully comfortable type of music.

The risk, however, is boredom and lack of enthusiasm. This is the point in many relationships where the song goes flat—either flat in pitch, as in off-key, or flat in terms of losing energy and motivation. It's like an old children's song that says, "Same song, second verse, a little bit louder and a little bit worse!"[60]

Depending on personality types and where people are in their life or career, some people can settle in and sing the same song in the same way for weeks, months, and years. The predictability makes them happy. If someone is close to retirement, or if their personal life is tumultuous and discordant, they may depend on the repetition of a familiar song to counterbalance the big change they're about to make or the chaos they're experiencing at home. They are not looking for the challenge and stress of new music and uncertainty. They appreciate the routine.

Others have low boring points and get antsy or annoyed singing the same song, second verse, a little bit louder and a little bit worse. It becomes a lot worse for them. I know some musicians who hate rehearsals: they learn the music quickly and resent having to go over and over certain parts for others who have more trouble catching on.

When I was in high school, I sang in a trio. By the time we had our three-part harmony mastered, I was sick of the song and didn't want to sing it anymore. I've always wondered about the actors who perform the same part in the same

---

60 This is the type of song that was annoying when I was a camp counselor for several summers. The kids would sing this on the bus over and over and end up shouting louder each verse. It was especially painful at 8:00 a.m.

play on Broadway for years. They say that every audience is different, but I suspect it's difficult to keep their delivery fresh and interesting.

So the dilemma in Stage 6, Finales, is how to accommodate the people who are comfortable settling into familiar music, as well as the others who need to mix it up with different songs or at least different arrangements. It's an interesting challenge to consider how to build on what you've learned in the first five stages. Then you can decide if you can maintain the song effectively, or if it's time for the finale, time to end the music and move on.

The Devil You Know

Often, people will stay in a bad job or even an abusive personal relationship out of inertia or fear of change. They adopt the attitude of the sixteenth-century Irish proverb, "Better the devil you know than the devil you don't know." You might consider it less painful to deal with a boss, teammate, or job description that you don't like but are familiar with than it would be to look for a new assignment or relationship that is full of unknowns and could be even worse.

There are times when it's valid to choose the lesser of two evils. You might decide that looking for a new job or asking for a transfer to a new department would be even more stressful than coping with your present situation. I recently had a young man say to me, "I really want to apply for a new job with a different company. But I'm moving in two weeks. I hate moving. It exhausts me and stresses me out. I'm going to put up with my current, crazy boss till I get unpacked and settled into my new house. Then I'll be able to focus better on applications and interviews."

When the current relationships or work environment are out of tune and unsettling, it's important to be honest with yourself and ask

- Am I tolerating the status quo, because I'm afraid I can't find anything better?

- Is the toll that this stress is taking on me really worth the security of avoiding change?

- Is my decision to stay a result of some rational analysis that maintaining the song for now is the most practical option?

- Do I have any optimism that I could improve relationships and reduce the friction if I stay?

- Am I staying put out of laziness, fear, inertia, and tolerance of the devil I know?

Once you reflect on questions like these, you are better equipped to make a more honest decision about the best course of action. Sometimes it's obvious: this song is over, and I need to get out! Usually, it's not that clear-cut or easy.

It can also be tempting to go to the other extreme and quit the music at the first sound of sour notes. Some people will quit a job (or a personal relationship) too quickly. They work their way successfully through the first three stages: Auditions, First Notes and New Songs. But as soon as the Clashing Chords begin, they adopt Leslie's Double Bind Theory as described in Stage 4. They assume things are awful and will never improve. They are not willing, able, or confident enough to do the hard work of resolving dissonance and fine-tuning the song, so they bolt.

In order to avoid hanging onto a song too long or giving up too fast, there are strategies, tools, and support options to help you decide if you can improve the music or need to accept that it's a Finale.

As counterintuitive as it may seem, positive changes, such as a marriage, a new baby, or a promotion at work, can cause as much stress as negative changes. Noted stress expert Hans Selye did a great deal of research about the impacts of positive *eu*stress and negative *dis*tress. His 1975 article discussed how similar our physical responses can be to both positive and negative stressors.

In 1967, Thomas Holmes and Richard Rahe also developed the Social Readjustment Rating Scale, more commonly known as the Holmes-Rahe Stress Inventory. It rated a variety of positive and negative life changes and correlated the magnitude of those changes with the likelihood of a resulting illness or injury. As an example, getting fired at work can have nearly the same stress rating and physiological impacts as getting married or retiring.

Strategies for Dealing with Sour Notes and Lagging Tempos

One approach to tuning up interactions in the Finales stage is to build in checkpoints that ensure the periodic review of your comfortable relationships. Often people call in organizational consultants when a team or company is in trouble: when profits are down, tensions are high, or the path forward is unclear. By contrast, high-performing teams and organizations don't wait until there's a problem. They schedule yearly or quarterly check-ins, just like you schedule regular oil changes for your car or teeth cleaning with your dentist. It's preventive maintenance.

In spite of all that you and your colleagues may have learned in the first five stages, it's tempting to get complacent about regularly using those skills to keep the music of your relationships vibrant, interesting, and in tune. Whether it's a formal retreat for a whole team, or periodic requests for feedback from individual colleagues, we all need regular, preventive maintenance. We don't want people waiting eighteen months to tell us that something is off-key.

Using Cooperrider's Appreciative Inquiry mindset, it's best to start off with these questions:

- What am I (or we) doing well?

- What have been our successes or improvements in the last week/month/quarter/year?

- What benefits did we reap from those accomplishments?

The subsequent questions might include

- In what ways did we mess up or miss the mark?

- What impacts did these shortcomings have on our goals? Our profitability? Our progress? Our relationships and communication?

- How can we leverage our strengths and successes to address what needs improvement?

- Therefore, what goals or priorities do we need to establish or revise for the next week/month/quarter/year?

- How should we measure our progress? How will we know if we're moving forward, or if we need to recalibrate our targets and methods?

- How will each of us feel and benefit when we see positive movement toward those goals and priorities?

We're either taking corrective action when a problem has been identified or conducting preventive maintenance to anticipate and address challenges before they happen. Both approaches are helpful in keeping a familiar song from veering off into sour notes or lagging tempos. They increase the likelihood that the relationship music will continue and stay strong.

Sometimes, when individuals and teams are willing to pause, reflect, and ask themselves these questions, they reach a different conclusion. If they are honest with themselves and with each other, they might decide that

- We've done all we can here,

- This song has played itself out and lost its energy, and

- It's time to move on or change the music.

One of my experiences of figuring out when and how to end the song was in a job that had been happy for several years. I had good relationships with my boss, peers, and customers. I had consistently achieved positive performance reviews and feedback. I liked going to work and felt challenged to learn new skills.

Then I had to take a few months off for a medical leave. I came back to a hostile environment. Some peers were understandably stressed, as they had been required to cover my responsibilities as well as their own during my absence. A few people accused me of malingering and unfairly taking time off.[61] Coworkers started excluding me from conversations and withholding information to which I needed access. Opportunities for interesting projects passed me by and were assigned to others. One colleague in particular, who had been a good friend, gave me the cold shoulder. When I asked her why she was angry and shutting me out, she would not reply and left the room.

---

61 I was insulted and felt like saying, "Do you want to call my physician and see my medical records?" Fortunately, I did not give in to that snarky temptation.

I spent the next year trying to mend fences. I kept my head down, worked as hard as I could, agreed to do whatever people asked of me, and avoided making waves. I also started eating Tums for the first time in my life. Stuffing my feelings and trying to make everyone else happy was destroying the lining of my stomach and making me miserable.[62]

After twelve months of Tums and tension, I decided the song was over. I'd done my level best to re-create the harmony that had existed before my leave. It wasn't going to get any better. Stick a fork in me: I was done. When I gave notice and went to say goodbye to each of my colleagues, they were shocked that I was leaving. "But I thought you were so happy here," was what I heard from many. Either they were not reading my cues, or I was disguising my discomfort in an effort to rebuild relationships.

The other irony is that after I left, friends asked me if I'd lost weight. The scale read the same, but a huge weight had been taken off my shoulders. I finally had figured out that I had done all I could, and I was relieved to move on to new music.

Compromise and Collaboration

Compromise and Collaboration are two of the five main responses to conflict in the Thomas-Kilmann model when addressing clashing chords. They may also be useful in Stage 6 when you are deciding if, when, and how you should end the song you've been singing. They are tools to consider as alternatives to a Finale. They can help you look for some common ground upon which you might continue the song effectively.

There are several situations that might motivate you to attempt Compromise or Collaboration before deciding to end the song:

---

62 Avoidance and Accommodation have never been my strongest suits.

- *Pervasive tension* in one or more relationships, like my Tums example, causes people to consider calling it quits. They begin to feel traumatized by the constant static between them and their coworkers. Before you make it a finale, ask yourself and your colleagues, "If you want A, and I want B, where could we meet in the middle, so that at least some of our needs are met and we feel satisfied with the agreement?" That would be a *compromise*. Or if you say, "Neither A nor B is sufficient for either of us. Are you willing to *collaborate* with me to look for C, a third option, that will better meet all or most of our needs at least some of the time?"

  Both of these approaches to ongoing friction in relationships presume that you and the others involved are willing to talk about what's stressful and look for solutions. The way others respond to your questions will tell you a great deal about the likelihood of improving the song moving forward.

- *Boring, tedious or repetitive tasks* are another condition that make it hard to get out of bed in the morning and head happily off to work. There was a time in one of my jobs when I had delivered the same seminar so many times that I was on autopilot. One day in particular, I must have been making sense, because participants were raising their hands, asking questions, and engaging me in conversation. I, however, was mentally absent. I wasn't sure what day it was, what topic it was, or what city I was in. I remember calling a break to look at my agenda and calendar to reorient myself.

I went to my boss and told him that my brain had started to atrophy. I asked him to give me some project or seminar that had the word *new* in front of it. I would have been happy to *compromise*, if he had said, for example, "Finish three more weeks of that program, and I'll give you time to design a new course." I would have been thrilled to *collaborate* with him or anyone to come up with ways to reinvigorate me and my job description. Instead, he said dryly, "I have you signed up to deliver six more months of that seminar. You're doing great work." Something inside me died when he said that, and I started thinking not if but when and how I'd end that job.

- *Invisibility and dead ends* are two related scenarios that make people question if they can continue the song harmoniously or if it's careening toward a finale. Sometimes, if people are not recognized appropriately and sincerely for their hard work and contributions, they start to feel invisible. Some of my coachees say things like, "I have the most seniority in my department. I work the hardest and volunteer for the most challenging assignments. But everyone else gets raises and promotions. I'm beginning to think my boss looks right past me to see everyone else and what they're doing."

Another common complaint when people get to this stage in relationships is feeling like the interactions, as well as the job duties, have hit a dead end. They see no opportunities for improvement, growth, new challenges, or enthusiasm. They've either decided from observation or been told by higher ups that they're at the top rung of the salary scale and that there is no path forward for them.

This ties back to the top three levels on Maslow's hierarchy of needs and Motivational Factors in Herzberg's model. Once someone's physiological and safety needs have been met, and once the Hygiene Factors have been provided, most people need and want acknowledgment. Some folks appreciate public recognition, such as the boss commending them in front of the rest of the team or giving them an award like top salesperson or innovator of the year. More introverted people might want to crawl under the table with public accolades but welcome a one-on-one conversation or an email from someone who has noticed and appreciated their efforts.

Intention and impact play a role here too. Let's say I give you a loud pat on the back and say, "Great job! Love your work! You're a terrific employee!" My intention might be to recognize your successes, but the impact may feel hollow and formulaic. You might want to know what was great about the job you did. What do I love about your work? What exactly do I think makes you terrific? If my feedback were more specific, you'd know what to continue and do more of. If you don't feel that the positive words are sincere, you won't be motivated to continue the music. It is difficult to find ways to either *compromise* or *collaborate* when you feel ignored or out of options to grow.

The Focus Map

In his work with top executives and large corporations, one of the many tools that Steve Vannoy developed is what he first called the Energy Circle. It was originally presented in his book about creating relationship harmony in families,

The 10 Greatest Gifts I Give My Children. He later adapted it to the workplace. It is used to solve problems and get results.

Further modified here, the Focus Map represents how we use all of our time and energy. It's a useful tool to increase awareness of what your experience has been, what you know or need to find out, and where you want to go regarding a specific issue or challenge. It helps you to access the positive energy that is needed to move you and your colleagues up and out of Gridlock, so that you can resolve issues and achieve goals.

Focus Map

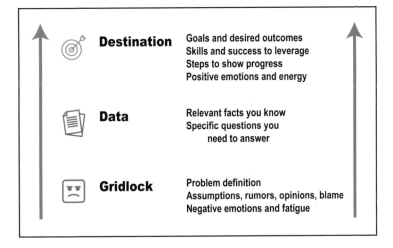

Destination
Goals and desired outcomes
Skills and success to leverage
Steps to show progress
Positive emotions and energy

Data
Relevant facts you know
Specific questions you
need to answer

Gridlock
Problem definition
Assumptions, rumors, opinions, blame
Negative emotions and fatigue

The Focus Map articulates how we use our time and energy
to solve problems, get results and reach our desired goals.

The bottom part of the map is called Gridlock. It is the place to acknowledge and record concerns: problems, reasons things are not working, and what or who you think is to blame. You can include the emotions that you and others have about what's not working: anger, fear, fatigue, cynicism, confusion, resentment, and lack of motivation to fix things. It may also contain assumptions, rumors, or opinions. This portion of the map is characterized by events and feelings that drain your energy. It's called Gridlock because if you keep your focus here, you will feel stuck, frustrated, and tired.

The middle part of the map contains Data: what you know are verifiable facts related to this issue, as well as specific questions you need to get answered in order to improve the situation. It is a neutral part of the map that neither depletes nor increases your energy.

The top part of the map is the Destination. It articulates where you want to go and how you want to be: what is working, what successes and assets you can leverage to address this issue, what solutions you might seek, and steps you can take to get there. This section of the map contains the positive emotions and ideas that increase your energy. It is tied to your optimism and desire to make progress.

It's important to recognize and validate all that's contained in the bottom part of this map. But if you spend too much time focusing on the troubling events and reactions, it wears you down and keeps you stuck in a state of "complaining, criticizing, and condemning," as my friend Lisa Marie likes to say.

Significant research confirms that we can only effectively focus on one thing at a time, and that we get more of what we focus on. If we devote most of our attention to problems—those listed in Gridlock—we usually get more problems. By contrast, if we acknowledge the concerns and then highlight what we know or what we need to find out, we can then shift our focus up to the Destination we want to reach. This, in turn, frees up our energy to address and resolve what we need to improve or shift. We can lower stress levels, raise confidence and energy, and build more collaboration to create better harmony in our projects and relationships.

The map analogy is perfect. It is possible to get in your car and start driving with the hope that you'll arrive someplace interesting and safe. Some people see this as an adventurous way to approach a vacation. It is similar to improvisational music, when the musicians don't know exactly how the piece will play out. Most of the time, however, we need to know where we are now, where we want to go, and have a plan of how to get there.

At work, we rarely have the luxury of just driving without identifying the desired destination and route. Even with improv music, there has to be some structure within which the musicians can experiment and improvise: which key, who takes the lead next, what tempo, and how we'll decide when and how to end the song. Otherwise, they would create a musical mess.

Take Singing Lessons—Who, Me?

One other strategy to consider in Stage 6 of Finales is to ask yourself what if any coaching, training, or education might augment your skills and experience. What additional knowledge would help you decide if there's a future with this particular song at work, or whether all the instruction in the world will not bring back the harmony?

Some employers have a contract with an EAP vendor— Employee Assistance Program. They provide counselors to help you for a limited number of free sessions around issues such as job stress, career advancement, money management, work-life balance, and controlling anger. A good EAP counselor will listen well and ask thoughtful questions to help you sort out your needs and options. EAPs are confidential. Your employer will not know why you were getting counseling.

Sometimes, your company will pay for continuing education courses to expand your job skills or finish a degree.

The challenge of learning new information and tools can be the perfect tonic to reinvigorate your current music and future assignments at work.

Discussing your options with friends or family members can also be helpful for some, and a perilous one for others. The success of this approach depends on how well the people close to you will listen and offer unbiased suggestions. If the advice comes with criticism or pressure, this may not be a productive route.

Mentors are another resource that many have found to be helpful. There may be a formal mentoring program that matches mentors and mentees within your organization. You might also be able to access an external leadership development program through the Chamber of Commerce, local universities, or other volunteer agencies in your community that would help you find the right mentor. That person can be a sounding board and someone objective to talk with who does not conduct your performance appraisal. They might coach you on new approaches to difficult situations where the music has gotten dissonant. They may introduce you to other people who could help to enrich the music and give you access to some new opportunities.

These are some of the many ways that you can broaden your perspective and add to your tool kit as you consider if this song that you've been singing can regain and expand its harmony, or if it's time for the final chord. What's important to remember is to not end the song as an impulsive move after a bad day. Be sure to calm down, get some distance from whatever was upsetting, and make your stay-or-go decision after rational reflection and weighing of the pros and cons.

Final Notes

Once you get to this sixth stage in a relationship, the hope is that you make a decision that is both lucid and graceful. You have many tools in your toolkit to bring you to a verdict, regardless of whether the music will continue, or if you choose to move on. Boredom and trauma may be avoided with sufficient variety and growth. Preventive maintenance helps you acknowledge some of the sour notes and prevent others. Compromise and Collaboration are useful in reducing tension, tedium, and lack of recognition. Resources like the Energy Map and learning opportunities from classes and coaches are valuable to recharge the music and make wise choices.

While no situation is ever perfect all the time, the goal is to create harmony in as many of your relationships as possible, as often as possible. Your awareness of these six common stages, as well as the skills and concepts that pertain to each one, will increase your ability to improve the music at work.

Rehearsals:

Application Exercises for Finales

Choose one of these exercises to help you apply the Stage 6 information to your current experience. Then decide if it would be helpful to try a second type of rehearsal.

1. **Schedule regular check-ins** with yourself to take stock of your current job satisfaction levels. It's helpful to set aside time in your calendar for a mini retreat with yourself to assess your

    - Current state—how your current position is going, and

    - Desired state—what you're planning and hope to achieve moving forward.

    Many people do this at the end of the calendar year, and others plan it around the time of their annual performance appraisal if their organization conducts yearly reviews for each employee. Some people do this quarterly, either by themselves to review their own goals, motivation levels, and quality of their relationships, or with their team to look at collective goals, progress indicators, and degrees of harmony occurring in the duets between individuals and for the team chorus overall.

    Questions to consider posing to yourself and others include these:

    - What goals for the quarter or year have I (we) achieved or to what degree has enough progress been made?

- What actions, attitudes, and other behaviors have helped me (us) succeed? What if any external forces have also supported my (our) advancement?

- Which goals need to be revised, abandoned, or reprioritized for later?

- What internal and external factors had kept me (us) from achieving those goals? (skills, information, time, budget, quality of communication and collaboration, staffing, customers, competition, economic considerations)[63]

- How can I (we) leverage past and current successes and skills to address any barriers or concerns about moving forward?

- What are my (our) priorities for the next ninety days or year? What's the level of enthusiasm and commitment to achieving these goals? Are they S.M.A.R.T. goals (specific, measurable, attainable, relevant/important, and time-bound)?

If your check-in is just for yourself, rather than your whole team, decide if it's best to reflect on these and other questions on your own. Sometimes, they may be part of a discussion with your boss and tied to a performance appraisal. You may choose to discuss them with a peer, a coach, a friend,

---

63 This is commonly called a SWOT analysis: strengths, weaknesses, opportunities, and threats. A SWOT looks at both the positives (strengths and opportunities) and the negatives (weaknesses and threats). Strengths and weaknesses typically address issues internal to your organization or team, or personal factors that you can control. Opportunities and threats refer to external variables that you may or may not control. I've never been fond of the terminology weaknesses and threats, as they're so loaded. If you come up with any alternative words that also form a nice acronym, please let me know.

or a family member who can be nonjudgmental and supportive as well as honest with you.

When people fail to make time for this kind of self-assessment, it's difficult if not impossible to gauge your achievements or the areas that need adjustment. Without this type of evaluation, you may wake up one day and say, "Oh my goodness, I'm stagnating or failing." Worse still, it may be your boss who has not provided ongoing feedback about concerns but who walks into your office with a shocking surprise: "I'm sorry to say that we're not happy with your performance, and I have to let you go. Here's your final paycheck. Please clean out your desk, and I'll escort you out of the building."[64]

2. **Draft a pros and cons list**. Similar to your shopping list in the Auditions phase, part of your regular check-in should go beyond goals, measures, and priorities. Create plus and minus columns on paper or in a computer document.

    On the plus or pro side, list all of the aspects of your current position and job duties that you like. What puts a smile on your face and motivates you to come to work each day? With whom do you experience the most relationship harmony and support? Who helps you laugh and roll with the punches?

    In the minus or con column, identify what stresses you out, depletes your energy, or distracts you from your priorities. With whom is there discord or a lack of engagement? Who do you find yourself avoiding, or who do you think is avoiding you? Which relationships need tuning up?

---

64   This really happens: an employee may get no indication that they're missing the mark, or that people are unhappy with their performance. Surprises are nice for birthdays but not for job appraisals or continued employment.

Then step back and analyze the two lists. Which one is longer? Is it the quantity of each list that is more important, or are there a few items on one list that overshadow several items in the other list? For example, let's say my list looks like this:

Pros: What's going well?	Cons: Where is there stress or lack of progress?
Meeting individual performance goals	Team is disorganized; poor communication
Boss is pleased, got a good raise	5 of 7 team goals not achieved
Love working with Sally and Max	I'm working 60+ hours/week; am exhausted
	3 members of team are hostile, hard to work with, and not carrying their weight
	Boss is not holding slackers accountable

Listing and comparing the pluses and minuses of your current position will help you decide if, when, and how to rearrange or end the song.

If "Working 60+ hours/week" and "Boss not holding slackers accountable" have lots of negative impacts for you, that might override the three pluses. Similarly, if the three pluses are important enough, they might help you cope with the longer list on the minus side.

3. **Look for opportunities to collaborate or compromise**. During the Finales stage, pervasive tension, boring tasks, and invisibility or dead-end positions are some of the most common causes of people ending a given song. Maybe you're experiencing one of these three or have identified other reasons that you're wondering if the song is over. If so, ask yourself, "Have I really done all I can to

improve this situation and reduce my frustrations with the current music?"

Review the suggestions in this stage to see if you can find opportunities to collaborate or compromise. You may be able to do this on your own with some reflection. It might be helpful to talk to your boss, a peer, or someone else to help you sort through your options. It's best if you explore all of your options before deciding that the song needs to end. This is a way to make sure you're not just

- Putting your head in the sand, eating Tums, and trying to cope (Avoidance), or

- Ignoring your own needs, meeting everyone else's, eating Tums, and feeling resentful or unappreciated (Accommodation).

4. **Identify your current and potential support systems**. Make an actual list, not just in your head, of specific people who now have your back, as well as people to whom you could reach out for support moving forward. While you have to take responsibility for your own actions, biases, and emotions, you don't need to tune up every song all by yourself. Often, that's impossible to do. If you're looking for harmony in your relationships, you're not singing alone in the shower.

Think about who at work has positive Emotional Bank Accounts with you—who wants you to succeed and will acknowledge your strengths. That person also needs to be someone who will give you honest feedback and useful suggestions for improving the music. Then add to the list any people who fit those criteria who are outside of work and possibly more objective: a coach, a former colleague, a friend, or maybe a family member.[65]

The next step is to identify people within your organization and in your personal life whom you've not approached in the past for advice and encouragement but with whom you feel comfortable asking for help. Many people are reluctant to ask for help. They believe it makes them look weak and incompetent. Research and experience have taught me that the strongest leaders and most successful employees are the ones who have the self-awareness and courage to develop networks of people to help them improve and enjoy the music over time. Asking for help, when not overused, shows that you have the confidence to be vulnerable and humble.

5. **Test out the Focus Map to maintain a forward focus**. Choose a situation where you feel stuck in a negative mindset but want to redirect your energy toward enhancing the music. Review the Focus Map model in this stage. Draw a circle with the three areas. Either alone, with colleagues, or a coach, jot down elements for each area of the map. Then use this map to articulate next steps for addressing this issue. It is another way to focus your energy to help you sort out if it makes sense to stay and revitalize the music or draw the finale to a close and move on.

6. **Review the skills** suggested for one of the six phases that you most want to work on first. Identify one skill, tool, or model to emphasize for a week or a month. Think about where and how to apply it. Consider how it might

---

65 Some people look to certain family members first since they know you well and care about you. Other people say that spouses, parents, and other relatives would be the last place they'd look for assistance: too much judgment, vested interests, or other baggage.

help to improve the harmony in one or more of your relationships that are currently in that phase. If there is someone who can observe you trying out new language or other behaviors, ask them to give you feedback. Give yourself some evaluation of what worked well, what might have been uncomfortable, or what backfired.

Use that to inform what you repeat or do differently on your successive attempts to use the new skill or tool. Remember: practice rarely makes perfect but often makes progress. It's like the thumb-crossing experiment in the first application exercise in Stage 5: if what you're trying out feels awkward at first, congratulate yourself. That means you're stretching yourself out of your comfort zone. Know that subsequent attempts will get easier and feel less awkward.

7. **Practice skills in low-risk situations**. It's likely that when you learned to drive, someone took you to an empty parking lot to let you start driving in a big, open space with room for mistakes. Many singers start their careers singing on a street corner for donations or in a small club where the patrons might not even listen to them. Both of these are examples of low-risk settings where you hone your skills and build your confidence.

    This is also a good idea for enhancing your relationship skills. Stores and airports are ideal places to practice. Unless it's a small, neighborhood shop that you frequent every week and know the owner, you'll likely never see the people again. For example, consciously practice influence skills when trying to get a different seat on an airplane or get on a different flight altogether. Practice the feedback model when you've hired a repair person to work on your house, they've shown up late and want to charge you more than the estimate they gave you initially. Even if you don't get what you want, you're intentionally pulling these tools out of your toolbox and increasing your competence. Then, when you need to use them with important relationships, you're more likely to succeed.[66]

8. **Revisit your self-assessment** in the Overture. If you filled out the quick rating of yourself with each stage when you started reading, look back at that now. See if there are any changes or improvements in how you see your comfort and skill levels with some of the stages. This might give you some idea of what you've learned and what you still want to work on.

9. **Make a playlist of songs that tie to each stage of *Harmony at Work*.** Use music, quotes, poems, or other references to remind you of the stage(s) of relationship development that you want to focus on. They can help you keep the tools and concepts front of mind as you work to change interpersonal habits and expectations. They also provide some entertainment and inspiration. Alternatively, just identify one song that you love that will inspire you to strengthen your skills and improve the music. Sample playlists to get you started are provided at the end of this book in the section called Additional Tools.

The Coda:
Conclusions and Refrains

What might Juanita and her friends have learned from *Harmony at Work*?

For starters, Juanita found out from the HR manager that it's okay to ask for help. Rarely can we figure out everything on our own. It's important to recognize when you need help and to consider who are the safe, smart, and reliable people in your orbit whom you can approach for that support. The HR manager also modeled for Juanita both the need to sort out what the issues are, and then to leverage your strengths to address the challenges.

Her lunchtime conversation with Sally, Alex and Omar was an example of how no work situation is perfect: everyone has their relationship challenges. They pointed out to Juanita that her successful auditions in the past included clarity about what she wanted and her ability to promote her own assets. Again, she saw the benefit of relying on others for encouragement.

In subsequent conversations with her friends, she was encouraged to

- Plan and practice for interviews and other challenging conversations,

- Have patience when building trust in a new relationship,

- Ask good questions to uncover and respond to hidden agendas behind negative behaviors,

- Set boundaries with others when they act inappropriately or take advantage of you,

- Remember that people often show their worst behaviors when under stress,

- Balance a receptivity to feedback with an effort to not take everything personally,

- Know that if you can work through disharmony constructively, you can eventually get on the same page of music with others, and

- Respect that people are motivated by very different situations and tasks, that one size does not generally fit all.

Action Plans, Follow-up, and Conclusions—Create Enduring Music

By now I hope you have some answers to the question, "Why another book on relationships?" You've looked at the typical stages through which relationships evolve. You've examined many of the theories that explain the complex underpinnings of how people interact. You have a sense of how challenging it can be to create and maintain harmony at work. Now what?

You've likely already had some successes with different elements of each stage. Consider what next steps you want to take. It might help to review notes you made for some of the application exercises in each stage. Analyze what has worked and what you've learned so far. Ask yourself, "How can I leverage my successes and build on my strengths to help me further develop my skills?"

Look at which stages and exercises you have avoided and ask yourself if that was because they were not relevant or useful to you right now. Or is it possible that you were avoiding certain action steps that seemed too daunting to address? If it's the latter, reflect on what you could do, or who might help you to make those exercises seem more approachable. Start with one step—that one step mentioned in the Chinese proverb about the journey of a thousand miles. Sometimes, we need encouragement with those initial, single steps in order to overcome our fear and gain some momentum.

For some people, it helps to set a goal and say, "I will try this one new behavior for a week or a month." Then stop and assess what impacts that has had. It's important not to take on too much all at once, because that may throw you back to feeling overwhelmed.

I had a client who was highly accomplished in her field but who had extremely low emotional intelligence skills. She was totally discouraged and felt as if she could never become proficient in all that she wanted to learn. She agreed that she should start small and just focus on one behavior. She knew that she was typically oblivious to others' nonverbal cues and only took note of the words they said. So I asked her to notice and jot down at least one nonverbal cue from one person in each meeting that she was in every day. Her task was to just notice and record. Since she attended many meetings a day, that gave her many opportunities to observe.

A week later, she called me, astounded: "This is amazing! I hope it's okay, but once I started paying attention, I noticed way more than one cue per meeting. There were so many nonverbal cues from each person!" Obviously, that was only the first step in strengthening her emotional intelligence muscles and creating more harmony at work. But she took that first step and had some success. That success helped to build her confidence and encourage her to take the next steps.

Books, seminars, and coaching can be interesting and entertaining. They are, however, totally worthless unless you create a plan, set some goals, and find a way to hold yourself accountable for progress. Use whatever format works for you. Some sample goal statements and action plan templates are included in the Additional Tools at the back of this book.

Choose one task that resonated most with you from the six stages outlined here: an application exercise to try or repeat, a theoretical model that you want to learn more about, or a conversation you want to have with someone to reduce the discord and increase the harmony. Also identify a support person—a family member, spouse, a friend, a mentor, a coach, or a colleague at work. Tell them about the goal or goals you are setting. Ask them for help and advice. Set regular times to check in with them to monitor progress, get encouragement, and revise your plan as needed.

Some people have enough internal motivation that they don't need the external accountability partner. For others, it's more likely that you will pursue a goal if someone whom you trust and like helps to hold your feet to the proverbial fire.

Do Try This at Home: Applying This Information to Personal Relationships

You probably know the familiar TV trope, "Don't try this at home." It is the disclaimer used when they show people doing incredibly dangerous or stupid things. By contrast, I encourage you: *do* try this at home. Many of the tools and theoretical models described in *Harmony at Work* apply just as well to relationships with family and friends outside of work.

I've learned things about handling personal challenges from successful work relationships and vice versa.

One way to build your confidence and interpersonal skills is to first identify tough situations that you've handled well and people with whom you've built trust and good communication. These can be current situations or successes from the past. Next consider what you did well in those relationships. Then ask yourself how you can transfer that insight and ability to use in the challenging circumstances at work now.

If, for example, you want to get better at feedback and listening with your colleagues in your office, practice the tools with people at home who will continue to love you, even if you don't communicate perfectly. If you find you can be assertive at home but wimp out at work, consider the assumptions you're carrying around in your head about the dangers of being as strong and confident at work as you are with friends and family. Similarly, if you create harmony well at work but have discord at home, think about how you can transfer your skills at work to apply to your personal relationships.

It's useful to consider the pros and cons of trying new approaches to the music of your relationships. Sort out which are valid, fact-based risks and which are expectations rooted in fear or history. Is it a fact that when people assertively ask your boss for a raise that they get fired or demoted? Or is that just what you worry might be the outcome? Find ways to check your assumptions, and if it is wise to proceed, think about how to prepare.

Sometimes it's helpful to have a rehearsal: practice a challenging conversation with someone you trust who can play the role of the other person. You may also practice by recording yourself and playing it back for review, or by looking in the mirror and assessing how you look and sound when delivering the message you want to share. If you notice that you furrow your brow when trying to look open and calm, or that you soften your voice and mince your words when trying to be assertive, that's useful feedback.

Other Books and Resources

You'll find a daunting array of other books related to the topics in *Harmony at Work*. The question becomes what to read next. Sometimes, the right book will be recommended by a friend, suggested in a blog, or described in a magazine article. More often, it's a challenge to search out the most relevant titles to help you expand your relationship harmony skills.

A list of Additional Resources is included at the end of this book to help you begin your search. Think about which of the six stages you want to learn more about now. Look for key words, theoretical models, and assessments mentioned in that stage. This will help you to focus your exploration. Also consider what kinds of professional resources you can access that would provide the most appropriate support to continue your learning. These include EAP services through your employer, continuing education, mentors, coaches, and counselors.

Patience, Courage, Optimism, a Sense of Humor, and other Sanity Preservers

When I was in elementary school, I'd often try to talk my mom into driving me to school when it was cold and raining. She'd usually hand me my raincoat and umbrella and say, "Put one foot in front of the other. You'll get there. You won't melt!" While I found that incredibly annoying at age eight, I now realize it was good advice for more than walking to school in the rain.

Your efforts to increase your harmony at work require just putting one foot in front of the other. It's a process, a journey.

The stages take time, patience, and courage. It's true that trust and harmony can be demolished in an instant by one false move or an inappropriate comment. It also happens on rare occasions that people meet, develop instant rapport, move through the relationship stages quickly, and go on to create relationship harmony with each other for a long time.

Most of the time, however, creating and reinforcing trust and good communication take way more than an instant. And once you start to create some discord, your repair efforts may take even more persistence. The tools in the last three stages can help to reinforce your determination and offer support. If you are not patient and determined by nature, it may be part of your learning goals to find ways to increase both traits.

Optimism is an interesting element in the dynamics of relationships. Research suggests that some people are hardwired to be optimistic by nature. Others instinctively tend to focus on the proverbial half-empty glass.[67] Studies have further shown that pessimists can train themselves to focus on the half-full part of the glass. But it's like Myers-Briggs profiles: even though people can learn behaviors outside of their preferences, they must expend more effort to use them. Pessimists can learn more optimistic behaviors, but it's generally more of a challenge than it is for the natural optimists who instinctively focus on the positives first.

Regardless of how you're hardwired, it's important to learn or preserve an optimistic attitude as you work on creating and maintaining harmony in your relationships. A client of mine was going through a stressful time at work that involved

---

67 My wonderful husband, ever the realist, dislikes this phrase. He says, "Half-full, half-empty—same amount of liquid." True, but the expression emphasizes which half of the glass people tend to focus on. That choice of focus has a profound impact on people's mood and behavior, since we get more of what we focus on.

278 | Harmony at Work

massive layoffs, unrealistic workloads, and pay cuts.[68] He's a very optimistic man, but he said to me, "I'm having trouble hanging onto my optimism: it's definitely being challenged." Hanging onto at least some optimism impacts your ability to practice these skills and increase your relationship harmony. When your optimism sags, reach out to others for support and encouragement. We all need reassurance at times.

A sense of humor can be a wonderful tool to have in your tool kit. Like patience, determination, and optimism, it may be instinctive for you to find the humor and irony in a tough situation. Some people develop a sense of humor based on the pain and stress that they've experienced. Other people don't have a clue about how to see the ironic or amusing side of a challenging situation. They only focus on the facts of a dismal scenario.

A friend of mine recently discovered that she had a golf-ball-sized brain tumor in the side of her head. At first, she was stunned when the problem was identified, but she switched gears quickly. Much to the chagrin of her surgeon, she joked with him about it when he gave her the diagnosis. When I asked her about the surgery, she said, "Yes, I'll be getting a very unique new haircut tomorrow. I can't wait to show it to you." When I asked her what time the surgery was scheduled for the next day, she replied, "The grand opening will be at noon." I was impressed that she could find humor while coping with such a serious medical problem. Her jovial attitude, while off-putting to some, was likely a factor in her successful recovery.

The good news about the ability to laugh and joke about discord is that it can relieve tension and help you keep even the toughest music in perspective. It can remind you and others to have a little fun as an antidote to the stress.

---

68 "Other than that, Mrs. Lincoln, how was the play?" (A sarcastic response to difficult situations, referring to President Lincoln's assassination. The phrase has been attributed to many different sources.)

There are also challenges to using humor as you work your way through the stages of relationship development. First, what is funny to me might not be the least bit funny to you. It could even be offensive or give the impression that I'm making light of a serious issue. A joke or an off-hand comment might cause you to step on an interpersonal land mine that you had no way of knowing was a sensitive issue. Two examples come to mind:

- I knew a woman whose first child was premature and who died five days after birth. Her hairdresser, who'd cut her hair for years, wasn't thinking when he told her a dead baby joke. She told him how offensive the joke was and never went back to that salon.[69]

- I was facilitating a seminar on public speaking skills. One of the assignments was an instructional presentation in which participants had ten minutes to teach the group a skill. One woman decided to teach the group a song—so far, so good. Then she asked each person to stand up and sing it solo, to check to see if they'd learned it—not so good.

  One participant froze and refused to sing. The "instructor" kept urging him to sing until he said, "When I was in elementary school, the music teacher said I couldn't carry a tune in a bucket and asked me to mouth the words to the songs for our concerts. So there's no way I'll sing for you!" While the instructor was trying to be funny and encouraging, she had no way of knowing what a sore subject it was for this gentleman.[70]

---

69 Personally, I can't think of any situation when a joke about a dead baby would be funny.

70 Once the group recovered from this painfully awkward moment, it provided a rich and useful discussion about the use of humor in learning environments.

A second challenge with humor is to be careful to not appear to laugh at others, only *with* others or at yourself. This is a perfect example of intention versus impact. My intention might be tension relief. But the way my comment lands on you might be mockery or embarrassment. It doesn't matter how noble your intention is. If it lands badly on someone else, your humor is doing damage to the relationship.

You can't control how people will react, and you aren't responsible for all of the emotional scar tissue that they bring to work with them every day. But you need to pay attention to people's reactions, to their nonverbals, to their responses and nonresponses. Be prepared to apologize if your joke or comment goes sideways. And on a good day, you can hope that an offended person will have the courage to give you feedback, so that at least you know to tread lightly around that topic in the future.

Another kind of humor that can get people in trouble is sarcasm. Some folks intend to be sarcastic. Others think they're being funny but come across to others as critical or caustic. Sarcastic humor most often comes from people who are angry or somehow unhappy with a given situation or relationship, or who feel insecure and need to put others down (consciously or unconsciously) to somehow elevate themselves.

As a result, it's generally a bad idea to make jokes or try to be funny when you are feeling any type of upset or threat. That kind of mood often creates a negative edge to attempts at humor. As the research on emotional intelligence indicates, the key is to be aware of when you're feeling off-kilter in some way, thus cuing you to keep your sense of humor dialed back in that moment.

In spite of these caveats about humor, maintaining a healthy sense of humor, along with strengthening your patience, courage, and optimism muscles are all useful tools to help you with every stage of relationship evolution. Laughing at the sour notes that we all sing at times can also help us get to the next step: figuring out what we've learned from the mistakes and trying the song again with more harmony.

Final Notes

People say that once you learn to ride a bike, you never forget how. They refer to other activities that are implanted in our memory and say, "It's like riding a bike, you just get on and go. You'll know what to do." Unfortunately, creating harmony at work is *not* like riding a bike.

I have outlined many theories and tools in this book that can help you create more harmony with more people more of the time. However, the techniques won't do you any good if you don't practice them—often. When you meet someone who seems to communicate and build trust effortlessly, it's possible they have innate abilities that help them to succeed.

It is, however, more likely that they consciously apply the necessary skills whenever they get the opportunity. And just like any other behavior, the more you use it, the more likely you are to increase your proficiency. This is especially true if you pay attention to your results, observe the reactions of others, and ask for feedback about your impact.

One more caveat: none of us gets it right all the time. Even professionally trained singers miss notes and timing from time to time. That's why they always rehearse. When a singer knows a piece of music 100 percent but is singing it with a new accompanist or ensemble, they still have to practice with the new partners to solidify the new relationship.

It's the same with harmony at work. While it's nice to be comfortable and unconsciously competent, there are times when you need to pay attention so you can be consciously competent. This type of focus helps to build trust, get agreement, and share information more effectively. You also need to notice when the clashing chords start, be humble enough to apologize when needed, and be brave enough to restart the song. You hope to learn from your mistakes and might need to sing in a different key or at a different tempo to improve your delivery.

If you're not careful, you may actually have fun exploring how to create more harmony at work, regardless of which stage of development you find yourself in with a given person or team. By being conscious of the six stages and the tools that support each one, you can build your confidence as you strengthen your musical muscles.

So review what you've learned. Decide on one skill or stage that you want to focus on now. Find some learning partners to be sounding boards, advisors, and support systems. Be courageous: try some new behaviors and approaches. Pick yourself up when you trip, admit your mistakes, and cut yourself some slack for not having perfect pitch with everyone all of the time. On a good day, laugh at your blunders.

Creating harmony at work is not a one-and-done, finite task. It's an ongoing process. Some days it's more challenging and tiring than others. Some days, it's a fascinating adventure that may include slow progress or pleasant surprises. I hope I have given you ideas, tools, and encouragement to enjoy making harmonious music with more people more of the time.

Glossary of Music Terms

aria: a song sung by a soloist, most often as part of an opera

baton: a thin wand used by a conductor to lead an orchestra or choir

chord: two or more musical notes sung or played together that create harmony

chorus: either the refrain, repeated in a song, or a group of people singing together

coda: the final section of a piece of music that brings it to a conclusion

crescendo: a gradual increase of musical volume

dissonance: two or more musical notes sung or played together that clash or create disharmony

duet: when two musicians sing or play instruments together, often creating harmony

encore: an extra piece requested by an audience after the expected ending of a concert

finale: the last piece of music played in a concert according to the published program

flats and sharps: symbols written into music that lower or raise the pitch of a note

fortissimo: very loud musical notes or phrases

major key: a series of notes that creates music that sounds bright or happy

measure: a specific number of musical beats, with each beat representing a particular note value

minor key: a series of notes that creates music that sounds dark, sad, or gloomy

off-key: a note that is sung or played incorrectly so that it is not in tune

overture: an introductory section of music played before the main part of a symphony or opera

perfect pitch: the ability to sing or identify exactly what note is being played or sung just by listening

pitch: higher or lower position of a single sound in the complete range of notes

refrain: the repetition of a phrase or section of a song; sometimes called the chorus

scale: a series of musical notes that defines the key in which the music is written

score: written sheet music for one performer or a compilation of multiple parts for an orchestra and/or chorus, allowing the conductor to see everyone's parts simultaneously

sight-reading: the ability of a musician to sing or play music accurately the first time they see it without practice or preparation

soprano/mezzo/alto/tenor/baritone/bass: different vocal parts for singers that range from high to low

tempo: the fast or slow pace at which a musical piece is performed

transpose: to change a musical composition from one key to a higher or lower key

unison: when musicians are singing or playing the same notes at the same time so that they sound like one voice

vibrato: the slight pitch variation added to a single note or series of notes for vocal or instrumental compositions

Additional Resources

Blanchard, Kenneth and Spencer Johnson, *The One Minute Manager* plus dozens of related books by Blanchard and other coauthors. These books are quick reads that use a story to demonstrate a few key behaviors that managers must use to be effective and create positive relationships.

Bramson, Robert M., *Coping with Difficult People in Business and in Life*. This book is decades old and still relevant. Bramson uses very few pages to delineate when and how to be assertive, how to respond to both attacks and reticence, techniques to deal with defensiveness, and tactics to move people from complaining to action.

Cain, Susan, *Quiet: The Power of Introverts in a World That Can't Stop Talking*. This best seller is an excellent description of the challenges introverts have in a world that rewards extroversion. It should be required reading for all extroverts so that they understand the perspectives and needs of their more introverted colleagues.

Clear, James, *Atomic Habits: An Easy & Proven Way to Build Good Habits & Break Bad Ones*. Clear provides specific tools to identify your current behavior patterns and build new, sustainable habits that support your goals. It will reinforce your efforts to improve the harmony in your work relationships.

Cooperrider, David and Diana Whitney, *Appreciative Inquiry: A Positive Revolution in Change*. This is a quick overview of Cooperrider's approach. It will help you understand how to leverage your successes, strengths, and interests to address current relationship and organizational challenges.

Covey, Stephen R., *The 7 Habits of Highly Effective People*. The models and metaphors in this enduring best seller provide excellent tools to help you create healthier, more harmonious relationships. His application exercises are also quite valuable and accessible.

Fisher, Roger and William Ury, *Getting to Yes: Negotiating Agreement without Giving In*. This classic best seller gives simple, straightforward advice about how to get more of what you want more of the time. Successful relationships always involve negotiation. These techniques will complement the resources in *Harmony at Work*.

Fritz, Robert, *The Path of Least Resistance: Learning to Become the Creative Force in Your Own Life*. Not your typical business book, Fritz describes a method for creating what you want in your life and compares it to the creative process of artists, musicians, and authors. He contends that once you make the conscious choice to pursue your goals, your life is profoundly changed. He also wrote *The Path of Least Resistance for Managers*.

Gallwey, W. Timothy. His Inner Game series on music, work, stress, tennis, golf, and skiing. Gallwey's Inner Game books explore the thoughts and emotions that drive our external actions. He provides specific methods to circumvent the self-imposed obstacles that decrease our performance.

Goldsmith, Joan Oliver, *How Can We Keep from Singing.* Goldsmith, a writer and choral singer, also draws parallels to music, self-awareness, and courage. She describes the "invisible instrument" that we all possess, which drives us to create, accomplish, and just show up. I love her statement, "One person's noise is another's music."

Kolbe, Kathy, *Conative Connection: Uncovering the Link Between Who You Are and How You Perform.* This is a good introduction to Kolbe's model of "conation" and describes how the way our mind is hardwired impacts our actions. She explains how we can best leverage our natural instincts rather than work against them. Later books include *Powered by Instinct: 5 Rules for Trusting Your Guts* and *Pure Instinct.*

Lencioni, Patrick, *The Five Dysfunctions of a Team: A Leadership Fable.* This wildly popular book uses a fable to explain how teams get into trouble and how to remedy those problems. The myriad of later books, workbooks, and licensed workshops demonstrate how much his pyramid of trust, conflict, commitment, accountability, and results resonates with readers.

Mauer, Rick, *Beyond the Wall of Resistance: Why 70% of Changes Still Fail—and What You Can Do about It.* Mauer explains how resistance derails the majority of organizational change efforts. He offers many strategies to anticipate and redirect the resistance toward achieving the changes you seek. His strategies apply to creating better harmony with individuals as well as teams.

Rock, David, *Your Brain at Work: Strategies for Overcoming Distraction, Regaining Focus, and Working Smarter All Day Long.* Among the myriad of books on neuropsychology and cognitive science, this is one of the most accessible. Rock uses a clear analogy to describe how our brains function, what wears them out, and techniques to allow us to use our brains more effectively to achieve more harmony and success.

Tieger, Barbara Barron and Paul Tieger, *Do What You Are: Discover the Perfect Career for You Through the Secrets of Personality Type*. The authors give a good overview of the Myers-Briggs Type Inventory (MBTI). They then tie information about a person's innate preferences to occupations that best match each of the sixteen profiles. This is a helpful resource for people in the Auditions stage who are contemplating not only a job change but also a new career.

Vannoy, Steve, *The 10 Greatest Gifts I Give My Children*. This powerful parenting book has direct parallels to how we seek to create harmony at work. It was the basis for Vannoy's later work-focused models and books, including, *Stomp the Elephant in the Office* and *Degrees of Strength*, both with Craig Ross. It is also the basis of his nonprofit, 10 Greatest Gifts Project, that trains parents and grandparents to build more honesty and self-reliance into every family, hence creating healthier future citizens. The parallels to work relationships are clear.

Wile, Daniel, *After the Honeymoon: How Conflict Can Improve Your Relationship*. Even though this book is focused on personal relationships, his approach to conflict applies completely to interactions at work as well. Wile explains how to take the inevitable clashing chords that occur from unexpressed emotions and difficult conversations and leverage them to strengthen the connections between you and others.

Additional Tools

Active Listening
Behaviors and Examples

Drawing Out the Speaker

- To initiate discussion

- To gain additional information

- To clarify the message with examples and details

- To help reassure and/or calm the speaker (acknowledging feelings and/or venting anger)

SAMPLE LANGUAGE

> Tell me some more about . . .

> I'm interested in your comment (perception, opinion) about . . .

> What would be an example of that?

> What has been your experience with . . . ?

> In what ways were you frustrated . . . challenged . . . your needs not met?

> What would it be like for you if (the problem were resolved, that support was withdrawn, etc.) . . . ?

> How did this situation first start? I'd like to know what's behind . . .

> Help me understand . . .

> What do you think would help you with this situation?

Paraphrasing What Is Said

- To repeat the speaker's words verbatim

- To reflect back the message in your own words

- To rephrase certain parts of the message to help direct or focus the speaker

SAMPLE LANGUAGE

> So what you're saying is . . .

> In other words . . .

> Do you mean that . . . ?

> What I'm hearing from you is . . .

> It sounds like you're (worried, excited, angry . . .) that . . .

> I get the impression that . . .

> It seems like . . .

Observing Emotions and Nonverbal Cues
(reflecting back what is not directly said)

- To check your own understanding or "read" of the speaker's emotions

- To mirror back to them their impact and the subtler messages they are conveying

- To help them clarify their own reactions

- To point out discrepancies between verbal and nonverbal cues

SAMPLE LANGUAGE

> It sounds like you're feeling (excited, scared, mad, etc.).

> You seem pretty (pleased, overwhelmed, etc.).

> I get the impression you are (confused, uncertain, etc.) by this situation.

> You say you're excited, but your face looks worried.

> Your voice doesn't sound as confident as your words do.

Summarizing

- To increase clarity and focus

- To help both the listener and speaker sort quantities of information

- To encourage the speaker to pause and reflect

- To wind down active listening and move to problem solving

SAMPLE LANGUAGE

> > What you've told me so far is . . .

> > Wait—let me see if I'm following you up to this point.

> > It sounds like there are three themes here . . .

> > It seems to boil down to this core issue . . .

> > I get the impression that we agree on these two main ideas . . .

Nonverbal Cues to Watch and Listen for in the Speaker

Remember that "reading" nonverbals is very subjective. It is your perception. So make your observations tentative and personalized to you. ("You seem to me to be . . .")

- Fidgeting, tapping toes, fingers, etc.

- Closed posture (arms and/or legs crossed, turned away)

- Lack of eye contact

- Frequent shifting of position

- Smirks, frowns, worried looks, wrinkled brows, questioning looks

- Frequent sighing, clearing of throat, nervous laughter, or prolonged silence

- Very loud, very soft, or strained speaking voice

- Any other tone or nonverbal cues that do not match the words spoken

IN ADDITION, THE LISTENER SHOULD STRIVE TO —

- Sit comfortably, conveying patience and openness

- Lean slightly forward to show interest, but not aggression

- Keep arms open and relaxed (vs. folded or crossed)

- Keep gentle eye contact (vs. intense staring or looking away)

- Use a relaxed, nonjudgmental voice tone, indicating concern and attentiveness

- Notice own volume and rate of speech to show patience, acceptance, and interest in the speaker

Keys to Assertive Behaviors as Distinguished from Submission and Aggression

	Submission	**Assertiveness**	**Aggression**
GOALS	accommodates others, avoids conflict, gives in, seeks approval of others, sacrifices own needs	meets own needs, considers others' needs, seeks cooperation, win/win build trust, is honest	meets only own needs, ignores others' needs, forces compliance, seeks power and control, dominates others
WORDS	apologetic, shy, rambling, vague, selfless, dishonest, cautious, tentative	clear, direct, objective, firm, specific, focused, uses "I" statements	blaming, critical, subjective, rude, condescending, uses "you" messages
TONE	weak, soft-spoken, hesitant, wavering, pleading, eager to please or accommodate	strong, assured, friendly, relaxed, calm, even-toned	curt, abrupt, cold, aloof, loud, shrill, or deadly quiet
FACE	scared, sad, fake smile, avoids eye contact, chin down, eyes up	expressive, open, engaged, attentive, good eye contact, balanced, level	tense, hard, mad, expressionless, flat, glaring, intense eyes, chin up, eyes down
OTHER NONVERBAL CUES	stooped or leaned back, fidgety, unstable, nods head often, wring hands/ shuffle feet	balanced, stands tall, relaxed, steady, natural gestures, feet planted firmly	stiff, rigid, strong, leaning forward, clenched fists, pointing finger, feet apart, hands on hips

Plan for Achieving Goals

Today's date:

Summary: (WHO) plans to do (WHAT) by (WHEN), as measured by (WHAT)?

Goal #_____	What do we want to accomplish?
Action Steps	What should we do using what resources?
Resources Needed	What people, materials, training or information do we need?
Time Frames	What are the interim and final deadlines?
Assessment	How will we know we have reached our objective?
Evaluation & Follow-up	Who? What? When? and Where?

Playlist of Song Titles for Each Stage

Auditions

"One Man's Ceiling Is Another Man's Floor" by Paul Simon

"Leap of Faith" by Bruce Springsteen

"Should I Stay or Should I Go" by The Clash

"The Music and the Mirror" from *A Chorus Line* by Marvin Hamlisch and Edward Kleban

"Somewhere (There's a Place for Us)" from *West Side Story* by Stephen Sondheim and Leonard Bernstein

First Notes

"I Can See Clearly Now" by Johnny Nash

"Here Comes the Sun" by George Harrison

"You Had Me from Hello" by Kenny Chesney and Donald Skip Ewing

"Hey, Look Me Over" by Cy Coleman and Carolyn Leigh

"Getting to Know You" from *The King and I* by Richard Rodgers and Oscar Hammerstein

New Songs

"New Kid in Town" by Don Henley, Glenn Frey, and J. D. Souther of the Eagles

"Brand New Day" by Sting

"Brand New Day" by Van Morrison

"Changes" by David Bowie

"Nothing Can Stop Me Now" from *The Roar of the Greasepaint* by Anthony Newley and Leslie Bricusse

Clashing Chords

"Gonna Be Some Changes Made" by Bruce Hornsby

"King of Anything" by Sara Bareilles

"Love Has No Pride" by Libby Titus and Eric Kaz, sung by Bonnie Raitt

"Something's Gotta Give" by Camila Cabello, Joe Khajadourian, Sarah T. Hudson, Alex Schwartz, Jesse St. John, and James J. Abrahart

"We Just Disagree" by Jim Krueger, sung by Dave Mason, formerly of the band Traffic

"Anything You Can Do (I Can Do Better)" from *Annie Get Your Gun* by Irving Berlin

Encores

"Three Little Birds" by Bob Marley

"Don't Worry, Be Happy" by Bobby McFerrin

"Start with the Ending" by David Wilcox

"Worry No More" by Amos Lee

"Let's Work Together" by Wilbert Harrison, sung by John Lee Hooker

Finales

"The Times They Are A-Changin'" by Bob Dylan

"Hit the Road Jack" by Percy Mayfield

"July" by Noah Cyrus, P. J. Harding, and Michael Sonier

"My Way" by Paul Anka and Jacques Revaux, sung by Frank Sinatra

"The Gambler" by Don Schlitz, sung by Kenny Rogers and Johnny Cash

"Let's Call the Whole Thing Off" from *Shall We Dance* by George and Ira Gershwin

End Notes

Stage 1

"The buck stops here" was a placard on President Harry Truman's desk. The expression is said to have originated from a prison warden in Oklahoma. It refers to the expression, "pass the buck," which means passing responsibility to others. This, in turn, supposedly comes from poker and the option to pass your turn to deal the next hand to the next player.

The term *Self-fulfilling Prophecy* was first coined by sociologist Robert K. Merton in his book *Social Theory and Social Structure* [1968 New York: Free Press, p. 477]. This, in turn, is built on the Thomas theorem [Thomas, W. I. (1928) *The Child in America: Behavior Problems and Programs*, New York: Alfred A. Knopf. p. 572], which says that "If [people] define situations as real, they are real in their consequences." In other words, if I believe you don't like me, I will unconsciously act in ways that cause you to not like me, thus reinforcing my initial belief, even if it was not based on fact.

A common misperception about the MBTI goes like this: Thinkers *think* that Feelers *can't think*. Feelers *feel like* Thinkers *have no feelings*. They're both wrong. Feelers think just as clearly as Thinkers do—they just use different criteria to make decisions. Similarly, Thinkers have just as many feelings as Feelers do—we all have emotions. The difference, per the MBTI model, is that Thinkers tend to express their feelings differently than Feelers do. The T-F scale in the MBTI model is not about someone's worth as a human being. It is about how they make decisions using which type of criteria. It is also important to note that T-F does *not* stand for True-False, as one of my clients, who had a Thinker preference, once suggested that it did.

Some people learning the MBTI get confused by the term *Judging*. When used in this model, it's not about being judgmental. Both Js and Ps can choose to be judgmental about themselves or others. Judging in this context refers to the methods a Judger uses to manage and organize themselves and others.

Job applicants are sometimes asked to take personality inventories even *before* they're hired as part of the screening process. Some, like the Kolbe Indexes, are legal to use for hiring in the US, as they've been approved by the EEOC as nondiscriminatory, valid, and related to job competencies. Others, like the MBTI, are *not* legal for hiring decisions to use in the US, as they can't be proven to statistically correlate directly with job performance. So if you plan to use assessments as part of a hiring process, be sure to check out their legality as a screening tool first.

Kolbe's use of the term *conative* comes from an obscure word, *conation*, that means "the area of one's active mentality that has to do with desire, volition and striving. The related word, *conatus* {koh NAY tus}, comes from the Latin verb *conari*, to try." From *1000 Most Challenging Words*. The Kolbe

Indexes are unique among personality inventories given their inclusion of conative activity.

Read descriptions of David Cooperrider's impressive background. Then read one of his books or articles and attend a workshop on Appreciative Inquiry. He's amazing, and his thinking and techniques are powerful. The wide range of where he's applied his models is also quite impressive.

Emotional intelligence (EQ) research has gotten much attention in the last two decades. The concept can be traced back to Darwin's work in the mid-nineteenth century and other psychological writings in the early to mid-twentieth century. Daniel Goleman brought the term into popular usage with his 1985 best seller, *Emotional Intelligence*. Unlike your IQ or cognitive, intellectual abilities, EQ is characterized by Goleman and others as being a variable measure of your ability to perceive, understand, and manage emotions—your own and those of the people around you. Your EQ is independent of your IQ, which is measured by standardized tests and school achievement. EQ experts believe that you can expand your EQ with feedback and coaching to increase your self-awareness and attunement to others.

Stage 2

One of many studies on the speed with which people form first impressions is by Janine Willis and Alexander Todorov, "First Impressions," *Psychological Science*, Vol. 17, No. 7, July 2006.

In *The Book of Lists* [Wallechinsky, Wallace & Wallace 1977 + later editions], one of their many lists of arcane facts was a list of people's greatest fears. According to their research, the third most common fear was acrophobia—fear of heights. The second greatest fear was fear of death. Surprisingly, the most frequently named fear, greater than death, was fear of public speaking. I find this amazing.

Studies on how long it takes for a habit to form and become ingrained cite numbers that range from 18 to 254 days. It varies on the individual and the type of habit they want to develop. Look for Phillipa Lally's articles and research, as well as James Clear's book in the Additional Resources section of this book.

"Methinks thou dost protest too much" is one of the few lines from Shakespeare that I can actually quote. The exact line from *Hamlet*, "The lady doth protest too much, methinks," is spoken by Queen Gertrude in response to the insincere overacting of a character in the play created by Prince Hamlet to prove his uncle's guilt in the murder of Hamlet's father. The phrase is often used to indicate doubt about someone's sincerity or honesty.

Albert Mehrabian's books, *Silent Messages* (1971) and *Silent Messages: Implicit Communication of Emotions and Attitudes (1981),* explain his research about how much of an average message is conveyed by nonverbal cues, as opposed to people's words and tone of voice.

Stage 3

Some of the questions suggested in the section, Make Commitments and Draw Up Contracts, tie back to the four Myers-Briggs [MBTI] dimensions: E-I [think out loud vs. reflect first], S-N [big picture or details], T-F [facts/standards vs. values/relationships], and J-P [structure/sequential vs. flexibility/spontaneity]. These questions are a quick way to predict someone's MBTI preferences without administering an assessment, for which you need a license to administer anyway.

The questions that ask about someone's strengths and best boss align with David Cooperrider's philosophy and methodologies of Appreciative Inquiry. It helps people focus on positives and successes.

Bravado is distinguished from *vibrato*, a vocal technique in which a trained singer produces a rapid variation or oscillation in pitch. When used correctly, vibrato can add richness and strength to the singer's tone. Some opera singers have lots of vibrato in their voice, which can make their tone sound wiggly. Ironically, vibrato can only be created from a relaxed, "open" throat. As someone who has spent years trying to add some vibrato to my singing voice, I find that the harder I try, the less vibrato I have [aka tense throat]. It's like conveying a sense of confidence: if you try too hard, you generally make yourself look insecure.

Stage 4

The Thomas-Kilmann Conflict Mode Instrument can be purchased from themyersbriggs.com.

The 7 Habits of Highly Effective People by Stephen Covey ©1989 and later editions, Simon & Schuster, pp. 188ff.

Stage 5

The term *synergy* comes from the ancient Greek word *synergos*, meaning "working together."

S.M.A.R.T. is an acronym that has been credited to both Peter Drucker (1954) and G. T. Doran (1981), though it is difficult to know if either of these two were really the first people to use the term, S.M.A.R.T. with reference to goals. It's a reminder to craft goals that are Specific, Measurable, Attainable, Relevant, and Time-oriented.

"Who's on First?" was popularized by the vaudeville comedians Abbott and Costello in the 1930s. It's quite funny and is worth listening to if you've never heard their routine. While it's intended as comedy, it's also a good metaphor for how confused some people can get at work about who's responsible for what, when, and how. This kind of misunderstanding can create many sour notes with either duos or whole choirs.

In the 1970s, a psychologist named Noel Burch from Gordon Training International created a learning model to describe how humans go through four stages of learning when introduced to a new skill. This model is known as The Four Stages of Competence. It is said to have evolved from management trainer Martin M. Broadwell's 1969 model called The Four Levels of Teaching. This is the origin of the terms *unconscious incompetence*, *conscious incompetence*, *conscious competence*, and *unconscious competence*.

Open-ended questions are ones that elicit more than a yes/no reply. They invite the speaker to give you more information. If you ask, "Were you mad about what he said to you?" you're asking a closed question, and the person can respond "Yes" or "No." When you open up the question by asking, "What about his comments upset you?" you're encouraging more information from the speaker.

"Nice Work If You Can Get It" is a well-known jazz song composed by George and Ira Gershwin in 1930. The phrase came from an English magazine. The song was used in the 1937 movie *A Damsel in Distress*, with Fred Astaire, Joan Fontaine, George Burns, and Gracie Allen.

The nineteenth-century slang expression "Fish or cut bait" refers to a fisherman who needs to either focus on actually trying to catch fish or stop and cut bait for others to use. While it's a colorful expression, this is not to imply that you should be messing with fish or bait while trying to make decisions in a meeting. Neither the odor nor the mess will promote harmony within the team.

In *The Nature of Stress*, Hans Selye differentiates "eustress" [positive stressors like marriage and job promotions] with "distress" [negative stressors like getting fired, financial problems, or death of a loved one]. He explains how the toll on our minds and bodies can be the same, whether something is eustress or distress.

In their 1967 article, "The Social Readjustment Rating Scale," T. H. Holmes and R. H. Rahe rate different kinds of stressors, both positive and negative, in terms of how much of an impact they can have on people's physical and mental health.

Acknowledgments: "It takes a village."

This book is dedicated to my wonderful husband, Mike, my amazing boys, Doug, Andy, and Eric, and my incredible daughters-in-law, Jodi and Michelle, who have taught me more about relationships than I can measure. Thanks for putting up with me all these years. I love you bunches.

My sister, Peggy, my brothers, Don and Dick, and their wonderful spouses, Bill and Nancy, have all been important parts of my harmonious network. As the bratty baby sister, I have learned from each of you in countless ways. Thanks for not giving me away to a passing circus when I was too young to protest.

Bob and Marcy Brower were my first significant non-family mentors, although they came to feel like family over time. I met them at age six when I was one of the first campers at their new day camp, Circle M, outside of Chicago. At age eighteen, I went back to their camp as a counselor for several summers. Much of the foundation of how I have worked and managed relationships ever since is what I learned from them. They provided unparalleled staff training and created

312 | Harmony at Work

miraculous harmony among staff, campers, and their families. I am forever grateful.

An important part of the huge "village" that has helped to make this book a reality is my bevy of faithful beta readers: Ed Bray, Kerry Clark, Marla Cohen, Michael Eber, Brett Feddersen, Linda Jalving, Mike Jalving, Peggy Kappy, Peter Milewski, Patrick Moody, Steve Niven, Catherine Rymsha, Nancy Sager, Craig Schaum, Joann Schaum, and Dennis Tallon. Your time, honest feedback, and periodic nudges to finish this book have been invaluable. I send you my emphatic appreciation.

Techno-challenged as I am, I could not survive creating any documents, much less this book, without the patient tutelage and repairs of Dan Prendergast, IT guru supreme. I so appreciate your calmly answering questions that I've asked you three times before, talking me off techno-ledges, and repairing what I have broken. My devices and I humbly thank you.

I had so much fun with the Playlist Posse who helped me brainstorm songs for the playlist that is mentioned in the ninth exercise in Rehearsals for the Finale chapter. Sample playlists are also provided in Additional Tools. Many thanks to Kerry Clark, Bill Creighton, Linda Jalving, Felice Morel, Dan Prendergast, Carla Sciaky, and Barb Wollan. Your musical knowledge is terrific.

Lorrie Tishler, my faithful office manager and copy editor extraordinaire, you have tolerated my office clutter, my forgetfulness, my grammatical errors, and all-around goofiness with incredible patience and grace for many years. In honor of my profound gratitude, I bequeath to you the honorary Red Pen Award. Thank you!

If you want a fabulous editor, you need to hire Sandra Wendel of Write On, Inc., who encouraged me, debated me, rolled her eyes at me, and taught me things that never would have occurred to me. Your skills have made the book immeasurably better. Your friendship and twisted sense of humor have helped me maintain my sanity. Thank you so much.

About the Author

Susan Spero has been an organizational consultant for nearly four decades. She founded Spero & Company Consultants, LLC, on April Fool's Day, 1987, which says a lot about her sense of humor.

Susan realized years ago that much of what impacts productivity and job satisfaction in the workplace ties directly to people's ability to create and maintain healthy relationships. She actually enjoys helping people sort out the messy conflicts that they often generate with coworkers. She appreciates the opportunity to provide tools and safe environments in which they can learn, grow, and produce more harmony.

Her international company conducts strategic planning, team development, leadership training, and executive coaching for corporations, nonprofit organizations, and government agencies that range in size from five to 5,000 employees. The company's tagline is "continuous people improvement."

Spero & Company's clients have included library systems, law firms, transportation districts, hospitals, housing authorities, manufacturing companies, universities, professional associations, energy and telecom companies, aerospace companies, home builders, public relations firms, regional and national nonprofits, churches and synagogues, and local, state, and federal government agencies.

Because music has played a major role in Susan's life, it became the metaphor for this book. She learned to play piano and guitar as a child and has loved singing in choirs and musical theater. Like most kids, she hated practicing. She led a small community choir for over thirty years. That experience helped her see the similarities between choir members learning to sing in tune with each other and team members finding ways to work harmoniously together in their careers.

She earned a bachelor's degree in education at the University of Michigan and completed a master's degree in psychology and counseling at the University of Northern Colorado. Prior to founding Spero & Company, she worked as an elementary school teacher and clinical psychologist.

She is certified in the use of many assessments, including the Myers-Briggs Type Inventory, the Kolbe Indexes, Genos Emotional Intelligence tools, and the Graham-Sloan Resilience Index. She is licensed to facilitate many programs, including Interaction Associates' Facilitative Leadership and Essential Facilitation, Executive Team Alignment, and Appreciative Inquiry.

She is a member of the Organization Development Network. Always an active volunteer, she has trained facilitators and chaired the Personnel and Search Committees for a local nonprofit. She was a board member of the Denver Child Care Consortium. She has coordinated projects for her homeowners' association, the 10 Greatest Gifts Project, Denver area school systems, and the Denver Metro Chamber of Commerce.

Susan grew up outside of Chicago and has lived with her husband, three boys, and a succession of cats in Denver, Colorado, since 1973. She speaks Spanish, French, and, on a good day, English. In addition to music, she loves travel, exercise, photography, chocolate, and any opportunity to laugh.

Made in the USA
Thornton, CO
07/08/22 16:19:30